I'LL DIE
BEFORE
I'LL RUN

The Story of the Great Feuds
of Texas

C. L. SONNICHSEN

illustrated with drawings by José Cisneros

University of Nebraska Press
Lincoln and London

The paper used in this publication meets the minimum requirements
of American National Standard for Information Sciences—
Permanence of Paper for Printed Library Materials,
ANSI Z39.48-1984.

First Bison Book printing: 1988
Most recent printing indicated by the first digit below:
                3   4   5   6   7   8   9   10

Library of Congress Cataloging-in-Publication Data
Sonnichsen, C. L. (Charles Leland), 1901–
    I'll die before I'll run: the story of the great feuds of Texas / C. L.
Sonnichsen: illustrated with drawings by José Cisneros.
        p.   cm.
    "Bison."
    Reprint. Originally published: New York: Devin-Adair Co., 1962.
    ISBN 0-8032-9192-2 (pbk.)
    1. Vendetta—Texas—History—19th century. 2. Texas—
History—1846–1950.   I. Title.
F391.C734   1988
976.4—dc19   CIP 88-14320

Reprinted by arrangement with the Devin-Adair Company,
Publishers, Greenwich, Connecticut

This book is dedicated with deep respect to the sons and grandsons of the feuding clans of Texas who have built good lives for themselves in spite of the troubles of yesterday.

Wake up, wake up, darlin' Corie!
And go get me my gun.
I ain't no hand for trouble,
But I'll die before I'll run.

—Smoky Mountain Ballad

CONTENTS

★

I'll Die Before I'll Run

THE THEORY AND PRACTICE OF FEUDING

For some reason feud collectors are as scarce in this country as fiddlers in heaven—probably on account of the hazards of the business. A feud specialist always wonders if he is going to be shot, and can be absolutely sure (supposing that he lives and stays out of jail) that he will never be allowed to finish a sentence when he gets into a discussion of his specialty.

His best friend will break in impatiently: "Just what do you mean by a feud, anyway?" he wants to know. "I've always understood that it was something that happened up in the Kentucky mountains or some such place between a couple of hillbilly families. Everybody forgot what started it, but they killed each other off anyway until only two old men were left, and they met out in the cow lot one morning with Winchester rifles and. . . ."

"Yes, I know," says the collector patiently. "That's what everybody believes. It's part of the folklore of the subject. But there is more to it than that." And then he makes, or tries to make, an explanation which goes something like this:

Nobody knows exactly what a feud is. The word usually suggests something bad and bloody, but it can be used to describe the conduct of rivals for the presidency of the Ladies' Aid Society or a habitual silence between husband and wife at the breakfast table. This confusion has lasted for something like a thousand years, and even the Oxford Dictionary can't be pinned down to a precise definition. Sometimes we talk about a "blood feud" or a "vendetta" to indicate that we mean a real shooting feud—the kind we are discussing here. "Any prolonged quarrel involving blood vengeance between families or factions" is a good enough definition to work with.

This leaves out several kinds of trouble which do not quite make the grade. Hard feelings should not be described as a feud, though a feud cannot exist without them. A "difficulty" (the Texas word for a fight) is not a feud, though a feud is a series of difficulties. A grudge murder is not a feud, though there are usually several grudge murders before a feud is finished. And a gang fight, a lynching bee, or a riot cannot by itself be called a feud, though these social embroideries usually decorate the annals of a feud historian.

And yet, in spite of all this scrambling for an exact definition of the word, the feud is one of the oldest of human institutions, one of the hardest to get rid of, and one of the least studied. It follows its own ancient rules. It germinates, grows, and sometimes flowers among all branches of the human family whenever conditions are just right. It will be with us until Time shall be no more, unless somebody finds a way of transforming human nature.

To understand what feuding actually is, and not what people think it is, some folklore has to be got out of the way. First we have to eliminate the notion that the Kentucky mountain feud, like the one in the *Trail of the Lonesome Pine*, is the model which all real feuds have to follow. There is a great deal of truth in John Fox, Jr.'s picture, but many of the basic implications are wrong—for Texas, if not for Kentucky.

For instance, we have picked up the idea, from Fox or somebody like him, that a feud is a family affair; that if it isn't a family affair it isn't a feud. One good look at the facts will show us that in Texas feuding can go on between groups bound together by any kind of loyalty. Political ties—economic ties (like those of cattlemen)—racial ties—any one of them can bind unrelated people together against a common enemy. Family loyalties almost always run up the temperature. But it isn't just a question of two families killing each other off—at least not in Texas.

Another common mistake is the presumption that a typical feud is caused by something trivial, like the famous razor-back hog which is supposed to have started the Hatfields and the McCoys, and that once the shooting starts the participants forget what caused the trouble and keep on feuding just because they like to feud. "Nobody don't know now what the first quarrel was about, it's so long ago; the Darnells and the Watsons don't know, if there's any of them living. . . . Some says it was about a horse or a cow—anyway, it was a little matter." [1] —So says Mark Twain in *Life on the Mississippi*, describing a feud on the border of Kentucky and Tennessee which he had heard about. A good Kentucky historian,[2] writing in the *Dictionary of American History*, picks up this venerable piece of folklore: "Bitter disputes have arisen between mountaineers over trifling matters," he says. "Livestock, women, politics and thievery have been the most common sources of strife." He does not explain why he classes women and politics as "trifling matters."

But even supposing that some insignificant irritation appears in the opening episode of a feud, it should probably not be spoken of as the "cause." When two people quarrel bitterly on Monday, the chances are that they were not any too fond of each other on Sunday afternoon. A spark can set off a powder barrel—but the powder has to be there. No man undertakes a war of extermination just because he hasn't anything else to do. His honor, his property, or his life must be in danger, at least to his way of thinking. If he wishes to retain his self-respect and the esteem of his friends, he has to do something about it. Usually he kills somebody, thus giving the other side a serious grievance too, and the ball opens.

A third piece of folklore which refuses to die is the notion that feuds take place only in isolated communities

among illiterate people. Quite often they do, but there is
no hard and fast rule for it. Isolation and lack of education are powerful helps in the successful breeding of
healthy feuds, and (all things being equal) there are apt to
be more feuds in the backwoods than in Chicago. However, there have been some healthy vendettas in Chicago.
There is a tendency also, not often pointed out, for feuds
to move out of the hills or the mesquite pastures and come
to town. The final battle is often fought around the courthouse; and before the last shot is fired, doctors, lawyers,
and the sheriff—members of old families, and the products
of education and culture—are apt to be mixed up in it.

Like their undeveloped cousins, the lynching bees, feuds
might well be separated into two types—the ones that
occur on a remote frontier where the law hasn't arrived,
and those that break out in civilized communities when the
law breaks down. Naturally the men of background and
culture would appear most often in the latter type, but there
were fine people among the frontiersmen too, and they were
often leaders in the demand for an application of folk law
or popular justice. The fact is, no rule can be laid down
about who gets mixed up in a feud. It can happen to anybody.

One further mistake is made in talking about these little
wars. We speak of them as "outbreaks of lawlessness"
when they are really no such thing. A family feud over
property or other cause of jealousy could be called lawless, but the typical feud in Texas is not as simple as that.
It usually starts when a group of people feel they have
been intolerably wronged and "take the law into their
own hands." This is not lawlessness. It is an appeal to a
law that is felt to be a reasonable substitute for legal
redress which cannot be obtained—sometimes to a law
that is higher or more valid than those on the statute books.

It seemed to Bancroft, when he wrote his monumental
work on popular tribunals, that the vigilance committee

(which he distinguishes from the unorganized mob) is the expression of a belief highly developed in America in "the right of the governed at all times to instant and arbitrary control of the government." It aims to "assist the law" and, "to accomplish its purpose, it claims the right to resort to unlawful means, if necessary. Therefore it is easy to see that the vigilance principle does not spring from disrespect for law." [3]

Bancroft might have gone even further and argued that the extralegal justice of frontier communities is really a return to the oldest code known to man—the law of private vengeance. "The matrix of all law is the blood feud," says William Seagle. In England it was not until the Normans came that murder was regarded as an offense against the state—that "the private avenger has been succeeded by the judge." [4]

It should be added also that feud troubles occur, usually, not among the rebellious and unrestrained, but among highly conservative people who cling to their ancient folkways. Strictly speaking, such people are not lawless—they are just operating under an earlier and more primitive code.

Any code is certainly better than none; popular justice is an improvement over no justice. But there is one major objection to the revival of feud law: the fact that all forms of self-redress, but especially hanging and ambushing, are both catching and habit-forming. Vigilantes, mobsters, and feudists are all alike in their inability to stop of their own accord. Once men take the law into their own custody, they seem unable to lay it down. Pride or fear keeps them going until they commit "outrages under the excuse of enforcing folk law." Then another party rises in righteous wrath, and only a higher authority or mutual extermination can stop the proceedings. A feud has no brakes.[5]

The word "feud" in this country has always been as-

sociated with the South, to the great resentment of the
majority of Southerners who have never even come
close to a feud. Unfortunately there is much truth in the
idea. Feuding is not limited to the South, or even to the
South and West, but it does crop up more often in Dixie.
Historians have always wondered why questions of personal and family honor should be so much more touchy
in Atlanta than in Albany.[6] The English cavalier tradition
has been held responsible, and so has the survival of the
codes of French and British army officers. It has been
suggested that the Scotch blood in the Southerner may
have had something to do with it. Mark Twain had a
theory that all the medieval ideas in Southern heads came
from the poisonous influence of the novels of Sir Walter
Scott.[7]

Charles S. Sydnor, a contemporary historian, distinguishes between the folk law of the frontier and the code
of the South—separate and individual things though "too
similar for easy distinction." The rural character of Southern civilization, like the isolation of the frontier, weakened
the force of law. So did the white man's power as an
owner of slaves. More important still was the "code of
honor," [8] the most powerful set of compulsions in the
Southerner's life. When the unwritten law conflicted
with the written law, he generally chose the former.

In Texas the folk law of the frontier was reinforced by
the unwritten laws of the South and produced a habit
of self-redress more deeply ingrained, perhaps, than anywhere else in the country. The grievances and abuses of
the bad days after the Civil War gave extraordinary scope
for the application of the old ways of dealing justice,
and even today there are many vestiges of frontier days and
the Old South in the Texan's attitudes toward crime and
punishment. For instance there is the matter of self-
defense. In other states a man has to "retreat" as far as he
can before he kills an attacker. In Texas he can stand

his ground. The lawyers say he doesn't have to retreat any farther than "the air at his back." [9]

The Texan's code which demands immediate and active resentment of an insult has produced the story which says you can tell where a man is from by the way he acts when you call him a liar. If he is from Texas he shoots you or knocks you down. If he is from up around Ohio he waves his fists and shouts, "You're another!" If he is from New England he spits on a grasshopper and remarks calmly, "Well, you can't prove it."

It would be possible to add a great many more contributing circumstances to explain why bad blood so often turned into blood feuds in Texas. The fact that everybody went armed, even little boys and preachers, had something to do with it. The ever-present whiskey barrel helped. The necessities which made the Texan a hunter of game (and sometimes of Indians) contributed something. Put all these together and it would be queer if somebody couldn't find a feud or two.

Feud production in Texas would probably not have been much above normal, even so, if it had not been for the War Between the States. Although crimes of violence increased all over the country from 1830 on,[10] the great feud of the Regulators and Moderators in East Texas in the 1840's was the only bad outbreak before the war. As soon as the soldiers came home after Lee's surrender, however, the fireworks started. Feud troubles rose to a peak in the seventies, slacked off in the eighties with the help of the Texas Rangers, and should have become rare by 1890. Instead of continuing downward, however, the curve jumped upward again in the nineties, and even since 1900 the old custom has been frequently revived.

Since the post-Civil-War period brought feud troubles in Texas to their climax of blood and hate, the greater portion of the pages which follow are devoted to the years between 1865 and 1900.

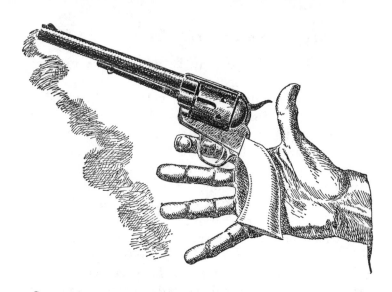

Strangely enough the feud history of Texas is almost unknown to the average Texan. Sometimes a man will know about the feud down at the forks of the creek in his own neighborhood, but the one in the next county has usually escaped him. Western reticence is at least partly responsible for this condition. The old time Texas pioneer was close-mouthed, particularly about other people's troubles and weaknesses, and besides, it was once dangerous to talk. As a consequence, only half a dozen of the biggest and bloodiest feuds are known, even by name, throughout the state, though there must have been at least a hundred of them, big and little.

Even now many good people will not discuss their local troubles, feeling that if nobody talks, the feud may be "lived down." It is hard to convince them that feuds are history, and important history—that few human actions, particularly if they are scandalous, can be sure of decent burial—that it is surely late enough to talk about the feuds of fifty, sixty, and seventy years ago.

Since there was feuding in every state in the South and West and in many places in the North—particularly in the "border states"—it is reasonable to suppose that at least some of the facts about Texas feuds would be equally true for Arkansas, Alabama, Kansas, or California. Allowances would have to be made for obvious differences, for instance the fact that Kentucky is mountainous and Texas is mostly plains, or that there are no Mexicans or Comanche Indians in North Carolina. Still, anything as ancient and honorable as the custom of feuding must have a pretty solid groundwork. Like marriage and religion and other serious things which have been around for a long time, its uses and satisfactions remain stable though the outward observances change. The pattern of American feuds is fairly stable too, whether the feudist uses a long Kentucky rifle or a short El Paso ice pick to carry out his urges.

The Sorrowful Sixties

O credit me, youth, that when men draw cold steel on each other in their native country, they neither can nor may dwell deeply on the offences of those whose swords are useful to them.

SIR WALTER SCOTT, The Monastery

Nor did she think, then, consciously of her parents or realize that, almost by instinct, she was reacting to the pattern of conduct they had laid down in her. She would be judged—she thought—would judge herself—not by the victory over any kind of circumstances, but by the spirit with which she confronted it. The obligation never to falter lay as heavily and inescapably upon a woman of her group as upon a man; always she had known that.

LAURA KREY, And Tell of Time

Now I will not cease to punish these men so long as I can find them. Peacock still hires men to kill me, and they must take the consequences.

BOB LEE

FROM REGULATION
TO RECONSTRUCTION

A hundred years ago Texas was still a new world, and to many a refugee European and land-hungry American, it looked like Paradise. From the piney woods and black-jack thickets in the east to the endless flowery plains and cedar-covered hills to the west its untilled fields and un-cropped pastures offered much to those who had nothing —freedom and elbowroom to men at outs with civilization. Through the twenties, thirties and forties the pioneers flocked in by ship and ox wagon, on horseback and on foot.

They came from everywhere—from the North, the East, the South, the Old Country. Southerners predominated, and gave their color to the folkways of the frontier; but the Texas border was a special environment and remade its sons to fit its pattern. Even in very early days the word "Texan" had a ring of its own—not always pleasant to sensitive ears. People in older states almost believed that Texans were born with horns and tails, and news-paper stories about horrible deaths and crimes of violence down on the border gave some flavor of truth to the idea. It was certainly a fact that most Texans would fight for their rights, and frequently had to, for along with the honest settlers came many a rascal who robbed and murdered as the spirit moved him.

There was naturally some feuding in such an environ-ment, especially among Southern settlers who never took anything lying down. The great feuds of Texas, however, were products of the Civil War. One big trouble and a few little ones are all the record shows before the sixties.

The big feud was the terrible war of the Regulators and

Moderators which flared up in the 1840's in the pine-clad hills along the Sabine River.[1] This region had long been a No-Man's Land where horse thieves, counterfeiters, nigger stealers, and land-sharks threatened to outnumber the honest men. Traffic in fake land titles was probably the most prevalent form of villainy, but no kind of meanness was neglected, and there were men about who would cut a throat for pennies. Apparently the crooks were banded together in a rogues' fraternity which had enrolled many outwardly respectable citizens—including judges and officers of the law.

In 1840 Charles W. Jackson, bitter over a political defeat, let it be known that he was going to expose the ring. Eventually he killed a member named Joseph Goodbread, and when Goodbread's friends pushed the prosecution vigorously, Jackson protected himself by organizing a group of "Regulators"—the good old American term for vigilantes brought together to regulate, or set right, an intolerable situation. His excuse was the alarming growth of cattle stealing in the neighborhood, and one of the first activities of the Regulators was the whipping of some suspected cattle thieves.

These night riders soon became so high-handed in their methods that a counter-organization was formed—the Moderators. This name was also traditional. Moderators used to be called together to put the brakes on Regulators when the latter became overenthusiastic about their business. In this case the skirmishing between the two factions continued for four years while the country went to ruin. Crops were neglected, good people moved away, and at one time miniature armies of several hundred men were marching and countermarching about Shelbyville. Furthermore the feeling was spreading to adjoining counties and involving more and more people; just before the end it looked as if the thing might go on forever.

It took "Old Sam" Houston, the President of the

Republic, to stop it. He rode into San Augustine one day, got out a proclamation ordering everybody to go home, and called out the militia in four counties to back up his orders. The Moderators surrendered—the Regulators dispersed—but the leaders of both factions were assembled and brought to San Augustine where Houston was waiting for them. Under his stern eye they signed an agreement to suspend hostilities, and except for a few sporadic outbreaks the feud was over.

The Shelby War set a record which stood for twenty years. Texas was not particularly peaceful during the fifties, but conditions did get better.[2] Desirable immigrants came in. The Compromise of 1850 settled the western boundary and brought ten million dollars of badly needed cash into the treasury. And the thunder of approaching civil war caused some citizens to think less about their own personal conflicts.

They feuded occasionally. On the Upper Brazos the white settlers and the reservation Indians repeatedly attacked[3] and threatened each other in the "Reservation War" of 1858. Farther south there was the "Cart War" of 1847 between Mexican and American teamsters, and the "Cortina War" of the late fifties.[4] These were minor troubles, however; hardly feuds at all.

Then came the conflagration of 1860, forcing thousands of Texans into new patterns, taking away the securities and safeguards they were used to. Almost at once the willingness of these men to take the law into their own hands made its appearance. Governor Sam Houston, who was not a secessionist, refused to call a special session of the legislature to vote Texas out of the Union. Thereupon the leaders of the secession party invited the people to elect delegates to a special convention which would, in effect, take over the government. This was done, and the power which had come from the people was taken back by the hands that in theory had given it. The pattern is a familiar one to a student of Texas feud troubles.

The war itself produced many feud situations, for Texans disagreed among themselves about the basic issues almost as much as they disagreed with the Yankees. The majority of those who were opposed to dividing the Union fought manfully for the South after hostilities began. But some left the state, or tried to, and some hid out in the scopes of wild country like the "Big Thicket" in East Texas. The most violent Southern patriots could not bear to let such men go unpunished, and many were hunted down and killed. Much of the hunting and killing was done by the Home Guard organization, sometimes called the "Heel Flies." [5] Theoretically this force was composed of men too old or too young to join the regular army, but the membership sometimes included draft dodgers and thieves who came in for protection.

The Early-Hasley feud in Bell County was the outgrowth of trouble with the Home Guard. A very active band of Heel Flies made it hot for deserters and Union sympathizers all during the war, and sometimes used rough tactics with inoffensive citizens. One of them named John Early, who passed for a furious secessionist at the time, fell out with old Mr. Drew Hasley, abused him, and pulled a handful of hair out of his long white beard. About that

time Mr. Drew's son Sam came home on furlough from
the Confederate Army and took the matter up. The war
ended shortly after, and Early immediately started col-
laborating with the Union officials, so Sam had him and the
whole Yankee military government to fight.

Serious feuding broke out when Early and his new
friends arrested a number of the best citizens, including
Drew Hasley, for supposed complicity in the hanging of
three deserters during the war. The prisoners were never
even brought to trial, but they were confined in an un-
healthful prison in the dead of winter and the elder Hasley's
health was so broken that he did not last many years after
his release.

Sam Hasley, his brother-in-law Jim McRae, and some of
their friends, resentful over this outrage, formed a faction
with the avowed intention of wiping out the Early party,
which included Dr. Calvin Clark and Chief Justice Hiram
Christian of the Military Commissioners Court of that district. For a time Hasley and McRae had to be cautious and
work under cover, but they forced Hiram Christian to leave
the county in haste and gave many a nervous moment to
the Union men. Finally in the summer of 1869 a posse was
formed for the purpose of wiping out the whole Hasley-
McRae band. With John Early in the lead they crept up to
the headquarters of the "outlaws" and killed McRae. This
broke up the clan, but the feud was not finished. Judge
Christian was run down and killed in Missouri, and Dr.
Calvin Clark was finished off in Arkansas before it was
all over. What happened to Early and Hasley the record
does not say.[6]

Not all the policing during the years of conflict was done
by the Home Guard. Secret bands of Regulators, working in the shadows, added more than one lurid chapter to
local history and sometimes promoted a feud. Typical of
such episodes was the Franks case, which sprouted in San
Antonio in the summer of 1863.

A vigilance committee had been organized, led by one Asa (or Ase) Mitchell—fiftyish, stout, prosperous, and a pious pillar of the Methodist Church. He was one of those good men so well known to history who wish to make other men good and are willing to shoot, burn, or hang them in order to do so. San Antonio was full of rascals during the war and no doubt something needed to be done about them, but Mitchell was a little overconscientious. This became apparent one Sunday when he was preaching earnestly to a large congregation, calling down fire from heaven on the sinners of San Antonio. It was a warm day and he perspired freely. Pretty soon he reached into his tall white hat, sitting on the platform beside him, for his handkerchief. A general gasp went up when a coil of rope came out too.

Mitchell's vigilantes, though Mitchell himself was not immediately concerned, were respnsible for hanging Old Man Franks to a chinaberry tree just outside the San Antonio jail in July, 1863. Franks was under arrest for allegedly killing two Mexicans who had come to buy some of his stock, but the vigilantes were not willing to leave him to the orderly processes of law.

Franks had several sons who were unable to take any action at the moment, but they found out who the lynchers were and bided their time. After the breakup in 1865 they are supposed to have evened the score with seven men. Three got away to Mexico.[7]

People like Sam Hasley and the Franks boys, full of

war-born grievances, feuded furiously in the sixties. Two of the major vendettas of Texas—the Lee-Peacock and the Sutton-Taylor troubles—were war products also and were big and bloody enough to deserve chapters to themselves.

THE HUNTING
OF BOB LEE
The Lee-Peacock Feud

Bob Lee was the sort of man a sensible desperado would have let alone. His people were frontier stock, having settled on the line between Hunt and Fannin Counties in northern Texas in the 1830's, and Bob was well able to take care of himself. When the war broke out, he went to fight for the South and became one of the most dashing cavalry captains in General Nathan Bedford Forrest's dashing band of raiders.[1] After the surrender he rode proudly home and immediately found himself a marked man.

The trouble with Bob Lee was that he looked too prosperous. His horse and saddle were better than those brought home by most of the soldiers. He wore a fine black suit and a hat with a plume on it. Though he was not a highly educated man himself, he liked to be with cultivated people and did not have to apologize for his manners or conversation.[2] Furthermore he had money and liked to spend it like a gentleman. There was a story current in the country that old Daniel Lee, Bob's father, had brought a pot of gold with him when he came from Virginia to Texas by way of Missouri. The family was certainly a little better off than its neighbors, and the sight of a twenty-dollar gold piece in Bob's hand was enough to make certain people think he must be rich.

It happened that there were a good many of these certain people in the neighborhood. The "Five Corners" district, where Grayson, Fannin, Collin and Hunt Counties approach each other, is a wooded country even today, and in Civil War times it was spotted with impenetrable patches of brush and timber—the Mustang Thicket, the Black Jack Thicket, the Wild Cat Thicket, and so on—where deserters, slackers, Union sympathizers, thieves, and renegades hung out. Many of these minus quantities remained in the country when it was all over, and for a while the Union authorities took them at their own valuation as loyal citizens. After a while even the Yankees learned better.

When the Union League for the protection of negroes and Northern sympathizers came to Texas, it set up a control point at Pilot Grove, about seven miles west of Bob Lee's farm home in the northern part of Hunt County. By 1876 there was much bitterness between the officers of the League and the ex-Confederates, of whom Bob Lee was the most haughty and uncompromising. There was also bad feeling between Lee and a group of civilians known as the "Lick Skillet Men" (Pilot Grove was sometimes called Lick Skillet)[3] who sided with the Yankees. The real leader in this group was a forceful and ambitious man named Lewis Peacock,[4] who headed a sizeable clan of friends and supporters living to the west of the Lees in the near neighborhood of town.

It is hard for us now to form any idea of the rift which divided one neighbor from another in those unhappy times. Grayson County was one of the few places in Texas where the population was pro-Union at the outbreak of war. Furthermore, Union sympathizers from Kansas and other places had settled there.[5] There was great bitterness between the tried-and-true Southerners and the "scalawags" who collaborated with the Union forces. Hatred is a weak word for it.

A good many of the old families of the neighborhood were in sympathy with Bob. In particular there were the Dixons—Irish Jack Dixon, who ran a freighting business with his sons Billy, Simp, Charley, and Bob, and their

half-brother Dick Johnson.[6] These and many more were
with Bob Lee to the bitter end, but Peacock had the Yankee
rifles on his side and believed that he could at least hold
his own. All through 1867 and 1868 there was killing and
waylaying, and the last man did not die until 1871.

Bob Lee told his story of what happened in a letter to
the Bonham *News*, dated June 26, 1868, his indomitable
personality standing out in every line:

Lee Station, Fannin Co,
June 26, 1868.

Editors Texas *News:*

If you will permit me the use of your valuable columns, I
would like to give you a true statement of what is known as
the Pilot Grove Difficulty, notwithstanding there has been
no killing in Pilot Grove at all except Dr. Pierce. But to
begin:

I was raised in this state, and enlisted in the Southern
Army, and fought the best I could, until the surrender, when
I laid down my arms and returned home to live, as I thought
in peace the balance of my life. But how badly I was disappointed you will soon see. A short time after my arrival
home, one night when I was sick in my bed, I was arrested
by a party of men: (Israel Boren, Lewis Peacock, James Mad-
ison, Bill Smith, Sam Bier, and Hardy Dial) wearing the U. S.
uniform, and was told by them that I would be carried to
Sherman to stand trial for offences committed during the
War. Of course, I surrendered and was perfectly willing to
yield myself. After we had proceeded a short distance from
my home another party (in citizens dress) fell in with us.
Among these citizens I recognized a party known as "Doc"
Wilson and several other thieves. Well as we proceeded to
Sherman "Doc" Wilson began to hint to me that I should
buy out and not go to Sherman. Now, you can imagine my
dismay, when our entire party, U. S. soldiers and all, halted
in Chocktaw Bottom this side of Sherman, went off the road,
and stationed a guard over me apparently with a view of
staying some time, in the meantime "Doc" Wilson still per-

suading me to buy out and escape the punishment at Sherman which he presented as very severe. I repeatedly begged to be taken to Sherman, sick hardly able to sit up, surrounded man. Now then I was in Choctaw Bottoms surrounded by a band of thieves. After keeping me thirty-six hours, my sickness growing worse all the time, and I begging them to take me to Sherman, I finally agreed to accept their offer and obtain my release. I agreed to give them my mule, saddle and bridle, a $20 gold piece which I had in my pocket, and executed my note to "Doc" Wilson with my father's name for security for $2000 in gold payable on demand and to leave the country for ever. Having no pen and ink Wilson made a pen of a toothpick and ink of gun powder and water mixing it in my brother's hand. (He came with me when arrested.) Now after being arrested I thought to try the civil law on these scoundrels, and to prevent me from doing so they have ever since tried to kill me. One day about twelve after this occurred, I was in Pilot Grove and met Jim Maddox, a friend of Peacock's, and I told him that if he desired to fight me I would loan him a pistol, but the coward said he did not want to hurt me and proposed taking a drink, saying he was sorry he had done what he did. After drinking with him I told him I wanted to be let alone and he said all right. However he went out of the grocery store, borrowed a pistol from a friend, slipped up behind me while I was making a contract with a negro to do some work, and shot me in the face. He then left me on the ground for dead and bragged that he shot Bob Lee's brains out. I was in a very precarious condition for some time and would have perished but for the timely aid and skill of the late Dr. Pierce. I may add here that the excellent gentleman (soon after my recovery) was called to his gate and brutally murdered in the presence of his family by one of the clan, Hugh Hudson. The Doctor's death is attributed to his kindness in taking care of me in his house and nursing me. Still the civil authorities take no notice of these things. I have done everything I could to procure peace; I have even tried to buy it with money; and I have done every way in my power to do right and be peaceable; still I am hunted by a squad of U. S. soldiers assisted by a number of horse thieves who come to my house, throw fire in the beds, drag my children by their feet over the floor and insult my wife. Yet the U. S. troops stood by and said not a word.

These "Good Union" men were principally deserters from the Southern Army and lay in the bush during the war, the lowest of God's creation; and these good Union men, "truly loil," are biasing the judgment of the men (U. S. troops) who should protect us impartially. I further wish to say that Elijah Clark, a young man, was taken from his horse, which he had bought from one of these thieves, by the gang and was tied and murdered on the prairie, the U. S. troops being present. Also William Dixon was followed some twenty miles from his home, at Hog Eye, and taking refuge in a mill kept thirty men at bay. After flirting with death and firing many times at Dixon, the party told him if he would surrender they would not hurt him. When Dixon came to the door of the mill and threw down his pistol they riddled him with bullets, the U. S. soldiers being present at the time. They robbed his pockets at the time, turning them inside out, and even took the dead man's spurs.

In conclusion, I would like to say that Hugh Hudson received his reward of $300 from the "Clan" for killing Dr. Pierce, and has since died. Wilson and Maddox have left this country for a new field in Southern Texas. Nance, Baldock, Bud Favors and several others have been killed while pursuing me. Sanders and Peacock have been wounded, the latter twice. Now I will not cease to punish these men so long as I can find them. Peacock still hires men to kill me, and they must take the consequences. I trust the U. S. troops will cease their interference and I will clear the country of this band of thieves. Finally I am perfectly willing to surrender myself to any impartial civil authority at any time, but will not give myself up, unarmed to thieves and robbers. I am sorry to take so much of your valuable time and space, but a great many people, even the military, have no idea of the true origin of all this trouble, so I give you all the particulars. I remain yours,

Robert Lee[7]

This, of course, was just one side of it. There must have been some reason for the sentence of outlawry passed against Bob Lee at Union headquarters, but it is too late now to learn the details.

Some parts of Bob's statement can be filled in, however. The party which arrested him had heard a rumor that a reward had been offered for their captive. They stopped in the bottoms of the Choctaw Creek, four miles from Bonham, while a messenger went into town to see about it. To their chagrin they found that the rumor of a reward was unfounded, and apparently they felt that it was somehow Bob Lee's fault. They reimbursed themselves with his gold watch, twenty dollars in gold, and the two-thousand-dollar note.

When he was free Bob "thought to try the civil law" on his persecutors, which means that he not merely refused to pay, on advice of counsel, but had the kidnappers arrested. "The jail was broken open," however, and "the leaders escaped," as the newspapers told it.[8]

Jim Maddox, whose bullet had glanced off the bone behind Lee's ear, was one of Peacock's men, and his action made a full-grown feud of the trouble. There was so much feeling that anyone suspected of having anything to do with either side was in danger, as Dr. Pierce found when Hugh Hudson called him to his door and shot him for harboring and nursing Lee. The doctor came out to Hudson, rested his arm on the horse's neck and talked for a few minutes in what appeared to be a very friendly fashion. As he turned away to return to the house, he was shot in the back. This happened on February 24, 1867. Dr. Pierce died three days later. Officially, it was stated that Pierce had accused young Hudson of stealing horses, but everyone knew the real reason for the murder.[9]

Before a month had passed two men tried to waylay Bob at his own house. A newspaper story copied by the Dallas *Herald* from the McKinney *Enquirer* is all that remains to tell what happened:

"We learn that a few days since, two men called at the house of Bob Lee in the eastern part of the county, and after firing at him several times, made their escape, thinking probably they had killed him. Lee, however, was not hurt. His brother arrived a little time after, when the two traced the would-be assassins to Farmersville, and attacked them, killing one and wounding the other. We did not learn the names of the parties, or any of the particulars." [10]

It was a cold and rainy spring that year, and food was scarce all through the region. Hardship did not soften hard feelings, however, and the killing went on as usual. In January, Hugh Hudson was murdered under somewhat mysterious circumstances.[11] Hugh was the Peacock man who had shot Dr. Pierce down at his front gate—for $300, they said. In February, it was Elijah Clark's turn.

As G.B. Ray, the regional historian, tells the tale, Lije came courting Hester Dixon. He was more or less on the Peacock side and Hester's family were strong Lee supporters. Undoubtedly a wise man would have done his courting elsewhere, but Lije couldn't let the forbidden fruit alone. He asked Hester to go to a party with him, and when she gave him an emphatic No, he lost his temper. As he left the house, boiling inwardly, he met Hester's sixteen-year-old brother Billy. They had been boyhood friends, but Lije was too angry to remember that. He saw that Billy had left his pistol in the saddle holster when he tied his horse at the gate. Lije jerked the gun out and took a pot shot at its owner.

Ironically, Lije had forgotten to pick up his own pistol when he left the house. Billy snatched it off the table by the door and shot Lije off his horse as he rode away.[12]

The whole neighborhood knew that Billy would have to pay for his deed sooner or later, but the reprisal came more quickly than anybody expected. Two or three weeks after Lije was buried, a posse of Peacock's men caught Billy and his older brother Charley on their way to Jefferson with a load of cotton. They had a wheel to fix and were off guard when the men rode up on them. Charley was spared, but Billy died with bullets in his back as they marched him off with his hands in the air.[13]

It was now the Lees' turn to even the score. Several skirmishes probably took place as they stalked their enemies. There was one brush at Pilot Grove in which Peacock was wounded—probably in April, 1868. On June 15, there was a real battle.

It happened at the home of old man Nance, a Peacock ally, who had a place with a big horse corral. The Peacock clan members are said to have used the corral for meetings on dark nights and may have been doing so on this occasion. Newspaper stories say that they were working horses when the Lee men jumped them. Dow Nance and John Baldock were killed, and a man named Dan Sanders was fatally hurt. None of the Lee party was hit.[14]

As the feud blazed higher, the good people of the region grew more and more alarmed. After the killing at Nance's corral, the McKinney *Enquirer* remarked with deep feeling: "We do hope and trust that this last tragedy may close this long continued and bloody strife. For nearly three years this feud has been kept alive by these parties, and at short intervals fights have occurred in which many of our citizens have lost their lives."

The Union League officials were even more concerned, since it was their men who were being regularly buried. They sent off to Austin for help, and on August 27, 1868, General J.J. Reynolds issued a proclamation offering a thousand dollars to anyone who would deliver Bob Lee "to the Post Commander at Austin or Marshall, Texas."

Not content with this, Reynolds sent Lieutenant Charles A. Vernon to the seat of trouble. Vernon's report,

dated October 19, 1868, was a little plaintive about the difficulties being encountered. Lieutenant Sands, the local officer, had thirty-five soldiers and fifteen civilians in the field, but Bob Lee just had too many friends. "Lee seems to be the most popular man in this section of the country, and I am sure that the citizens of that neighborhood would not only give him all the aid in their power, but will even help him with force of arms if necessary. I have strong hopes that Lieutenant Sands will eventually capture this man. . . . He has at all times a portion of his command under a non-commissioned officer lying in the brush . . . and he has put Lee upon the defensive." [15]

Lee was indeed "upon the defensive." He never slept at home any more. His hideout was a tent in the midst of the Wildcat Thicket from which he never emerged until one of his family had made sure that all was safe. Well he knew that somebody would try to collect that thousand-dollar reward.

In December a soldier was killed near Farmersville. He was "one of a squad supposed to be in search of Bob Lee, guided by one Peacock, and the firing is supposed to have come from some enemies of Peacock, who also narrowly escaped. Another man was wounded." [16]

No other details of this passage at arms have turned up, but there was a bigger and better story in the spring of the next year. As Dean Taylor tells it, three "Kansas Redlegs" came into Pilot Grove about April or May, 1869, and word was immediately carried to Bob Lee that strange men were hanging around. He and his brothers deduced that Peacock had brought in outside help and they prepared to give the newcomers a hearty welcome. They stretched ropes across the road the men might be expected to travel and waited all night for them to appear. Nothing happened. Then in the morning, after the ropes had been removed, the Kansas killers came riding up in broad daylight.

A sister of Dr. Pierce (shot for aiding Bob Lee two years before) was teaching school in the neighborhood and boarding at the Lee home. She was with Mrs. Lee that morning when the shotguns began to boom down in the woods. Mrs. Lee was terribly frightened. "I know they've killed Bob," she said.

"You'd better go to him," advised Miss Pierce. "If they have shot him, you might be able to hear his last words."

"Will you go with me?"

"Of course I will."

They had gone only a little way into the woods when they almost stumbled over the body of a man lying across the road. Mrs. Lee would not go close enough to look at him, but Miss Pierce had the courage to place her hand on his heart to see if he was alive. Finding that he was quite dead, Mrs. Lee crept up and looked at him. "It's not one of Bob's men," she said with relief.

A little farther down the path they found a hat—then another dead man—then a third. The "Redlegs" had been cleaned out.

The women went on to the home of Dan Lee, Bob's father, but found that everybody had taken to the brush and there was nothing to do but start back. On the road they stopped long enough to place hats over the faces of the dead men and even to tie up the wounds of one of them who had been shot in the face and was still bleeding. Later these two women are said to have dug shallow graves and buried the victims, since none of the Lick Skillet men had the nerve to come out from Pilot Grove and do what was necessary.[17]

This triple killing was more than Peacock and his Yankees could stand, and they made up their minds to move heaven and earth to get Bob Lee. The military commander at Greenville, acting under orders from the headquarters of the Fifth Military District, extended the thousand-dollar reward to "each and every member of 'Lee's gang.' " [18]

On Monday, June 25, 1869, they got him.

The official announcements made it appear that it was strictly an army job done by "Capt. Charles Campbell and a squad of men, 6th Cavalry, who were attempting to arrest him." It was well known in the vicinity, however, that some civilians were taken along in a semi-military capacity and that Henry Boren, a near neighbor of Lee's and supposedly one of his friends, got in the first shot.

Lee was getting ready to leave for Mexico when it happened—some say that he was already on his way. His sister-in-law told Dean Taylor that he was riding down the road "singing a little song," perhaps enjoying the thought of safety at last. A quarter of a mile from his own house the soldiers and Henry Boren were lying in wait in a thicket. When Bob came riding down the road, erect and proud with his four six-shooters and his rifle, his gold watch and his plumed hat, they were ready. He fell from his horse with eight bullets in his body. Sixty years later his sister-in-law still had the shirt he was wearing, with the bullet holes in it. His horse ran home, riderless, and his family knew that what they had feared for so long had happened at last.[19]

With their leader gone, the rest of Lee's outfit broke up and vanished, with the exception of several men who did not vanish fast enough. These included the three Dixon boys, Charley, Simp, and Bob. Simp Dixon, described as a "notorious outlaw," was overtaken by a detachment of U. S. troops near Springfield in Limestone County. He escaped to the brush, fought off the soldiers till he had only one bullet left, then engaged them hand to hand until they shot him down. He was of the breed that would not run. Death overtook him on February 1, 1870.[20]

Next, Peacock and his men followed Charley Dixon, his father, and his half-brother Dick Johnson to Black Jack Grove (now called Cumby), where they had gone for a load of lumber. The Peacock party killed Charley and wounded Dick. Either before or after this they got Bob Dixon, but details are lacking. Meanwhile Dick Johnson escaped to West Texas to get over his wound and stay out of trouble.[21]

It was not long before he had to come back. Jack Dixon, father of the Dixon boys, buried them all and then lay down and died himself, leaving three daughters in the family home, alone and unprotected. According to legend, Peacock and his outfit sent word that they were going to burn these girls out of their house, so they appealed to Dick Johnson to come back and take their part. A man of Dick's time and place could not pass over a call like that and keep his self-respect. He came on home. This was about the beginning of the summer of 1871.

Dick joined forces with Joe Parker, another Lee sympathizer, and began to lay plans. Peacock was told that they were up to something, and made a remark that he ought to have kept to himself. Some say he made it about Parker, and some about Johnson. At any rate he declared publicly in Kuykendall's drugstore at Pilot Grove: "Well, some morning when he goes out after wood for a fire, I'll get him."

Dick and Joe determined to get Peacock first. They crept up to within sight of Peacock's house on June 13,

1871, and one of them climbed into an elm tree on the prairie where he could keep watch. In the evening Peacock came into his house (he was sleeping out now as Bob Lee had had to sleep for so long). He acted as if he meant to remain at home for a while so they determined to kill him the next morning. About daylight next day he stepped out-of-doors to get wood to build his breakfast fire and they shot him down in his own yard—a clear case of poetic justice.[22]

That was about the end of things. Dick Johnson moved to Missouri and was never arrested. Joe Parker was not so lucky, but he lasted until October. A posse caught up with him and a friend named Billy Graves three miles below Mount Pleasant. "His captors surrounded the stable where he and Graves had put their saddle horses; camped there in the fence corners till daylight, when Graves and Parker came to the stable, saddled up, and were leading out of the lot when they were called upon to surrender. Parker instantly clutched his pistol, but before he could draw, he was hit by a shot from a pistol and a double-barrelled shotgun. They both turned and ran, Parker shooting back at his pursuers. Graves fell on his face, hit in the back with a pistol shot. Parker soon sank down from exhaustion. He thought he was dying and gasped, 'Boys, you have killed the bravest man in Texas.' He then confessed to having killed Peacock and eight other men, and to stealing innumerable horses."

Just what happened as a result of this arrest is not clear. Parker was not finally surrounded and killed until three years later.[23]

All this happened a long, long time ago, but it was talked about for fifty years and more. Some fine folklore evolved from it. The story of Bob Lee's signing the note for two thousand dollars, for instance, was worked over until it had Bob drawing blood from his own arm for the purpose.[24]

Long after it was over, the Lees remained on guard. Dean Taylor, who grew up in the neighborhood, used to see them riding to town in single file, well strung out, with guns ready and no fear on their faces. They died, but they never ran.

THIRTY YEARS
A-FEUDING
The Sutton-Taylor Feud

It was an ancient farmer man,
  And he stoppeth one of three:
"By thy Colt's improved and Henry gun
  I pray thee tell to me
If you belong to the Sutton gang
  Or the Taylor companie?"

When I first wrote to you from here, I was not acquainted
with the geography of the county; I have since been told by
an old citizen of Clinton that it takes five large counties to
bound DeWitt, and it is an awful strain on them to hold it at
all.

Pidge, in the Daily Statesman, September 24, 1874.

★

The Root of the Matter

So many things went wrong after the war it was hard to
say which one was worst, but trouble with the Negroes
was what everybody seemed most afraid of. DeWitt
County, focus of the great Sutton-Taylor feud, was a
wooded, brushy stretch of country halfway between San
Antonio and the Gulf Coast, mostly given over to cattle
raising. Colored men worked its cotton patches and corn-
fields, however, and DeWitt County had its share of race
difficulty. In 1865, the Negroes in that part of Texas were

reported to be "rambling about in idleness, and will either not work at all, or demand four prices for what they but half do." They were accused of wholesale horse stealing, drinking, loafing, displaying weapons, and insulting their former masters.[1]

The Yankee soldiers were another thorn in the flesh. A squad was stationed at Clinton, a now-vanished town which was then the county seat of DeWitt County, where they watched the ford over the Guadalupe River and disarmed everybody who crossed, no matter who he was or where he was going.[2]

Even the crops failed in those terrible years. The Galveston *News* reported on October 27, 1866, that on account of the Negroes, the soldiers, "bad crops, and fears of trouble ahead, many people are talking of emigration. The opportunity to emigrate would be seized by many persons, but the failure of the crops have left them without the necessary means."

A consequence of the general depression was a noticeable decay of character and ideals, particularly among the younger citizens. This fact was noted by a weeping philosopher who wrote regularly to the papers from the little town of Concrete in DeWitt County, signing himself "Lunar Caustic." "So far as I can learn," he declared, "there is not a boy of American parentage learning a trade or reading for a profession west of the Colorado . . . our youth have souls above the mechanical arts, the little children as early as they can walk pilfer their mother's tape to make lassoes to rope the kittens and the ducks, the boys so soon as they can climb on a pony, are off to the prairie to drive stock; and as they advance toward manhood their highest ambition is to conquer a pitching mustang, or throw a wild beef by the tail. . . . This ennobling occupation—the branding and marking of stock, with the attainment of the lowest patois of the Mexican language sufficient to blaspheme fluently and express ideas so low and filthy that the most hardened would blush to have them translated into English—these are the acquirements of the large majority of our rising generation." [3]

What Lunar Caustic said was more than half true. Poverty and discouragement were doing their work, and many a boy who might have been a doctor or a lawyer or a preacher in the best tradition of his family took the easy way and, with no more capital than a rope and a branding iron, started out to build up a herd and a fortune.

There was nothing fundamentally dishonest, of course, about cattle raising; but so many men would "brand anything with a hide on from a tambourine to a buffalo" that the word "cowboy" soon began to give off a heavy odor of wildness and sin. "Parents," advised a writer in the Denton *Monitor*, "do not allow your boys to load themselves down with Mexican spurs, six shooters and pipes. Keep them off the prairies as professional cow hunters. There, in that occupation, who knows but that they may forget that there is a distinction between 'mine' and 'thine'? Send them to school, teach them a trade, or keep them at home." [4]

All this warning and head shaking did no good, of course. Texas was meant to be a cattle state, and when the big herds began to swing northward on the cattle trails after 1867, the boom was on.

The rustling business boomed too. Many a man made a living and got a good start in life by stealing other people's cows; but horse theft was still more profitable. A horse meant money then. Government agents came to Texas in the sixties to buy saddle stock and paid for their purchases in real gold coin—something the younger Texans had never even seen. In Gonzales in 1867, prices ranged from seventy to a hundred dollars a head "and the consequence was an increased circulation of gold on our streets and a little less horse." [5]

Man's Best Friend being so useful and valuable, horse theft naturally became the unpardonable sin in Texas—and yet the business flourished. In some counties it was "almost impossible to keep a good horse." [6] It is not surprising, then, that when horse owners got their hands on a rustler, they were prepared to take very stern measures.

The defeats and difficulties of the post-war years produced the tough Texas cowboy of the seventies and eighties. Sometimes he came from a cultured family, but trouble and turmoil were all around him; he took up the rough life of the cattleman's frontier and reverted to the manners of an earlier time.

In DeWitt County the young men were probably no more wild and pugnacious than elsewhere, but they had a reputation for being a little extra rugged. Sore in defeat, resentful of the new Negro citizens, humiliated by their conquerors, and desperate over the stealing of their stock, they were ripe for trouble in 1866. When they clashed openly with the Yankee military authorities, the feud put up its first red leaf.

The sons of Creed Taylor were the ones to get into trouble.

★

Creed Taylor's Boys

All the Taylors would stand up for their rights at the point of a gun. There was a large tribe of them living in DeWitt County in the sixties—all sons and grandsons of Josiah Taylor, an ex-Virginian who is said to have been a relative of General Zachary Taylor. Josiah first came to Texas in 1811, joined McGee's filibustering expedition in 1812, took his bullet-scarred body back to Virginia when the expedition went to pieces, and did not return to Texas to settle until the late 1820's.[1] In 1830, he gave up the struggle, leaving five sons—Pitkin, Creed, Josiah, William and Rufus—on the Taylor ranch just below the present town of Cuero. Pitkin, Josiah, and Rufus continued to farm on the tract of land granted to Josiah's widow. William made his home not far away. But Creed was made of his father's metal and moved about freely, settling in Karnes County on the Ecleto but never able to stay away very long from the cedar-clad hills of the extreme frontier. In the late sixties he was ranching on the edge of the Indian country near Fort Mason.

The best way to describe the Taylors is to say that they were American pioneers. They had small opportunity to acquire refinement and culture, but they were much respected by Indian war parties who had occasion to test their shooting ability. They did not have the reputation of being interested in other people's cattle when such distinction was rare. Undoubtedly they were clannish and quick to resent a wrong to any member of the tribe. Furthermore they were Southern to the core and too high-spirited to stay out of trouble with the Yankee army of occupation after the surrender.

A few months after the end of the war, Creed Taylor's two sons were put on the "wanted" list by the Union authorities. They immediately went on the dodge, sleeping out at night, changing their camping place frequently, coming in to the house only when they were sure the coast was clear. Around them they gathered a band of eight or ten young men who were likewise unpopular with the authorities, and they were known as the "Taylor gang" or the "Taylor party," depending on how the speaker felt.

They were an interesting pair, those Taylor boys. Hays, the older, was named for Captain Jack Hays, in whose ranging company their father had served in the early days. He was the quiet one, good-natured, courteous, friendly. Doboy (the census taker in 1850 put his name down as Phillip, but he always went by his nickname) was the fire eater. He was always starting something that Hays had to finish for him. Hays never questioned anything his brother did, always admired him, and always backed him up—with bullets if necessary. Both of them were good-looking boys, rather short but well and strongly built, with black hair and keen dark eyes. Hays was single, but Doboy had married "a very handsome girl of good family." Because of the disapproval of the girl's parents and the watchfulness of the Yankee soldiery, the wedding took place on the prairie with the bride and groom on horseback, and their honeymoon was spent in Doboy's outlaw camp.[2]

The cattle-gathering business, along with the constant danger of arrest, was responsible for the Taylor boys' change of address a year or so after their trouble began. Their new headquarters was somewhere in the limestone hills near Fort Mason where the deer and the antelope played, and also the Indian. A garrison of Yankee soldiers was stationed at the Fort and apparently there was no love lost between them and the Taylors. Major Thompson, the post commander, was especially unhappy with them. Tom Gamel, who was living near Mason at the time, says Hays had run the major out of a saloon once just to show him who was boss. It is doubtful if Hays would have done such a thing, but that, or something else, caused the trouble to break loose in November of 1867.[3]

Half a dozen different versions of the story are in existence. The one that got back to J.B. Polley, who lived within five miles of the Creed Taylor place on the Ecleto and knew the family well, said that one day when Doboy was whooping it up in a saloon at the northeast corner of the square in Mason, Hays got tired of the noise, picked up a newspaper, and went outside to read. He sat down with his back against a hitching post, and just about that time a file of soldiers came up. One of the privates knocked his hatbrim up and asked him what in hell a damned old rebel could find to interest him in a newspaper. Hays pulled his hatbrim down and went on reading.

By now Doboy and one of his friends had come out to
see what was going on. Doboy said to the sergeant in
charge of the detachment, "You had better call off your
man pretty damn quick or that quiet fellow there will kill
him."

"Oh, I don't think he is as bad as all that," replied the
sergeant scornfully.

Encouraged by this conversation, the private took hold
of Hays' hatbrim a second time and jammed it down over
his eyes, and thereupon Hays got off the ground and shot
him dead. The sergeant was killed by one of the Taylors'
friends.[4]

At that moment Major Thompson drove up in an am-
bulance with his wife. The newspapers reported the story
from here on, and as they told it he ordered the arrest of
the Taylors, telling them that he wished to investigate the
matter, and if the soldiers were to blame he would see
that they were punished. This did not suit the Taylor boys
at all. In that day and time an earnest Southerner often felt
that he would be shamed in the eyes of posterity if he
allowed any Union official to arrest him. Besides, surrender
would mean giving up their guns and putting themselves
at the mercy of their enemies. They refused to give up.
So the major took a pistol from one of his men and tried to
make the arrest himself. It was the last mistake he ever
made.

The Taylors seem not to have been much disturbed by
all this blood and excitement. They rode out of town without haste. Hays even came back after the grub sacks they
had thrown over an oak limb out in front of the saloon.
The place was soon swarming with angry soldiers, but by
then there were no Taylors in sight.[5]

It was time now for an older head to take charge. Creed
Taylor had followed his sons out to the frontier without
giving up the ranch in Karnes County, and it was he who
began coolly to lay plans for getting out of the country.

His first move was to give George Gamel a horse to show him and his boys a safe path to Fredericksburg, as George's brother Tom noted when he wrote his memoirs many years later. Back on the Ecleto the Taylors stood at bay, and the soldiers were not far behind them. The Galveston *News* for December 3, 1867, brought its readers up to date on the state of the skirmishing:

> Military in Karnes.—We understand that the expeditionary forces that recently left this city went no further than the vicinity of Ecleto, the residence of Creed Taylor, who was himself away from home, only his wife and his son's wife being in the house. The party related that the old man had been hung and the boys soon would be and that they had an idea of burning the house down, which, however, they did not do. A very fine race horse belonging to Mr. Taylor was taken from the pasture and carried off; other horses, it is said were taken from the neighborhood, but for these receipts were given. Bacon was taken from the smoke house. These statements are given to us in such a manner that we place reliance upon them. . . . When the murderers of Major Thompson are caught we shall be in favor of their trial by military commission. . . . But to prey upon the property of their father and his family . . . is something we think highly censurable.

Creed Taylor's race horse, Dobbs, was famous in those parts and had been coveted by the Yankee officers for a long time before they found an excuse to take him. Legend says that Creed made strenuous efforts to get him back and finally succeeded, but not until after the horse was ruined.[6]

From this time on the Taylor boys were outlaws in the eyes of the authorities. A big reward—some say it was five thousand dollars—was offered for them, and they had a skirmish or two with men more brave than prudent who had a use for the reward money. One of these, Captain Littleton of Helena, was shot from ambush on his way home from San Antonio. Nobody could say for sure that the Taylor boys had killed him, but they got credit for the deed. Captain Littleton had let it be known that he meant to try to get the Taylors—had said, "I will do it or die"— and no further explanation of his demise seemed to be needed. A friend of his named Stannard died with him, and the double killing finally stimulated the military authorities to serious action.[7]

By this time some of the postwar confusion in Austin had been taken care of. General Reynolds, after being out of his job for a while, was back in the saddle as military commander. He was an efficient officer and was well aware that he was going to have to do something about the crime and disorder which was rampant all over the state. In the spring of 1869, he took the first step toward the elimination of outlaw bands, including the Taylor party, by casting about for some likely tools to use.

He found two of them. They were among the best-hated men in Texas in the sixties, though that was a distinction they had to share with a good many others. Their names were C.S. Bell and Jack Helm. For a time Bell was the more notorious of the two. He is described as "a fine specimen of physical manhood, being over six feet high, with blue eyes, light hair, full, flowing beard, and well educated. His literary intelligence was above the medium order, and he was for a long time a contributor to the columns of Bonner's New York *Ledger*. His articles were chiefly stories of the war, in which he figured conspicuously as a Union spy and scout." [8] There is evidence to show that Bell was a swaggering, overbearing bully, but for some reason the authorities decided to use him, and in the spring of 1869 he set out, armed with apparently unlimited authority, to arrest the bodies of people the officials did not like.

His first assignment was to go after Creed Taylor's boys. This was not a job to be undertaken lightly, and

Captain Bell did not feel like tackling it alone. Before he made any important moves, he joined forces with a strange character named Jack Helm, the mere mention of whom was once good for a shudder anywhere in South Texas.

Helm is hard to trace. He had worked for cattle baron Shanghai Pierce down on the coastal plain before he became an officer, but nobody knew where or what he had been before that. Victor Rose, who was acquainted with him, describes him as of medium height, thickset and athletic—not bad to look at. His character was less prepossessing than his looks. An extremely ignorant man, he was nevertheless convinced of his own wisdom and always able to explain why anything he did was the equivalent of an act of God. When anybody mentioned his exploits in his hearing he would swell out his chest and remark with humorous self-appreciation, "I God, I'm the man, ain't I?" [9]

Helm took occasion, after he had been operating for a while, to explain in the columns of the Victoria *Advocate* how he got started: "About the first of June I was duly summoned by the military authorities, through Captain C.S. Bell, special officer, to assist in arresting desperadoes in Texas known as the 'Taylor party.' We found this party near the rancho of Mr. Creed Taylor, and attempted to arrest them. We succeeded in wounding one, Spencer by name, the others effecting an escape. I now proceeded in company with Bell to the city of Austin, where I received emphatic orders to arrest the party." [10]

Apparently Helm made a good impression in Austin, for from now on Bell begins to drop out of sight and Helm becomes the leader of the "loyal" party, which was usually given the well-deserved title of "Regulators."

Back in DeWitt County he went about organizing a band of helpers by calling in Sheriff George W. Jacobs and instructing him to summon a posse of citizens "with such equipments as Captain Jack Helm might require, and ordered to report to him whenever directed." The posse was organized and ready to go by the third of July. How many of the men were in sympathy with Helm's ideas and how many went because they thought they had to cannot now be known, but the posse numbered about fifty when they rode south in the direction of Goliad County.[11]

Through the months of July and August there was a reign of terror in the cattle pastures between DeWitt County and the Gulf. The Regulators, backed by the might of the Union leaders, ranged over Bee, San Patricio, Wilson, DeWitt and Goliad Counties seeking whom they might devour. The Galveston *News* for September 23, 1869, reported "great excitement" and declared that "during the months of July and August they killed twenty-one persons and turned ten others over to the civil authorities." A great many of those killed were shot down while "attempting to escape." Not all of these victims were Taylor friends or relatives, but some of the most important ones were—the Choates, for instance. This family lived in San Patricio County, a long way from the Clinton neighborhood, but they took the Taylor side. Helm suspected them of harboring some of the men he was pursuing, and on August 3, 1869, he surrounded their house, killed old man Choate and his son Crockett, and shot up a neighbor named F.O. Skidmore who survived seventeen bullet wounds and retained enough spirit to write an account of the affair for the Victoria *Advocate*. A paragraph from his letter will show the kind of thing that was going on:

> They conducted themselves in an extremely boisterous manner while at the house, appropriating whatever they desired, as if they had killed a robber chieftain and had a right to appropriate his effects. They left me nothing, not even my

clothing and pocket change. They stole my saddle, six-shooter, and other things of less note. I cannot say what was taken from the house. Helm talked in a braggadocio style to Dr. Downs, the attending physician.[12]

A complete list of Captain Helm's company is not available, but among his prominent supporters in the Choate business were Captain Joe Tumlinson and Captain Jim Cox, both prominent citizens of DeWitt County who were active on the Sutton side of the Sutton-Taylor feud in later years. These men and others of the posse may have been persuaded that they were actually in pursuit of cattle thieves, as Helm always loudly maintained they were, and there can hardly be any doubt that some of Helm's victims needed killing. By hanging or shooting everybody he could get his hands on, he undoubtedly included some cattle thieves. Undoubtedly he also scared a good many more out of the country. But even the good people who were on his side hesitated to defend him, and the newspapers of the period, at first friendly to him, grew very restive as reports of wholesale shootings and executions came in. "This thing of putting down civil government," said the Galveston *News* on September 14, "and then employing 'regulators, under military authority,' to hunt up and execute people, according to their own notions, is not the best thing in the world."

Captain Helm was pretty sensitive to public opinion and had already published a card in the Victoria *Advocate* of August 19 explaining that an "erroneous impression" had got abroad—that he sought to molest no one, and that "to the honest, law-abiding citizen he offers protection." [13]

What he meant by "protection" may be deduced from his next move against Creed Taylor and his boys. It was a full-dress raid organized by Helm and Jack Bell in collaboration. The latter was encamped near Yorktown in DeWitt County when Helm returned about the middle of August from shooting up the Choates in San Patricio County, and together they determined on a double attack, each proceeding by secret and separate ways to Karnes County in the hope of catching the Taylors unaware. Fifteen of Helm's men were detailed to accompany Bell, who slipped out of camp under cover of darkness. Helm stayed behind in order, as he said, "to attract attention while Bell could operate." The next morning he himself set off by a circuitous route and had arrived within seven miles of the Taylor ranch on the Ecleto when he got word that the engagement was over. Bell's men had made a successful attack.[14]

Again there are variant accounts of just what happened. Tom Gamel, the Taylors' friend out in Mason County, heard that they were gathering a horse herd to drive to Louisiana at the time the blow fell. They were certainly getting ready to leave the country. As usual they went off at night to sleep in the pasture lest they be surrounded, and Helm made use of this habit to surprise them. He came up to the house after dark, placed a guard over the women to keep them from giving the alarm, and settled down to wait. In the morning, before day, the Taylor men rode in. Doboy and a friend named Westfall were first. Doboy already had one foot on the ground when his wife, hearing the sound of hoofs, screamed as loud as she could to give warning. Doboy took his foot off the ground and got out of there in a hurry, the bullets whistling past his ears. He was unhurt except for a slight wound in the arm.[15]

Hays was not so lucky. He charged the soldiers hidden behind the yard fence and was killed. The Galveston *Weekly Civilian* for September 2, 1869, told how it happened: "Hays, seeing his father, Creed Taylor, standing on the gallery, cut off from them, exclaimed to his companions, 'I will not leave my father there; I will go to him,' and at once charged the party, wounding five of the men and being himself literally shot to pieces."

Helm had broken camp on August 20, and the engagement with the Taylors happened on Sunday morning, August 23. On the twenty-fifth Doboy and a number of henchmen rode through Austin at midnight, well mounted and well armed, asking no odds of anybody. Next morning Captain Bell arrived, hot (but not too hot) on the trail. A week later he was back in town with a report that he had chased the fugitives to the wilds of Coryell County, north of Austin, where they had broken up and eluded him. He was either inventing a story or was very badly fooled, for Doboy and his friends Kelleson and Cook showed up in Crockett, more than a hundred miles east of Coryell County, on August 31.

It was their last stand. On September 7 they appeared at the town of Pennington, sixteen miles south of Crockett, and there a party was organized which came up with them the next morning at the house of William Conner on the Neches River. Doboy seems to have been completely surprised, but he refused to surrender, retreating to a log house for shelter and leaving Kelleson dead on the ground. After some brisk firing he and Cook gave up (out of ammunition, probably) and the posse started to take them back to Crockett. On the way, when dusk made accurate shooting difficult, they made a break for it and got away, leaving a bloody trail behind.[16]

It took two more years for fate to catch up with Doboy. He may have left the state for a while. Bell went as far as Georgia in pursuit of him but had nothing but the trip for his pains. In November of 1871 Doboy was living at Kerrville, or at least was making the place his headquarters. Creed Taylor by this time had moved out to Kimble County not far to the north, and the family may have reassembled in the new home.[17] Helm and Bell were no longer on Doboy's trail, and he had ambitions to get a job and settle down to a more or less peaceful life. The job he wanted was the agency for a New York firm of cattle buyers, but unfortunately the New York firm preferred the services of a man named Sim Holstein. Doboy was very much embittered over his defeat and went to work on the successful candidate. On the evening of his death, according to contemporary accounts, he called Holstein out of his hotel and engaged him in conversation over the gate. In the midst of it the explosion occurred. Since somebody may have heard it a different way, we had better let the *Express* tell it:

> Suddenly Taylor drew his pistol and fired at Holstein but overshot him—Holstein sprang over the gate, and before Taylor could shoot again, wrested his pistol from him and felled him to the ground with it. Taylor regained his feet, but was immediately shot down a second and third time. Then Taylor ran toward his house, calling on his friends for assistance. Another shot from Holstein brought him to the ground. His friends were prevented from doing anything by the determined attitude of Holstein. Taylor . . . survived six hours and died at 11 o'clock the same night. He was sensible to the last, and spent his last hours imprecating and cursing the man he had attempted to murder.[18]

It would be good to know more about Holstein. A man who could jump a fence under fire, take a Taylor's gun away from him, and kill him with his own weapon must have been one in a million.

With Doboy and Hays dead, Jack Helm, by now a captain in the State Police organized by Governor E.J. Davis, was able to concentrate on the Taylors who remained in DeWitt County, and before long the Sutton-Taylor feud proper was blazing away.

★

Bill Sutton Takes a Hand

William E. Sutton was the product of ancestors who came from England to Virginia a century before he appeared on the scene. His grandfather was a Marylander who served in the Revolutionary War and settled in Tennessee afterward. When the migration into Texas began, he caught the fever, packed up what he had, and came on down. At the time of William E.'s birth (his tombstone says it was on October 20, 1846) the family was living in Fayette County a day's ride north of Clinton, but by 1850 the Suttons were established in the Clinton neighborhood.

About all we know of Billy Sutton's youth is the fact that he saw service in the Confederate Army (Company A, Waller's Battalion) while still in his teens. When the war was over, he began life on his own in the little town on the banks of the Guadalupe.

By now he had developed into a good-looking young six-footer, gentlemanly and agreeable in manner, with blond, curly hair and blue eyes. He was not quarrelsome. A contemporary who knew him well said of him that "he was as honest and upright and law abiding as was the average man of that violent day. He was not a trouble maker, but he feared no man and would never, never run." [1]

They say he had a hearty laugh and liked to crack jokes. When asked what the "E" in his name stood for, he would say he didn't know, but "W.E.S." meant "Watermelon, Eggs, and Sugar."

In the crucial year of 1868, still unmarried, twenty-two-year-old Billy was living in a small house near Clinton and working at whatever turned up—ranch jobs, probably, with occasional stints as a peace officer. Being a law man at that time and place meant cooperating with the Yankee authorities. This was a good way to ask for trouble, and before long trouble came.

Somebody was stealing cattle in the neighborhood—a great many cattle. The tide of thievery which rose after the Civil War did not pass DeWitt County by, and the men of the countryside rapidly lost patience. In March of 1868, a gang of rustlers made an extra-large haul and headed north while the sheriff rounded up every able-bodied man in Clinton and prepared to go in pursuit.

As Bill Sutton's grandson, Ralph Calhoun of Victoria, heard it, Bill was passing a little time in one of the Clinton saloons when the sheriff came in for recruits, bringing the news that a very fine horse with a silver-mounted saddle had been run off with the rest of the stolen stock. Bill was a deputy sheriff and immediately prepared to join the posse.

"Bet you don't catch the man on that fast horse," commented one of the bystanders.

"Boys, when I come back I'm going to be riding that silver-mounted saddle," Sutton promised.

The posse pushed along fast on the trail of the rustlers until they came to a place where the gang had split up and ridden off in two directions. There was nothing to do but divide the posse and keep going. Bill Sutton took half the men and the sheriff rode off west with the remainder.

The trail led Sutton due north to Bastrop, where he caught up with the fugitives on March 25. What happened next got into the Galveston *News* for April 2, 1868:

On the 25th ult., as we learn from the *Advertiser*, Bastrop was the scene of considerable excitement, caused by the appearance of a posse from Clinton, DeWitt county armed with authority for the arrest of horse-thieves. Two of a gang of fourteen thieves had arrived in Bastrop a few days previously. The citizens from DeWitt seeing one of these on the street, called to him to surrender, but he tried to escape and was shot and killed. His name was Charles Taylor. James Sharp, another of the thieves, was arrested and taken to De-Witt. Two Germans from the country, father and son, named Longee, were accidentally wounded during the firing —not dangerously, however.

Another squad of citizens are in pursuit of other members of this gang of horse thieves.

On April 7 the *News* printed the sequel to this bad business:

We have learned from reliable authority that the squad of eight citizens under command of Mr. Sutton, who killed Charley Taylor in this place Wednesday, 25th inst., and captured his associate, James Sharpe, and started with him to DeWitt county, after passing Lockhart, riddled their prisoner with bullets, a short distance from that place and left the body on the roadside. We have heard no further particulars of this horrible affair, except that the citizens of Lockhart buried the deceased soon after the act was committed.

Back in Clinton, Sutton stepped into the saloon he had started from and the same man who had talked to him in the first place asked if he had brought back the silvermounted saddle. "Go and look under my slicker if you want to know," he answered. And when they looked they saw that the saddle had been placed on Sutton's horse.

The Suttons say that this episode was the start of the feud. The Taylors vigorously deny it. Charley Taylor, they declare, was no relative of theirs, not even a friend of the family, the identity of names being entirely misleading.[2]

The question "Who was Charley Taylor?" was debated away back in the seventies. In 1874, when the feud was making headlines all over the country, the Indianola correspondent of the Galveston *News* interviewed two men from DeWitt County (names not given) as to the causes of the trouble. His story states in one breath that Charley Taylor was "no relative" of the DeWitt County family, and in the next identifies him as a nephew of Buck Taylor and Pitkin Taylor.[3] Six years later (in 1880) Victor Rose, once editor of the Victoria *Advocate*, published an anonymous pamphlet called *The Texas Vendetta* in which he speaks of Charley Taylor as "a distant relation of the family of Creed Taylor." [4] Rose's pamphlet, now extremely rare, is generally reliable.

The Taylors and their friends don't mind admitting that the killing of Charley Taylor and James Sharpe "while trying to escape" was the kind of thing that got them stirred up to feuding pitch.

The way the Taylors tell the story, the real beginning of trouble was the killing of Buck Taylor. Buck was the son of William R. Taylor, a brother of Creed, Pitkin, and the rest.[5] Buck was often spoken of in the late sixties as the leader of his clan. When his cousins Hays and Doboy were in trouble with the Yankee troops at Fort Mason, they were said to belong to "the Buck Taylor party," and various scraps of information turn up which show that Buck (or William P.) was in demand among the Union authorities. It was not the Yankees, however, who finished him off on Christmas Eve of 1868.

There was an entertainment that night with exercises to be held in the courthouse at Clinton, and everybody who wasn't sick in bed planned to go. Lewis Delony was a little boy at that time, and it was his hard fate to be left to turn out the calves while his folks went on ahead. His friend Tobe Kelly stayed to help him; and as soon as the job was done, they scampered for the courthouse.

Nearly seventy years later Lewis wrote down what he ran into in the next five minutes: "The Courthouse was built in a big square of ground, and was fenced in with a plank fence on all four sides of this square. There were steps (or stiles) to go over the fence. These steps were open at the ends so a person could crawl under them. When we came down the street, we heard some loud talking, and as we passed the first saloon we saw a crowd of armed men in there. We hurried to get to the steps, when a man ran out of a saloon just ahead of us and shot at some one coming out of the saloon back of us. We ran under the steps at the square and waited until the battle was over. Dick Chisholm, a young man about 20 years old, who lived just across the street from our house was shot down and killed, within ten feet of us. I heard him say 'My God I am killed.' Another man was killed close to us by the name of Buck Taylor. As soon as the shooting was over, we ran to the court house and up the stairs. Just as we got to the head of the stairs, some one asked, who was shot. I said Dick Chisholm is killed. I heard a scream and saw Mrs. Chisholm his mother fall in a faint." [6]

Why was Buck Taylor killed? The Suttons say that a bunch of Taylors came to the saloon to tell Bill Sutton not to let the sun go down on him in DeWitt County again—that he called out, after they had delivered their message and turned to depart, "If you're going to start shooting, why wait till sundown?"—and that everybody opened up at once.

As the Taylors tell it, Buck Taylor drove a horse herd east that year and as a courtesy included a few head that Bill Sutton had for sale. Later, Buck found that Sutton's stock had been stolen and angrily taxed him with it. Sutton denied everything, but on that evening in 1868 he called Taylor out for what was supposed to be a friendly talk and led him into range of waiting rifles. Alfred Hays Day, official historian of the Taylors, goes on: "Dick Chisholm heard the shots and ran out to see what had happened. He was met with bullets and likewise slain in cold blood. When we had fully investigated these murders, efforts were made to bring Sutton and his henchmen to trial, but ended in failure." [7]

These conflicting stories show how hard it can be to trace a feud to its source, but there is more complication still. Some people still swear that the Suttons and Taylors started their feud in another state and brought it to Texas with their other essential furnishings. Captain Lee Hall, the famous Texas Ranger, heard that "the trouble started in the Carolinas, flourished in Georgia in the forties, and was brought to Texas with the household goods of the Taylors and the Suttons, who, oddly enough, elected to settle in DeWitt as neighbors." [8]

There may be a grain of truth in the legend. In 1905, not long before he died, Creed Taylor revealed to readers of the San Antonio *Express* that he was born in Alabama in 1820. Apparently the family came to Texas through the deep South and took its time on the road.[9] Possibly they got into difficulties en route—and possibly the story is an interesting bit of folklore.

★

The State Police

E.J. Davis got the blame for it. The idea had occurred to the Constitutional Convention of 1868-1869, but naturally, feeling the way they did about Governor Davis, most Texans were certain that anything he suggested was bad no matter who thought of it first.

In April of 1870 he asked the legislature to pass a bill establishing a State Militia to handle major disturbances and a State Police to take care of local difficulties. Both forces were to take orders from the governor, as "Commander-in-Chief of all the military forces of the State," and in case of "war or public danger" the laws might be suspended by his order. This simply meant that Davis was appointing himself absolute dictator, and a howl of protest went up.[1]

Among those who bitterly opposed the measure was Senator Bolivar Pridgen, of DeWitt County, elected by the Republicans and radicals but not completely sold out to the Davis gang. "I cannot, I will not yield my assent to a proposition so monstrous in its teachings as to confer upon Governor Davis the right to commit murder at his mere discretion," he thundered.

The only effect of the Senator's speech was to make him some important enemies and to involve him in the Sutton-Taylor feud. On July 1, 1870, the bill was passed and organization of the State Police force was begun. It was composed of a chief (Adjutant General Davidson, who later decamped with $34,000 of the State's money), four captains, eight lieutenants, twenty sergeants, and 225 men. One of the four captains was Jack Helm, who was sent back to the southeastern counties where he had operated with such bloody consequences before.

It was his plan to recruit his force in the counties where he was to work, and very shortly after his appointment he came to Gonzales to pick up volunteers. The editor of the *Index* asked him if he expected to take criminals or suspicious characters this time. "Oh, no," replied Helm, shocked at the very idea. "My men will be selected from all the counties in my district, not exceeding two or three from any one county. . . . I will not receive anyone indicted for crime, nor any who have not the business capacity to make a report." [2]

This was fine talk, but it meant nothing—Helm's new posse turned out to be a dead ringer for his old one. The old Southerners still refused to have anything to do with him and he was forced to recruit from the same group he had drawn on before. And his most potent fighters were soon to become known as the leaders of the Sutton faction when feuding broke out.

One was Captain Jim Cox, the patriarch of a large family living on a farm near Yorktown. He had settled in

DeWitt County before the war, migrated to California during the years of struggle, and drifted back with his accumulated children afterward, burying his first wife, who was a Wofford, somewhere beside the road. Captain Cox and his enormous beard had been conspicuous features of Helm's first group of Regulators, and now he reappeared as a leader in the second. There was a very good reason for his being there: it was about the only safe place for him with a county full of Taylors looking for his scalp.[3]

Even better known than Captain Jim was old Joe Tumlinson, a famous Indian fighter with a record that went back to the days before the Texas Revolution. He was living four miles west of Yorktown, not far from the Cox place, and his house was a rendezvous for the Helm-Sutton party. Old Joe was not much to look at. He was sixty-three years old at this time—bald headed and weather-beaten, and in the habit of wearing a pair of green spectacles which cast a sinister shade over his rough-hewn features. In spite of his glasses, said a newspaper correspondent, he could "see with his naked eye farther than any hawk this side of the Rio Grande; when he gets on his spectacles there is no telling what he can see." He usually carried three or four guns and bestrode a famous horse named Gray Eagle on which he would "ride a race over any kind of ground," and was guaranteed to "beat the best cowboy in Western Texas." [4]

The third of Helm's chief henchmen was Bill Sutton, in some ways the most notable of the lot. His agreeable personality has already been noted. After two years of guerrilla warfare he had added the cunning of the hunted to his equipment. The Taylors admitted that he was the hardest to catch of any of his party.

There is some doubt as to just when and where Captain Helm began operations. Jack Hays Day thinks he led his men on a hundred-mile jaunt west to McMullen County where they killed Buck Taylor's cousin, Martin Taylor, and his father-in-law Dave Morris. In mid-July Helm is said to have been present in Matagorda County when his old employer Shanghai Pierce ceased to be troubled by two Lunns, a Grimes, and a Smith, all suspected of killing cattle for their hides and tallow.[5] On the night of July 23 Helm, or somebody like him, turned up in Karnes County where a posse surrounded the house of one Pasqual, told him to come out, and wounded his little son when he refused. After that came the Kelly affair.

There were four of the Kelly boys living near the Taylors just south of Cuero. Pitkin Taylor's daughters had married Henry and William. Their brothers Wiley and Eugene were naturally Taylor sympathizers. In the same neighborhood lived John and Will Day, sons by a previous marriage of Pitkin Taylor's wife, Susan. They stuck together, as kinfolk did then, living on short rations sometimes, but never short on family loyalty and family pride.

Across the line in Lavaca County, on the road north to Hallettsville, was a little town with the lovely name of Sweet Home. About the middle of August a traveling company of performers presented an entertainment there (the papers called it a circus) and among those present were the Kellys—all four of them and their families, apparently. During the course of the performance something displeased the Kellys and they shot out the lights, breaking up the show. They said it was because the spectacle was indecent and unfit for their families to see. The other side contended that it was a case of too much bottled happiness. After the fireworks they went home, but Helm's State Police were soon on their trail.

On the morning of August 26, about daylight, three men rode up to Henry Kelly's gate and sat there looking the place over. Mrs. Kelly, old Pitkin Taylor's daughter, was up and busy about the house. Henry had just risen too. Pitkin, who was sleeping in the house, was still in

bed. Amanda Kelly recognized John Meador, who was on good terms with her husband, and a character from Clinton known as "Doc" White who had been a member of the posse that killed Charley Taylor in 1868. The third horseman was a stranger but they later found that he was a Hallettsville peace officer named Simmons. She remarked to her hsuband that there were three men at the gate and he immediately went to the door. "Step out here a few minutes," said one of them. "We want to see you." Like a fly responding to the invitation of three hungry spiders, Henry went out to the gate and found they wanted him to go with them to Hallettsville, the county seat of Lavaca County, thirty-five miles away. Undoubtedly Henry thought they wanted him for the Sweet Home business and agreed at once to go, but said he would have to catch up his horse. Going back to the house for his hat, he emerged with his six-shooter and cartridge belt, but they told him to consider himself under arrest and leave the pistol at home. When he laid it down, one of them picked it up and hung the belt on Doc White's saddle.

By now Pitkin Taylor was up and out, and while Henry went for his horse the old man engaged Doc White in conversation. White told him that things were desperately bad in Lavaca County—that they were having the same thing as martial law over there and many people were being outlawed.

As soon as Henry Kelly was ready they got started, first dropping by Bill Kelly's house a few hundred feet away where Sutton was holding Bill under arrest. This gave Amanda Kelly, who was extremely worried by now, time to hitch up and drive ahead four miles or so to the house of her half-brother John Day, where she waited anxiously for the posse to pass. It was her plan to go along with them as far as Sweet Home. John Day added to her fears by warning her that the boys were in serious danger, and when she heard a shotgun go off down the road, she could stand it no longer. She and her mother-in-law, Mrs. Delilah Kelly, got into the buggy and backtracked down the highway. They met the posse riding along quietly, strung out over a hundred yards of country road.

In a few minutes the men came to a place where a woodland trail wound off through the blackjacks and brush. Doc White insisted that this was the shortest way to where they were going and made the party turn aside. Henry Kelly protested. "Why are you going through that way? It is nearest to go by the house. My wife wants to go with us and her child is at the house. Let's go by there so she can get the baby."

White said, "No, it's nearer this way."

"Go by the house and get the child," Kelly told his wife, "and meet us in the flat above William Day's."

Mrs. Kelly later told, in a sworn statement, how she drove off up the road but grew so fearful of what was going to happen that she went back and ascended a little

hill from which she could see posse and prisoners. They were halted in a little clearing and William Kelly was filling his pipe. "After preparing his pipe," she said, "he dismounted from his horse and took out a match, and was squatting down with one knee on the ground, and engaged in striking a match on the bottom of the boot of the other leg, when William Sutton shot him. William Sutton was sitting on his horse at the time, and I saw him as he suddenly raised his gun, and pointing it downward in the direction of William Kelly, fired it off. William Kelly in his doubled up position sunk to the ground. In an instant another gun fired and I saw Doc White with his gun to his face, pointed in the direction of Henry Kelly and smoke between them, and Henry Kelly instantly fell from his horse. A general firing at the bodies on the ground by the party then ensued, and the ground where the bodies lay and vicinity, was so enveloped in smoke as to completely hide the men and bodies, too, from my vision. After the firing ceased, and when I was screaming and making towards the bodies, I saw the men escape in the brush."

Mrs. Kelly made her statement on October 13, and it was sworn to before a justice of the peace two days later, supported by numerous affidavits. The affair looked so much like cold-blooded murder that the authorities could do no less than bring in the members of the posse for a hearing. Helm seems to have been brought in too, though he was probably occupied in arresting the other Kelly boys when the shooting took place.

They were all turned loose. Though accused of a major crime, they were allowed to testify in their own defense, and their plea that they had shot the prisoners in the act of trying to escape was held by the grand jury to be valid.[6]

The decision caused tremendous resentment, and baying far out in front of the pack was Senator Bolivar Pridgen, who risked being shot in order to say exactly what he thought about the killings. "Unwarranted, inhuman, and outrageous" were the mildest words he used. Helm and his policemen, he asserted, "had the country completely terrorized." [7]

The state press was generally aroused—even the Republican papers. The Austin *Republican* reminded its readers that Sutton and White were still under indictment for the killing of Charles Taylor at Bastrop two years before and declared that Senator Pridgen was "entitled to the thanks of the public for ferreting out and exposing the infamous wretches who under the name of 'State Police' are engaged in taking the lives of the good citizens of Texas."

The governor himself could not long ignore the public clamor and at the suggestion of Adjutant-General Davidson he first suspended and then discharged Helm from the force.[8] There was much rejoicing over this happy event, but it was a little premature. Helm had been elected sheriff of DeWitt County at the last election and was still in a position to do plenty of harm. The main result of his removal, so far as the feud went, was to push Bill Sutton out in front. The Helm-Taylor trouble became the Sutton-Taylor feud.

It took one final outrage, however, to drag the thing out into the open and bring it to full development. This was the murder of Pitkin Taylor. Just when it happened is not clear. Pitkin's tombstone says he died in March of 1873, but the carving of the date is not finished, as if the carver had some doubts about the matter. For some reason the event was not noticed in the newspapers, and only the Taylor version of it has been told. Their story is that Bill Sutton and four of his men got hold of the bell of one of the Taylor oxen one day, probably in the summer of 1872, and at night crept into Pitkin's cornfield, rattling the bell to get the old man out of the house. Out he came in his night clothes and was shot down in his tracks. His daughter, the widow of Henry Kelly, tried to go to his assistance and almost fell over one of the assassins crouched in a fence corner. Clearing him at a bound, she made for John Day's house a quarter of a mile away and came back with help, but too late to do more than pick the old man up and try to make him comfortable. He lived for something like six months, and finally just gave up and died.

It was at his funeral that the Taylor boys made up their minds to wipe out their enemies at any cost. The reason appears in Alfred Hays Day's account of the funeral:

It was a grim and tragic scene. The burial plot was near the river on a shaded knoll. Around the open grave the relatives of the murdered man were assembled. Among the mourners were young Jim Taylor, son of the deceased, and five other youthful kin of the slain man. In hideous contrast to this grief-stricken group, across the river while the funeral services were being conducted Bill Sutton assembled his cut throat gang in bold mockery. With raw drink and coarse jest and wild firing of guns they celebrated the death of Pitkin Taylor while he was being lowered into the grave.

Hearing this hilarity, Jim's mother, who had borne up well under her grief, broke down and wept. If there had ever been a doubt in young Jim's mind what he should do about the slaying of his father, it was cleared up then. If ever a man was provoked into taking the law into his own hands Jim Taylor was justly provoked; if ever a man had reason to see that Justice was meted out, Jim Taylor was inspired by that reason.

Putting his arm protectingly about his mother, he vowed to her: "Do not weep mother. I will wash my hands in old Bill Sutton's blood!" The five other youthful relatives likewise pledged themselves to the same cause.[9]

It would be interesting to hear what Bill Sutton would say about his part in this scene, but he has been lying in the Victoria cemetery for over eighty years, and there is nobody left to tell it his way.

The old Taylor cemetery tells no tales either. It lies

across the fields off the main highway about four miles from the town of Cuero and a mile or so from the old Taylor homestead. A few Taylor kinsfolk have been buried in it in recent years, and Pitkin's tombstone still stands up against wind and weather while Pitkin himself sleeps the long sleep beneath in the shade of a hackberry tree, his wife Susan and his son Jim beside him. There is no gate in the barbed-wire fence around the plot, for pilgrims to that lonely spot are very few. Across the Guadalupe River, flowing past only a few yards away, the trees and underbrush have grown up thick and green. Whatever happened on the other side to infuriate the Taylor boys, there are no footprints left to tell about it now.

A month after the funeral the State Police force was laid away also. A new Democratic legislature passed a bill to abolish it, over the governor's veto, on April 22, 1873. The whole state of Texas rejoiced over the news, but the sighs of relief were deeper and longer in DeWitt County than anywhere else. The only unhappy feature of the situation there was the fact that Jack Helm was still around—was, in fact, the sheriff—and there was no telling what he would do next.

★

The Young Men Take Over

The nursery of the feud in the early seventies was really Major Carruth's school in Clinton. The major was a Confederate veteran who had set up his establishment in a big two-story building; and everybody, Suttons and Taylors alike, went to him for instruction. That the feud never broke out on the school grounds is probably a tribute to Major Carruth's firm hand and personal courage. That it festered in youthful minds was inevitable.

Lewis Delony tells about one boy who was to play a feudist's role later. His name was Jake Ryan, and at the mature age of nineteen years he was a pretty determined character—so much so that the major had to bring matters to a showdown. Jake fought like a wildcat, but the major was too much for him. Next day Jake stayed home, but along toward noon, five men, two of them Jake's half-brothers, rode up to the schoolhouse and told Major Carruth to come out. He came out into the yard, stopped, and asked them what they wanted. As Delony tells it, "They told him that he whipped Jake, and that they were going to hang him for it. One of them got down his rope and started to ride to Major Carruth. The major told him to halt; if he came any further toward him he would kill him. The man stopped. Major Carruth said, 'I want to explain why I had to correct Jake.' He then told them what kind of talk and swearing Jake used toward him in the school before all the girls and boys.

"In the meantime we boys gathered around our teacher, and were going to protect him the best we could. I was about twelve years old at that time. I had a pocket derringer. It shot once at a time. Some of the other boys had pistols, and some of them were sixteen or eighteen years old. About this time several men came running up the street with guns in their hands, when these men saw them, they rode away." [1]

By the time of Pitkin Taylor's death, the boys in Major Carruth's school were young men, all full of fire and vinegar. In 1873 they took over the feud.

Bill and Jim Taylor, Pitkin's sons, were the new leaders of the Taylor party. They were good-looking fellows, bold and athletic and sociable, at least among their friends. Bill was high-strung and irritable and apt to get into scrapes because of his temper, but Jim was under better control. In a happier time and place neither of them, probably, would have done anything particularly out of line, but this was not a peaceful time or place, and the Taylor boys had bloody hands before they were really grown men.[2]

Their object in life was to get Bill Sutton, and they wasted no time in going after him. About four months after Pitkin was laid away under the hackberry tree, they had their chance.

In the spring of 1873 the new community of Cuero was springing up across the river from Clinton on the route of the Gulf, Western, and Pacific Railroad, drawing business, people, and even buildings from the county seat. Among the bright new frame structures in Cuero was Banks's Saloon and Billiard Parlor. This was supposed to be an improvement over anything of the kind in that part of Texas, and life was incomplete for any man or boy who had not sampled its delights. In time Bill Sutton made a pilgrimage over there. It was the break the Taylors had been waiting for. On the night of April 1, 1873, Jim and Bill, with their cousin Alfred Day and perhaps some others, rode quitely up to the front of the saloon.

They had an exciting five minutes. Several of them pushed their gun barrels through the door and opened fire. Sutton was shot down. The lights went out. While everybody inside was running and shooting and wanting to know what the hell went on there, the Taylors rode away without being molested. Sutton wasn't even sure who was in the doorway shooting at him. He said he knew it was a kid because the gun kicked him down, so he filed charges against Alfred Day and a junior member of the clan named Scrap Taylor.[3]

It took him a couple of months to get over his injuries, but by the middle of June he was ready to appear in court and the case against the boys was called for trial in Clinton. On the sixteenth he got into a buggy, being unable yet to ride on horseback, and set out with a bodyguard of his friends—Horace French, Doc White, John Meador, and Ad Patterson. The Taylors were waiting for them down the road. John Meador was hit in the leg and French's horse was killed, but that was all the damage. Being young and overanxious, the boys fired too soon.[4]

A posse set out to scour the country for the bushwhackers, but as usual no trace could be found. Sutton's case against the two young Taylors also seems to have come to nothing. At least there is no record of anything further being done about it.

The date of the affair at Banks's saloon is given by John Wesley Hardin, who seems to have prided himself on his memory for dates when he wrote his autobiography. It was shortly after this fight that he joined the Taylor party, rode with them for about a year, built up an enormous reputation as a gunman, and went on in a very short time to become Texas' leading desperado. He was supposed to have killed a couple of dozen men, though he was only twenty years old at this time; his coolness and bravery under fire were almost legendary; and his sleight of hand with his pistols was something to tell stories about. "He is the man," said a humorous reporter, "who can make Catherine-wheels of a pair of six-shooters and drop a man with every barrel. With a good retriever to go in the chaparral and get them out when killed, he can bag forty per day, and has done it scores of times."[5] Just why Billy the Kid has beaten John Wesley out for first honors (or dishonors) in the nation is hard to say, for Hardin had more on the ball in every way than the buck-toothed little rustler from New Mexico.

At the time he joined the Taylors he had already had as much experience as most hardened old desperadoes of thirty-five. He had been in and out of jail for years, sometimes for things he thought he had to do; sometimes for killings which seemed to other people a little impulsive, to say the least. Over a year before, he had married Jane Bowen and had shown some signs of settling down in the vicinity of his cousins Gip and Manning Clements over in

Gonzales County, but his good resolutions were punctu-
ated by long rides with the law on his trail, arrests, escapes,
and periods of meditation behind the bars.

There was kinship between the Hardins and the Taylors,
John Wesley's cousin Jeff Hardin having married Creed
Taylor's daughter Mary,[6] though the family feeling was
not strong enough to bring Wes into the feud until the
summer of 1873. In fact he himself speaks of traveling
about the country in June of 1872 in company with
Captain Jim Cox, who had ridden with Helm's Regulators
and was hated by all the Taylors.[7] A year later, however,
things were different. The two factions were intent on
exterminating each other—were running each other
through the woods and down the roads all over the
country—and were making every effort to enlist as many
fighting men as possible on either side.

In April of 1873 Hardin ran up against the recruiting
officers. He was on his way from Gonzales to Cuero and
had "followed the furrow" as far as Mustang Motte near
Yorktown when he encountered a man on a gray horse,
armed with a rifle and two six-shooters, who turned out
to be Jack Helm. After announcing himself as the sheriff
of DeWitt County, Helm offered to shake hands, but
Wes would not shake with him. Instead, he pulled his gun.
We have only Wes's word for the conversation that followed, but here it is:

"You are armed, defend yourself. You have been going
around killing men long enough, and I know you belong
to a legalized band of murdering cowards and have hung
and murdered better men than yourself."

"Wesley, I won't fight you, and I know you are too
brave to shoot me. I have the governor's proclamation
offering $500 for your arrest in my pocket, but I will
never try to execute it. If you will spare my life, I will be
your friend."

The upshot was that they had two meetings at which

Helm tried to persuade Wes and his friends to join the Sutton faction. At the first conference Wes said he wanted to be neutral but agreed to think it over and come back for another talk. On April 16, 1873, he and his cousin Manning Clements, with Manning's brother-in-law George Tenelle, rode over to Jim Cox's house for a final meeting with Cox and Helm.

As Hardin tells about it, Helm and his henchmen offered to help Wes get out of trouble if he would join them, but when they added that his relatives Clements and Tenelle would have to be killed, he refused to listen to any more and warned all the Suttons present to stay out of his country. "When they had gone," he adds, "I told Manning and George just what had passed between us and George remarked that it would not be a week before the murdering cowards made a raid on us." And sure enough along toward the end of April, 1873, Helm and fifty men rode over to Gonzales County looking for trouble. Hardin and his friends had gone on a cow hunt, so the party succeeded only in scaring the women who had been left at home. The visit was enough, however, to needle Hardin into action. With Clements and Tenelle he met Jim, John and Scrap Taylor and together they agreed "to fight mob law to the bitter end, as our lives and families were in danger." [8]

The way to "fight mob law" in those days was to get behind a bush and pick off the opposition as rapidly as possible, and this system was immediately put into operation.

Captain Jim Cox was under indictment in Karnes County—probably in connection with some of his State Police activities—and in May or June of 1873 he rode down to Helena, the county seat, to answer the charges. Joe Tumlinson rode with him; along with a newcomer to the district named Chrisman, and a third party whose name appears variously as Griffin, Wallace, and Ragland. On the way home the party had just crossed the San Antonio River in the northern part of the county when old Indian-fighting Joe Tumlinson began to wag his head from side to side and sniff the wind for an ambush. The tradition in the Cox family is that he decided to head for a different cross-ing in order to play it safe. Captain Jim laughed at him and kept on; as a result he and Chrisman were mowed down by men in hiding, while Tumlinson and the other man, some distance in the rear, had a chance to escape.

Jack Hays Day says it was Jim Taylor, Scrap Taylor, Alfred Day and Bud Dowlearn, returning from a horse-buying expedition to the Choate ranch, who came upon the Cox party by accident. John Wesley Hardin hints that he was there too, but says coyly, "As I have never pleaded to that case, I will at this time have little to say." [9]

Not many days later the Taylors got Jack Helm.

The climate was now becoming a little warm for the Helm faction. Sutton had gone to Victoria to live. Helm himself had edged over into Wilson County to the west where a new post office called Albuquerque had been set up. He was working in a local blacksmith shop on some sort of "agricultural implement" which he had invented—supposedly a cotton chopper.[10] Humanity, however, was never to profit by his labors, because Hardin and Jim Tay-lor rode over and ended them—permanently.

The story usually heard is that Helm recognized Taylor the minute he came into the blacksmith shop—that he started to run crazily around the inside of the building—and that Jim pursued and pumped lead into him. Hardin says they fought—Helm with a knife and Jim with a pistol. Hardin joined in with a shotgun, and that was the end of Jack Helm. Hardin's version at least relieves Helm of the charge of dying like a coward, no matter how many other black marks he may have accumulated.[11]

Things were moving faster now, and the very next day after Helm was killed, the Taylors marched on Tumlinson

—though it may be, as Hardin asserts, that Tumlinson was just getting ready to march on them. At any rate, when the Taylors reached Tumlinson's stronghold, they found him all forted up in his house with a little army of fifty men overflowing onto the galleries. It was already dark when the thirteen Taylors arrived, and at first they thought it might be possible to creep up close enough to eliminate a few of the men sleeping on the galleries before they were detected. The dogs smelled them and raised an alarm, however, and three Taylor men were sent back to town for reinforcements while the remaining ten settled down to the job of holding the Suttons in their fort. By daylight they had seventy-five men on the ground, and when Deputy Sheriff Dave Blair showed up with a posse to help the besieged, he was unable to do anything against so great a number.

The skirmishing went on all the next day and the following night, and then another group of citizens appeared on the field of battle with the purpose of making peace. Hardin's account gives these anonymous arbitrators credit for "preventing a collision," and inducing the factions to agree to a truce. The newspapers got a different story. The Gonzales *Enquirer* heard that "On Monday night last Wesley Hardin, accompanied with some 35 or 40 men, well armed, marched to the residence of Joe Tumlinson, in DeWitt County, surrounded his house and held him in siege for two nights and one day. In the meantime Joe Tumlinson and party, numbering 15 men, and strongly fortified, managed to send a courier to Clinton for the sheriff to hasten to his assistance. After summoning about 50 men the sheriff started for the 'seat of war,' where he arrived on Wednesday morning and found Hardin's men formed in line of battle. A brief conference with the parties revealed . . . that a compromise had been arranged . . . and the two parties were ready to proceed to Clinton, a distance of 16 miles, and sign documents to that effect. The line of march was at once taken up, Hardin's men leading the column, the sheriff's posse following, and Tumlinson's party bringing up the rear. Arriving at Clinton, Hardin halted on one side of the town, and Tumlinson on the other, while the sheriff's men marched directly into town. After signing the documents and having the same recorded in the clerk's office, both parties quietly dispersed to the intense gratification of . . . peace-loving citizens.

"Our informant states that it is the general belief that the conditions of the treaty will be rigidly observed, and that the relentless war . . . is at an end." [12]

The general belief was quite wrong. One of the laws of feuding seems to be the principle that a truce holds only long enough for the signers to take cover. In this case the guns were allowed to cool off for about three months. Toward the end of December they blazed again, and Wiley Pridgen, a brother of the ex-senator, fell dead in the doorway of Jim Pridgen's store in Thomaston. The killer was officially unknown, but gossip said he was avenging the death of Neil Brown, whom Wiley had killed in a private feud.[13]

The Taylors had no doubts about who was responsible, however, and the day following they gathered for another attack. They heard that Sutton and some of his men were in Clinton, holed up in the courthouse, and they headed for town on the run. The big battle might have been fought then and there, but again the citizens, led by Judge H. Clay Pleasants, begged them not to endanger others while they carried on their private fights, so the Taylors pulled out for Cuero. Immediately the Suttons left the courthouse, hot on their trail. The two gangs skirmished all the way to Cuero, where the Suttons took up a position in the old Gulf Hotel, and the two parties aimed pot shots at each other for a day and a night. Then old Joe Tumlinson appeared with reinforcements and it was the Taylors' turn to stand a siege. They went to earth in a stock pen, and it began to look as if these moves and countermoves might go on indefinitely.

By now, however, the inhabitants of Cuero were beginning to feel very much bored with the whole business. They descended on the belligerents and talked them into signing another armistice, hollow as these treaties must have seemed by now. They all signed, as usual, though Jim Taylor is supposed to have made an exception of Bill Sutton when he agreed to lay off his erstwhile foes. Somebody suggested that it would be a good idea to let Jim and Bill fight it out individually, but nothing came of the suggestion.

As soon as the parties had loped off to catch up on meals and sleep, the good men of Cuero got together and made some agreements of their own. They organized the Cuero Protection Club, announced their firm intention of dealing very vigorously with anybody who tried to make a private battleground out of Cuero, and installed a huge alarm bell for use in an emergency.[14] Possibly because of their efforts there were no further pitched battles or prolonged sieges in the town, but terrible deeds were done all over the county and the killing went on without interruption. One Johnson was killed in Clinton; a McVea was slaughtered in Cuero; a third man named John Krohn was seriously wounded—all within the space of a week in the first part of January,[15] 1874. And Bolivar Pridgen's old Negro, Abraham, was killed by prowlers, supposedly because he would not give any information about his master's whereabouts.[16]

It is impossible for any of us now to conceive the depth of terror and hatred in that distracted region. No one's life or property was safe. A man had to be on one side or the other lest both sides make war on him. Hard characters had been enlisted by both parties—men without a drop of mercy in their make-up. You might ask why people didn't move away and avoid the trouble. The answer is that all the people who put a high value on their safety had already left. The ones remaining were the breed who wouldn't run.

★

Bill Sutton Checks Out

In the winter of 1874, Bill Sutton's luck ran out. He was a brave man, but a cautious one, and up to now his wits had been a match for anything the Taylors could think up against him. Even John Wesley Hardin pays tribute to his instinct for staying out of tight corners. Since the fight at Cuero, he had had two horses shot out from under him, and he had done a disappearing act once (says Hardin) when John Wesley made a special trip to Victoria to look him up. Sutton's skill in taking evasive action gradually improved the tactics of his enemies, however, and finally they caught up with him.

There are so many versions of what happened at this point in the feud that nobody can be sure of all the details, but these facts are agreed on: Sutton had gathered a trail herd, Kansas bound, in the early days of March, and he himself was planning to get out of DeWitt County. Some say he was tired of fighting, others believe that he was merely following his stock to the northern market and had every intention of returning as soon as his business was finished. Still others have handed down the story that his good friend and former battalion commander R.M. Weisiger, a breeder of race horses, was shipping some of his stock to New Orleans and Sutton had agreed to act as his agent.[1]

At any rate on the eleventh of March he appeared on the streets of Indianola with his wife and his friend Gabriel

Slaughter, and just before sailing time he went aboard the steamer *Clinton,* outward bound for New Orleans.[2]

Gabe Slaughter makes only this one brief appearance in feuding history, but his case is interesting because it shows how a feud could reach out and lay its deadly finger on the lives of men and women for whom the trouble had very little personal interest.

Gabriel was a fine young man whose father, John E. Slaughter, had come to Clinton from Kentucky before 1853. The Slaughters were kin to Judge H. Clay Pleasants and to Dr. Joseph Weisiger of Clinton, and ranked with the most highly respected families in the county. Mrs. John Slaughter and her daughter Miss Susie Slaughter added a good deal of tone to Clinton society, though there were not many people in that Texas town who were considered, either by the Slaughters or themselves, as in the same bracket socially.[3]

Just why Gabriel Slaughter went along with Sutton and his young pregnant wife is another subject for debate. S.R. Weisiger, grandson of the race-horse breeder, says that Gabe had been engaged to help handle and dispose of the livestock. Sutton's kinswoman, Mrs. Tim B. Cobb of Del Rio, has heard that Slaughter was to have gone to Kansas with Sutton's cattle and that Bill Meador was to have made the trip by boat. At the last minute, she says, Gabe became ill and Meador was sent with the herd in his place.[4] If this story is true, what happened to Slaughter was intended to happen to Meador, who had actually been involved in the feud. However the pieces of the puzzle fitted into place, Gabe was on the deck of the *Clinton* with Sutton and his wife as the crew made ready to get the ship under way.

Undoubtedly Sutton had made careful preparations to keep his motions dark. He knew that the Taylor boys were determined to prevent him from getting out of the country, and he must have done everything he could think of to throw them off the scent. It is believed in DeWitt County that a Victoria banker notified Bolivar Pridgen of Sutton's plans, and Pridgen notified the Taylors. This story may be true, for Pridgen's brother Wiley had been killed in a private squabble with Neil Brown and his son, Sutton supporters, and Pridgen was bitter against all Suttons and their connections.

At this point John Wesley Hardin re-enters the story. His father and his brother Joe were now living in Comanche, Texas, out on the edge of civilization far to the northwest of Dewitt County. Few people in the Clinton-Cuero region knew them by sight, and it seemed to Wes a lucky break when Joe Hardin came down to visit him in the first days of March. The grapevine (started by the Victoria banker and encouraged by Bolivar Pridgen) had brought word that Sutton was at Indianola. Presumably he was trying to get away, though nobody knew just when or how he meant to do it, so Wes persuaded Joe to go down there and see what he could find out. Joe agreed, and drifted over with Alec Barekman, a cousin of his from Comanche. They made friends with Sutton, who was a sociable person, and soon found out that he had taken passage on the *Clinton* for the eleventh. The word came back, and at once the Taylors began to get ready. Jim and Bill Taylor went by secret ways to Indianola and "six or eight" of their henchmen, names unspecified, filtered in behind them. They readied two good horses to be used in the escape, and on the afternoon of the eleventh they were prepared.[5]

From the Taylor point of view the whole performance was delightfully simple. It was ironical how smoothly everything went off, considering how hard Bill Sutton had been to catch for so many years. There he stood on the deck, unsuspecting, talking to his wife and Slaughter as the crew cast off. It was about one o'clock. He saw the two young men coming down the dock, hurrying, almost at a run. His descendants say that Slaughter recognized them and said, "Here come Jim and Billy. Hadn't we better get our guns?" and that Sutton replied, "No, don't worry. They are too much men to do anything now." [6]

Either because of misplaced confidence in Taylor manhood or because he was caught completely off guard, Sutton was shot through the head and heart before he could even reach for a pistol—assuming that he was carrying one. Jim Taylor did the shooting. Meanwhile Gabe had tried to help Sutton and had been fired on by Bill Taylor. They were dead shots, those Taylor boys. Slaughter dropped with a bullet in his brain.

A minute or two after the shooting started, Jim and Bill Taylor were racing back along the dock. At the stock pen where Hardin's men were branding cattle, they got their horses and headed west. Nobody offered to molest them. [7]

Next morning they turned up at Bol Pridgen's house in Thomaston. The ex-senator was so glad to hear of their success that he organized a party. "It was an occasion for great rejoicing," says Alfred Day, the Taylor's cousin. "Though Pridgen had a negro cook, he sent for more, bought two turkeys and a lavish meal was prepared. Needless to say everybody had a good time."

From Pridgen's place they rode on with full stomachs to the Hardin headquarters in Gonzales County, where Wes was gathering a herd to drive to Wichita, Kansas. Jim intended to go along when the cattle started north in April. Bill planned to remain in Texas, lying low.

Mrs. Sutton came back to Victoria with her unborn child, her husband's body, and her grief. She lived there until she died, an old, old lady. Her descendants continue to make the best lives they can for themselves near Bill Sutton's grave. They have not been feudists, and enjoy an excellent reputation even among Taylor sympathizers.

Mrs. John Slaughter and Miss Susie Slaughter went back

to Kentucky. They kept in touch with their friends in Clinton, but they never came back and Miss Susie never married. Feuds cast such shadows on innocent people sometimes.

★

Bloody Harvest

Feudists have short memories for their own trespasses and long memories for the trespasses committed against them, and the Sutton murder aroused the Sutton clan to the highest pitch of resentment. From what happened later it is certain that some of them, at least, must have resolved on wholesale revenge.

The mantle of Sutton fell on the muscular shoulders of a young man named Reuben or "Rube" Brown, who was serving at the time as city marshal of Cuero. He had many friends and is described as a fine figure of a man. Victor Rose says he was "liberally educated, and almost a perfect specimen of physical manhood." [1] His first job was to run Bill Taylor down and arrest him. About the second of April, 1874, he managed to do this, though no details of how or where he did it have ever been published. He was smart enough to send Bill off to Galveston at once for safekeeping, and Wes Hardin complains in his autobiography that "we never had a chance to rescue him." [2]

Meanwhile the herd of cattle Hardin had been gathering was well along in its journey up the trail, and a second herd had been placed in charge of "Doc" Bockius (always pronounced *Brockus*) and started likewise. Bockius might as well have a word here. He was a little man of mysterious antecedents—a nonpracticing physician who kept the post office in a double chimney in his home at Sedan, eight miles south of Smiley in the southern part of Gonzales

County.³ He seems to have been a modest and friendly man who might easily have been forgotten, but his later adventures were weird enough to give him a place in local legend.

As soon as Bockius had gone with his men and cattle; Wes and Jim got into a two-horse buggy and set out, expecting to visit Hardin's parents, brother, and wife at Comanche and catch up with the herds later. They reached Comanche late in April and lingered around the local gin mills until Hardin killed Charley Webb, a deputy sheriff from Brown County, and brought the Fates and Furies down upon their heads. Hardin called it self-defense but the citizens of Comanche called it murder. The town rose up in hysterical anger. A mob hanged Joe Hardin (who hadn't done much of anything except to be John Wesley's brother) along with several of his cousins, ran Wes and Jim Taylor all over the country, and made things so hot for them that they were glad to get away with their lives.⁴

There is no use in following the ins and outs of the chase. The point of most interest for us here involves the foreman and hands who had escorted the cattle belonging to Jim and Wes up the trail as far as Hamilton in the next county to the east of Comanche. Doc Bockius, the foreman, had come over to Comanche to report to his owners just in time to be arrested with Joe Hardin and his father at the time of the Webb killing, and the rest of the cowboys were rounded up as soon as the officers could get over to Hamilton, though they had done nothing at all but drive those cows. The names of the men were Scrap Taylor (a cousin of Jim and Bill), Kute Tuggle, and Jim White. There were three other men with the herd—Alfred Day, Ples Johnson, and Pink Burns—but they got away under cover of a heavy storm after they had been arrested. The first three, declaring they had not done anything and were not afraid to go back, set out under guard to answer to charges of having stolen the herd of cattle they were caring for. The charge was made by Dick Hudson of Cuero, a prominent Sutton peace officer who will be heard from again. Hardin declares that on the twentieth of June he received a letter from Ranger Captain Bill Waller warning him that the three prisoners were on their way back to DeWitt County and if they were interfered with in any manner "he would kill my father and little brother, and probably my wife and child, whom he now held as hostages." The prisoners, including Doc Bockius, were deposited in the Clinton jail without any trouble.

This was the opening the Sutton party had been waiting for, and they did not hesitate to commit one of the worst outrages of the entire feud—they hanged those three boys.

There was very little against them. Alfred Day says that Tuggle had never carried a gun and was not involved in the feud, and that Jim White was a newcomer from Mississippi. Scrap Taylor, of course, could not deny his name.

On the night of June 20, 1874, a mob gathered around the courthouse where the prisoners were confined (the jail being full). It was a rainy night and black as the bottom of a cellar—a perfect time for a deed of darkness. The guards made a feeble effort to do their duty. Jim Wofford, who was in charge at the jail, threatened to shoot the first man who came up the steps, but a voice behind him remarked that he would fire only one shot, and that quieted him. Then the leaders of the mob threatened to burn the courthouse down if the prisoners were not turned over to them, and no further resistance was made. Thirty or thirty-five men rushed in; the three boys and Bockius were led out into the blustery night.[5] Next morning one of Judge Lackey's boys found three of them hanging in the pasture next to the cemetery. He had gone to school with Scrap Taylor and Tuggle, and it took him a long time to recover from the shock of that morning vision.[6]

It might be added that the Sutton party allowed word to

get around that they had hanged the men near the cemetery so as to make less work for their friends.

Bockius was the only one who got away, and his escape has passed into the folklore of DeWitt County. The story says that the little doctor, who was a Mason, made a distress signal as he was being hustled along, and someone in the crowd took pity on him, putting his own hat, which was of a peculiar shape, on Bockius's head and pulling him back into the crowd. Then Joe Sunday, who weighed three hundred pounds, took little Bockius up behind him on his horse with his slicker around both of them, and there was hardly an extra bulge to indicate that the horse was carrying double. In that way they smuggled him out of town, and he took care to disappear thereafter until it was safe to come back.

Joe Sunday was a great character and storyteller and used to laugh himself into a quivering jelly over this episode, always concluding in his nasal voice, "Hit were my schemery."

A week later, on July 8, they got George Tenelle. George is not one of the men whose names have been handed down to posterity crowned with feuding laurels, but he died the way so many did—alone, surrounded, unafraid, and trying to fight back. He was regarded by the Suttons as a leader, perhaps because he was one of the few middle-aged men left in the field by this time, but more probably because he was trusted by Hardin and the Taylor boys and had been with them on several occasions when pistols and blood had been drawn. Since the affair on the deck of the steamship *Clinton* had started the Suttons on their career of extermination, George had grown a little weary of the feud, and they say in his home country that he had made up his mind to pull out for Mexico. Apparently his plan of action became known, for on July 8 the sheriff of Gonzales County, armed with papers from San Antonio, summoned a posse of nine men and started for

Tenelle's home, which was located in the southern tip of Gonzales County fifteen miles west of Cuero. It was not necessary for them to cover the whole distance. George had already left home—may have been camping out for safety for some time—and hoped to be on his way to Mexico very shortly. He had stopped in at John Runnells's place on Five Mile Creek, ten miles east of the present town of Smiley—tied his horse in the bottoms and gone to the kitchen for something to eat—when the posse caught up with him. Tenelle heard them as they were surrounding the house, ran to a nearby cornfield, jumped the fence, and tried to get to the woods at the lower end while concealed by the stalks of corn. At the far end of the field he found his escape cut off and went to earth behind a brush fence where he was shot to death.[7]

The posse gave out that he had been repeatedly summoned to surrender and had refused; also that he had snapped his hammer on a defective cartridge five or six times and was ready to shoot a good one when he was killed. The Taylors smiled derisively at this story, knowing well what would have happened to George if he had surrendered—the same thing that had happened to Bill Sutton on the deck of the *Clinton*. They looked much grimmer when the story came to them, as such stories will in killing times, that the posse had come to the house, after George had been carried back and laid out on the floor, and had trooped in to see if the victim were really dead. When they were sure he was done for, they laughed and whooped for joy and rode off firing their pistols.[8]

By now affairs in DeWitt County were obviously drawing to a head, and the entire state, not to mention numbers of people in other states, sat up and took notice. With typical wry humor they commented, the Austin *Statesman* proposed that in view of the crowded condition of the penitentiary, district judges give prisoners convicted of horse stealing the choice of going to jail or to DeWitt

County. The saga of Wes Hardin grew, also, and correspondents wrote in to their editors such stories as this: "He kills men just to see them kick, and on one occasion charged Cuero alone with a yell of 'rats to your holes!' and such a shutting up of shops has not been seen since the panic. . . . There is a reward of eighteen hundred dollars for him, and it will be well earned when he is captured. He is said to have killed thirty men and is a dead shot." [9]

The governor began to receive frantic requests from citizens to send them some Rangers, for God's sake, since that at least a hundred and fifty men on a side were getting ready for a pitched battle. Some estimates of the forces that would be involved once open warfare broke out ran as high as two thousand men, all told.

So along toward the end of July, Captain McNelly set out for DeWitt County with a group of forty Rangers, about ten of whom were volunteers fresh from Austin and due for surprises when they found what they were in for. They met McNelly at his home in Burton and the entire force slipped into Clinton before the factions knew they were coming.

It was high time. Bill Taylor was about to go on trial at Indianola and there was talk about either rescuing him or lynching him. It goes without saying that there were plenty of men available who had the nerve and the inclination to do either. Besides, court was about to convene in DeWitt County and hope was growing that the officers might, with the help of a few Rangers, get some indictments returned for a change. The whole county had taken sides and drawn in dozens of people from adjoining counties. Every man was a walking arsenal. Night riding and waylaying were attempted or expected every night. If somebody from outside did not straighten these things out, the only possible ending was the extermination of one side or the other. Captain McNelly, as he wrote back to Adjutant General Steele on August 3, found the citizens "very much pleased with our presence." [10] This was undoubtedly an understatement. The citizens felt about him as a drowning man does about a life preserver.

There was a young man along with McNelly's troop whom it would have been a pleasure to know. He was strictly an amateur at the ranging business and seems to have gone along primarily to get material for a newspaper column, for he made many jokes about his inexperience, fear of firearms, and general timidity. "The captain said he would shoot the first man who ran away from the fight," he wrote back to the Austin *Statesman* just after the arrival of the company at Clinton on August 1, "and I look upon my death warrant as already signed and sealed."

Signing himself "Pidge," this reporter wrote half a dozen long and humorous letters to his paper from the seat of conflict,[11] thereby throwing much light on the manners and customs of feudists in DeWitt County when times were really rocky. "They have a cute way to carry six-shooters around here without breaking the law," he commented. "Every man carries his coat tied behind his saddle, and in its folds is a peace preserver of the Smith and Wesson persuasion."

Joe Tumlinson was the man causing most of the excitement. At the moment he and his Suttons were "wrathy," as Davy Crockett would have put it, to kill John Taylor and Bolivar Pridgen. Pridgen was very prudently out of the country, but John Taylor, an uncle of Jim and Bill and Tumlinson's near neighbor, had a big horse ranch on his hands and didn't feel like leaving. On August 5, he came to the Ranger camp for protection, and with him came a brother of Kute Tuggle (lately lynched with Scrap Taylor) and a Clinton citizen named King.

Pidge described Taylor as reminding him, on foot, of "an old sun-dried bucket about to fall to pieces," but admitted that on horseback "his powers of endurance are almost incredible."

One reason for John's visit was a desire to help with the cases against the Suttons which were to come up at that term of court. On August 6, he went with a squad of Rangers to Yorktown after a witness who could testify against Tumlinson in the matter of the murder of Bol Pridgen's Negro. They located their witness without difficulty, but on the way back they were stopped by a band of armed men—something like fifteen of them. "Who are you?" demanded one of the fifteen.

"Who are you?" returned Sergeant Middleton, whose great virtue does not seem to have been originality.

"*Cuida'o!*" shouted the man in the road. "Look out! Give 'em hell, boys!"

In the fight which followed, the Rangers managed to get behind a fence and stand off the attacking party with the loss of two horses and a bullet through Ranger Turner's shoulder. The witness from Yorktown disappeared with dramatic suddenness. In a little while the attackers stopped the fight, pretended great surprise at finding their opponents were not Taylors, did what they could for the wounded man, and turned over some of their own horses to replace the ones they had shot. Captain McNelly reported to the adjutant general next day that they were "commanded by old Joe Tumlinson," and that they were after the witness who ran off. "But I caught him this morning and have him in camp," he added. "They are all alike Taylor & Sutton equally turbulent treacherous and reckless." [12]

On August 8, he went into more detail about the situation: "I feel entirely able to whip Tumlinson with the men I have if it must be a fight but will need more men, fifty men cannot overawe these people; they have been in the habit of overriding the officers of the law so long that it will require more force than I have, to 'bluff' them. We cannot expect help from the citizens, they had rather pay out half of all they own than obey the summons of the sheriff. The firing on my men the other night was done for the purpose of killing a witness whose evidence would convict them of cold-blooded murders, 'Joe' Tumlinson included. At the first fire the witness fled and on their approaching my men their first words were, 'By God boys, he is gone. 'Twas he who ran off through the fields.' His death would relieve them of many fears."

McNelly and his men had never seen criminal proceedings conducted as they were in Clinton beginning on the third of August. "The Tumlinson organization were in Camp near the County seat during court term, and subsistence furnished them by the sheriff, under the pleas of being prisoners but they were never disarmed. No effort was made by the Judge of the District or the Attorney for the State to have them disarmed or dispersed, although I told them that orders to that effect would be gladly received and promptly executed."

Tumlinson's trial, which was scheduled for August 14, apparently went off according to the old pattern of intimidated witnesses, courtroom packed with armed supporters, and a general atmosphere of contempt for anything but the will of himself and his supporters (who, it must be confessed, usually included the county peace officers).[13] Pidge reported at the end of the month that "Court has adjourned, and Tumlinson's trial is postponed till next term."

Encouraged by this success, the Tumlinson or Sutton party made up their minds to do something about the impending trial of Bill Taylor at Indianola on September 24. They called a meeting at Indian Motte, circulated a public letter quite openly, as McNelly reported to his chief, with the intention of "going to Indianola to see that 'Taylor' gets justice. It seems to be the impression that they will kill him before the conclusion of the trial." [14]

The Taylors were ready to take up the challenge. It was rumored that Wes Hardin and Jim Taylor were coming back to take a hand, and McNelly said, "If they come I will kill all my horses or have them." [15] He sent a detachment of Rangers, including the trembling Pidge, to surprise Hardin at his home one morning before daylight. They were relieved to find nobody at home.

The excitement spread even to Austin. Governor Coke ordered the adjutant general to go to Galveston and take command of the Lone Star Rifles and the Washington Guards, volunteer military companies of the type which flourished in many Texas towns after the Civil War. Surrounded by these gallant and gorgeously uniformed warriors, Bill Taylor took the steamship *Harlan* for Indianola. Reporters noted that he had a "quick eager eye" and was dressed in cowboy fashion—on his head "a white felt hat, well worn, and under his chin a cord . . . in order to secure it on his head while careering over the plains after cattle." [16]

At ten o'clock next day the case was called, and Taylor's lawyers asked for postponement. In such trials delay was a favorite tactic, and many a case was "worn out" by putting off trial. It was hard on the prisoner to stay in jail for years, but he usually felt that it would be still harder to be hanged.

The postponement, in this case, was granted, and very shortly after Taylor entered the courtroom, he walked out of it on his way back to his dungeon.

He sailed for Galveston at three o'clock on the steamer *Morgan*. The Indianola brass band escorted him and his guard to the boat with martial music, and practically everybody in town came along so as to be present in case anything happened. Nothing did happen, for a wonder. Bill went back to jail and waited another year for an act of God to get him out.[17]

Meanwhile the disappointed clansmen left behind at Indianola, both parties of them, proceeded to get the fight out of their systems as quickly and conveniently as they could.

One episode occurred on September 25, when Corporal Ellis of the Rangers was getting ready to bring witness John Taylor back to Cuero. They had boarded the freight train which ran from Indianola to Cuero when Rube Brown, marshal of Cuero and a leader of the clan since the death of Sutton, attempted to climb the steps in order to attack Taylor. The Rangers, of course, were doing all they could to keep the factions apart, but Mr. Brown insisted that he was coming aboard. Corporal Ellis insisted that he was not coming aboard. Only the drawn pistols and firm attitude of Ellis and his men prevented a ruckus. McNelly reported: "They have apologized to me for it and said they were drunk, but I constantly fear a recounter under just some like circumstances." [18]

The "recounter" was postponed from day to day. A deceptive calm settled down over DeWitt County while everybody waited for the December term of the district court. The lull was partly due to the floods which swept the country, held up Captain McNelly on his way back to Clinton with his family, and made it necessary to go from Clinton to Cuero by boat. "It is now predicted that this country will be unhealthy," commented Pidge, "but I had supposed it had been so for some years. They say that congestive chills will now be very prevalent, but they can scarcely be worse than the Winchester bullet fever, a disease which has been raging here for years, and which has carried off some of the best citizens in a very sudden manner."

Pidge likewise revealed a sudden impulse on the part of both Suttons and Taylors to confide in the Rangers: "Joe Tumlinson has just sent to camp for a guard to keep the Taylors off. A guard is now at Taylor's to keep the Suttons off, and we have to mount one in camp to keep them all off."

He noted also, when he went to church in Clinton, that there were no old men in the congregation—"not a silvered head could be observed, and I suppose that old people are never seen in DeWitt. If they are not killed they hide out in a country above here called 'the brush,' where the words of the gospel will never reach them unless used as wads for a double-barrelled shotgun."

But the most wonderful thing of all was the conversion of Captain Joe Tumlinson. "Now, Lord, let Thy servant depart in peace," marveled Pidge. " 'Uncle Joe' has been convicted, converted, baptized, and received into the church, and is considered by his friends to be sincere. Some of the Taylor party, however, express some doubts about it."

A few days later Tumlinson lay down on his bed and died. The Masons buried him, and Pidge wrote to his paper about Captain Joe's last fight with the Indians at Indian Motte in 1844.

This took a good deal of the wind out of ex-Senator Pridgen's sails. He had been trying to get at Tumlinson and his men from a safe distance (Galveston). Once he came as close as Indianola but the Tumlinson bunch ran him out somehow, and he went back to Galveston where he persuaded a U.S. deputy marshal to accept twenty-seven writs for service back in DeWitt County. These arrived in early November, about the time Old Joe got religion, and before anything could be done with them, he was dead.[19]

When District Court convened early in December, McNelly reported that the session was "quieter than it has been for years," but added that "the Dist. Attorney is drunk most of his time and when sober is of no earthly account." [20] Apparently it was still impossible to clean up DeWitt County and the purgation by blood had to go on for a few more weary months. The Rangers left, admitting they had not done much good, but their presence at least delayed the next bloodletting. The spring and summer of 1875 were comparatively calm.

★

Last Battles

Like many another historic spot on this planet, Indianola has more attractions for the imagination than for the eye. Hardly a trace is left on the low, weedy shores of Matagorda Bay of the thriving little port of a hundred years ago, through which a great part of the lifeblood of Texas immigration and commerce flowed. On September 15, 1875, it was struck by one of those terrific storms which ravage the Gulf Coast at intervals and from which the natives reckon time. The town never recovered from the ruin which followed, though it took a second storm in 1886 to deliver the final blow.

On the fifteenth, Bill Taylor was back in his cell in the Indianola jail, brought there for another trial. He hoped he was going to get loose this time, and was eager for the trial to begin. Like the rest of Indianola's permanent and transient residents, he was not much concerned when a storm came up from the east and began to rattle the windows and send waves crashing higher and higher on the beach. September storms were to be expected on the coast —it was not unheard of to look out on flooded streets and people going about their business in rowboats. It would all be over pretty soon.

But it was not over pretty soon. All that day and the next the wind constantly increased in violence until it was a screaming torment to everybody. Great seas began running into the town, smashing everything in their path. Buildings near the waterfront crumpled like cardboard and the water was soon filled with pitiful fragments of houses, their late occupants sometimes clinging to them and crying for rescue. Before it was over, upward of three hundred people had lost their lives.[1]

In the jail along with Bill Taylor were three other prisoners, one charged with rape and two with cattle stealing. Before long the cells began to fill with water and there was a good chance that the prisoners might be drowned. District Attorney Crain became concerned about this and went down to the jail to see how things were going. He wore only his pants, shirt, hat and shoes, and before he arrived the pants and shirt had been almost blown off him. He found that the jailer had resisted all pleas to release the prisoners because he was afraid he could not handle them once they got outside. Mr. Crain thereupon went and got the keys and let the men out himself.

The only place in town where there was any chance of safety was the new courthouse, a concrete structure which was built on the highest ground. They all made it over there, but Crain's hat blew off on the way. Bill Taylor took his own hat off his head and put it on Crain's. As he did it he laughed and said, "Bill Crain will never prosecute me." As it turned out, he was a good prophet.[2]

In the midst of that horrible uproar and overwhelming danger Bill Taylor proved himself a man. He sallied out into the waves again and again to bring back a man or woman struggling in the shadow of death. When, about 3 A.M. of the seventeenth, the wind suddenly shifted to the northwest and blew the water back into the Gulf faster than it had come in, there were almost a hundred people on the little hill, and many of them owed their lives to Bill Taylor.

As soon as he could, Sheriff Fred Busch rode from his home a mile away to the courthouse, tied his horse to the fence, and approached the battered crowd gathered around it. While he was talking to the survivors, Blackburn, one of the prisoners who had done his part in the rescue work, snatched the sheriff's gun from its holster, held him and his deputies up, and escaped on Busch's horse with Bill Taylor behind him.

A little way out of town they met Guy Michot, a Negro,

on horseback. Bill stopped him and said, "Get down. I've got to have that horse. I'll send him back and pay you for the use of him after I get to where I'm going."

"Naw suh! Nobody rides this horse but me. You nor nobody else can have him."

"Do you know who I am?"

"Naw suh, I don't know who you is, but if you was the Angel Gabriel you couldn't have this horse."

"I'm Bill Taylor."

"Yas *suh*, Mist' Billy. He's your horse."

According to legend Bill rode the horse away and really did send it back and pay for its use. It must have been a good animal, for he was not in the clutches of the law for some time.[3]

Where he went and what he did are still matters of mystery, but he may have made one public appearance during his retirement. On the night of November 17, as Rube Brown, marshal of Cuero, was dealing monte for some Negroes in the Exchange saloon, he was killed by five men who entered unexpectedly and opened fire. Two of the Negroes playing at him were seriously wounded. The Dallas *Weekly Herald* expressed what was in the minds of everybody: "The general supposition is that it was Bill Taylor's crowd, as Brown was the officer who arrested him previous to his escape at Indianola during the flood, and it is stated that Taylor sent Brown word that he would kill him." [4]

Things rocked along about as usual for a month or two after that with one Negro lynching[5] and several assorted skirmishes to break the monotony. The acts of violence during these months included the death of Billy Buchanan, who was killed by the Taylors because they thought he was leading them into an ambush, and the wounding of Joe Bennett when a party fired from hiding on him and Bill Taylor.[6]

Then, on December 27, there was a big shooting. The

Sutton and Taylor historians give diametrically opposite accounts of how it came about. The most anybody can be sure of is that on that date Jim Taylor and some of his friends rode into Clinton and left their horses at Martin King's stable. The Taylors say Jim had come in to give up and stand trial. The Suttons think he was planning to burn down the courthouse. Sheriff Weisegar decided he had better have help in either case, so he sent to Cuero for Deputy Sheriff Dick Hudson and a posse. With the arrival of this gang on the scene a number of young men, who had not previously figured in the feud, made their debut. Some of them who were to become better known were Curry Wallace, Bill Meador, Kit Hunter, Buck McCrabb, John McCrabb, Bill Cox, Jake Ryan, Joe Sitterlie, and Ed Sitterlie.

There seems to be no doubt that Martin King betrayed his Taylor friends by locking up, or otherwise detaining, their horses when the posse rode into town. Jim Taylor, Mace Arnold, and a man named Hendricks were unable to reach their mounts. They ran through Martin King's house and tried to get to an old log building (it had been the first DeWitt County courthouse) in the orchard. As Jim Taylor ran around the corner of the house Kit Hunter leveled down on him. Jim stopped, dropped on one knee, and fired just as Hunter pulled the trigger. Jim had his right arm broken and Kit got a bullet through his hat. In those days so many people wore breastplates that it was common practice to shoot for the head, as Jim did. He tried to get over the fence to join his men but never succeeded, for by then the air was full of bullets. Hendricks and Arnold (who was sometimes known also as "Winchester" Smith) were riddled as badly as he was. The three bodies were laid out in the courthouse and eventually turned over to the relatives for burial.[7] Jim Taylor was returned to the earth in the old Taylor cemetery, where he still lies. His tombstone bears this inscription:

An amiable father here lies at rest
As ever God with his image blest
The friend of man, the friend of truth
The friend of age, the guide of youth

He would have been twenty-four years old on his next birthday.

The entire personnel of Dick Hudson's posse was tried for his murder at the next term of court, but technically they had the law on their side—they had acted under the instructions of the sheriff and his deputies. So they got off.[8]

Jim's death left the Taylors without a leader, and really marks the end of the Sutton-Taylor feud proper. The two sides continued to fight, but over new grievances and with new alignments. Bill Taylor, who might have returned to lead the clan, stayed on the dodge out in West Texas until he was picked up by the Rangers at Coleman on April 15, 1877.[9] It is not easy to follow his movements from then on, but he spent some time in the Austin jail, where John Wesley Hardin (recently brought back from Florida by the Rangers) saw him. In June of 1878, he was tried at Indianola for killing Sutton and was acquitted. A little later he was taken on a change of venue to the now-vanished town of Texana for his last trial. Judge Lackey of Clinton defended him and he was acquitted of the charge of killing Slaughter.[10]

How such a verdict was possible may well puzzle a non-Texan, but it was no surprise to anyone at that time. If a case dragged on long enough witnesses dropped out of sight, evidence was no longer easy to get hold of, and people got tired of having the old skeleton hauled out of its mortuary wrappings.

A year later he was in more trouble. The Rangers arrested him again after a difficult chase and put him in the Cuero jail. According to Captain Lee Hall (who had succeeded McNelly) his friends tried to burn the town down in an attempt to free him, but did not succeed. Finding himself under indictment for horse theft, assault to murder, and forgery, he lost his nerve (again according to Lee Hall) and told the Rangers everything they wanted to know. "He has made a clean breast of everything and told on all his friends, giving their hiding places and plans of operations for the future and says he will decoy them into any trap I may set." [11]

Hall thought the plans included bank robbery, but apparently he had no evidence, and one gets the impression that he had a special grudge against Bill which predisposed him to believe all the rumors that were floating around. Somehow Bill got out of it all and lit out. In January of 1881, Captain Roberts reported to the adjutant general that Bill Taylor was out in the hills of Kimble County "raising cain with the inhabitants" and that the Taylors and the Gormans were "marshalled in warlike attitude." On the Gorman side was old Dick McCoy who had fought the Taylors in DeWitt County and it looked as if the old feud might be revived on alien ground. [12]

The difficulty apparently died down, and that is the last we hear of Bill Taylor. According to his DeWitt County relatives, he moved to Oklahoma, worked as a peace officer, and was killed in the performance of his duty by an unnamed desperado. [13]

★

The Brassell Murder

Times were stormy in 1876. The feud was almost burned out, but as usual things seemed most hopeless just before they began to improve. Captain McNelly passed through Cuero on his way to the King Ranch in April, and wrote back to Adjutant General Steele that he had had to stay over for a couple of days because of the "disturbed condition of affairs." The sheriff of Henderson County had raised a posse of Sutton men and tried to arrest a young Taylor sympathizer named Allen. A deputy sheriff of DeWitt County was killed and several others, including Allen, were badly wounded. McNelly waited to see if the thing was going to develop into a major battle and did not leave until the town was quiet again.[1]

In the fall trouble flared up once more with the perpetration of one of the worst crimes of the entire feud—the brutal murder of Dr. Philip Brassell and his son George.

The Brassells were fine, well educated people, originally from Georgia, where the doctor had been a member of the Constitutional Convention of 1866, and of the legislature from '68 to '70. In 1870 he moved to Texas for his health. He was a victim of chronic bronchitis and catarrh, according to his descendants, and of tuberculosis, according to newspaper stories of the time. He brought with him to his new home at Shiloh or Shiloh Mills, three miles east of Yorktown, his wife, a grown daughter Nancy, his older sons George, Theodore and Shehane (nicknamed Bant), and four other children—daughters Jenny and Len; sons Jeff and John.[2]

The Brassell family found itself in the midst of a community of strong-willed people, many of whom were prominent in the Sutton party. Among these neighbors were some of the Cox family, sons of Captain Jim who had been bushwhacked in 1873 by the Taylors. There was also Dave Augustine—an older man who was pretty well thought of in the community, but no friend of the Brassells. One story says that Dave ran against Dr. Brassell in a school election and was beaten, which caused the bad blood between them. At the time the trouble broke out Miss Amanda Augustine and Miss Nancy Brassell were the teachers of the Shiloh School.

From all available evidence it would seem that the real cause of trouble was Dr. Brassell's oldest son George. For some reason, perhaps connected with an earlier stage of the feud, George had been out of the country for several years. Old men still say that he was suspected of complicity in the waylaying of Captain Jim Cox and that there was a price on his head, though there is no evidence to show that such a thing was true. It is a fact, however, that deadly enmity had developed between the Cox connections and George Brassell, and there must have been a reason.[3]

In the fall of 1876, George came back. He must have known that this meant trouble. A possible reason for his act is the fact that his father was in poor health and perhaps wanted to see him. Some back-stage activity went on after he returned which has never been completely revealed, though a few bits of gossip still float around the Cuero neighborhood. There seems to have been a fight in which George Brassell and Bill Cox were mixed up at a dance in the Shiloh schoolhouse. Lewis Deloney says he met Bill Cox the next day (a Sunday) on his way to Cuero to have his gun fixed. He complained that it had hung fire the night before. Probably it was at this dance that the episode of the saddles occurred. It was a queer thing, but true in all places where the feuding instinct flowered in Texas, that both sides would go to parties and behave with the utmost politeness to each other unless something drastic happened. At the Shiloh dance the evening went off all right, but during the festivities somebody stepped outside for a few minutes, took a shingle out to the chicken house, got a good load of chicken droppings, and smeared the saddles of a number of the young Suttons. They found out about it when they mounted and were about to start for home. Dave Augustine and Bill Meador blamed the Brassell boys and did not propose to take it lying down.[4] In Texas in 1876 an insult could not be laughed off and real trouble developed.

At the trials for murder which followed—there were a

good many later on—it developed that a man named Hardin, another neighbor of the Brassells, also had a grievance against them. He had even got out a warrant charging that Theodore Brassell and William Humphreys had threatened his life. Hardin lost his nerve, however, and refused to cooperate with a posse which came out from Cuero on September 15 to arrest the two boys. A deputy who rode out on this wild-goose chase testified later that there had been talk about a killing. One member of the posse suggested that they all go to the Shiloh church some night, and that each should pick out a man, march him off, and "bust him open." [5]

The following Tuesday, September 19, somebody did bust the Brassells open.

The story went round at the time that the Doctor had had a premonition of death. A correspondent reported to the Galveston *News* that he had already bought his funeral clothes and selected a spot for his grave, and that on this particular day he had given his wife the money to pay his burial expenses.[6] His grand-daughter, Mrs. Georgie Brassell Alford, doesn't believe it. He may have been ready for death, as a good man should be, but he certainly did not expect it to come so soon.

According to family tradition, Dr. Brassell made a night call that evening and came home a little before midnight, very tired. As he undressed, he told his wife that he had seen a gang of men just off the road near the house. Some were standing. Some were kneeling or squatting. He thought they might have been burying something. He could make out a strikingly marked pinto horse whose owner he knew, and he wondered aloud what they were up to. Still wondering, he got into bed.

Everybody else was asleep by now. Bant (seventeen) and Theodore (eighteen) were bedded down on the gallery; the younger children were inside. All the lights were out and the dogs were curled up under the house. It seemed that this was going to be just an ordinary night for the Brassell family. Then came a clatter of hooves as a party of horsemen rode into the yard, helloing loudly, raising the dogs and waking the boys on the porch. "Light up!" they shouted.

Dr. Brassell roused himself and called for lights also, and his wife lit two lamps before going to the door. She heard a voice give an order to surround the house, and then someone they called "Mr. Sheriff" was ordered to search the premises. A tall, heavy man with a handkerchief around the lower part of his face came in. Mrs. Brassell at first supposed that it was their neighbor, Deputy Sheriff Callaway. Nancy thought it was Sheriff Weiseger until she held a lamp close to his face and found that it was nobody they had ever seen before. The man, whoever he was, explained that they were a posse from Gonzales County in search of horse thieves, and that they were particularly anxious to catch William Humphreys—though they could hardly have expected to find him there at that time of night.

The men outside kept in the shadow so as not to be recognized, and several of them had handkerchiefs over their faces as an extra precaution. The Brassells knew well enough who they were however, and Nancy is said to have jerked the mask from the face of one of them just to make sure.[7]

Several of these men took Bant and Theodore to the smokehouse, where they kept them under guard. Others began bawling at Dr. Brassell to come out: "Old man, get up and come out of there! Come out, old man!" The Doctor came out as requested and the women and George came with him, George without hat, shoes, or coat.

Apparently finding nothing of interest in the house, the "sheriff" and his men likewise emerged and let it be known that they were going after the Ainsworth boys. All four of the Brassell men were going along as prisoners or guides, or

both. George was allowed to come back inside to get his clothes, and as he sat in a chair putting on his boots, his mother asked if he knew who the men were. "I know them all," he said, and named three of the boys who had been working as deputy sheriffs and fighting the Taylors for the past year. George seemed nervous and worried as he spoke.

When he was dressed and outside again, one of the posse asked him how to get out of the yard. He replied curtly, "You can get out the way you got in." His father remarked more gently, "Here is the gate. Don't tear down the fence." Those were the last words Dr. Brassell's family ever heard him speak. A minute later the men all vanished into the midnight darkness. Ten-year-old Jeff tried to follow his father and brothers but was driven back by a blow from a pistol butt.

It was about five minutes before the family heard the first shot; then came two or three more; and finally a whole fusillade followed by the sound of running horses and the noise of men whooping and hollering happily. The two Brassell women ran out at the first report, thinking they had heard Bant scream. Mrs. Brassell called into the darkness, begging them not to shoot any more. When the noise had all died away, she went back into the house and lay down on the bed with the terrified and hysterical younger children. It was the only thing she could do.[8]

Nancy found her own way to heroism. Though she was a little thing who never weighed more than eighty pounds, she got Swindler, the hired man, to catch a horse which she rode to Yorktown to summon help. The story of her night ride picked up voltage as it was handed down to later generations. One chronicler changed the gentle old horse to a "wild colt," and pictured Nancy as "calling wildly that her father and brother had been killed in the night." [9]

About an hour after the shooting, Mr. Humphreys and Mr. Ainsworth, neighbors, came to the house to tell Mrs. Brassell what she already knew well enough—that George and her husband were dead. Bant had got behind a cactus in a fence corner and had escaped to bring them the news. A little later Theodore showed up, alive and unhurt. He had saved his life by climbing a tree.

Bant later testified that the men had picked him out as the youngest and tried to send him home, but George had interfered. "Don't go," he said. Then turning to their captors he added: "If you're going to kill us, kill us all. And you might as well do it here and now, because I am not going any farther. You can take me to court if you want to, but you can't prove anything because I haven't done anything."

"No, you haven't done nothing but rob your neighbors," said a man whom Bant identified in court—and he shot George in the face. Bant also identified the man who shot his father a moment later.

Neighbors carried the crumpled bodies of the dead men into the house and they all sat around waiting for day. Somehow the news spread, and by daylight many people had come in. There was much indignation. Dr. Brassell, in addition to his claim on public interest as a good man and a servant of the community, was a high-ranking Mason and his death was a matter of concern to people all over the state. In DeWitt County the better citizens began to feel that this was indeed the last straw.

On the very day of the Brassell tragedy, September 20, the coroner issued a warrant for Dave Augustine, Jim Hester, William Cox, William Meador, and Jake Ryan; and the men were brought to the courthouse at Clinton. People noticed how young they were. Augustine was middle-aged and Meador was somewhat less than that, but Cox, Ryan, and Hester were not much more than boys. Cox would be twenty-three in December. Only Meador had a bad reputation. Augustine, in particular, had been regarded as a reputable citizen up to that time.

They were all bold and confident in their bearing. Meador was said to have boasted on the streets that he could prove anything in the Clinton courts—that he could say hell was an icehouse if he wanted to and could make it stick. And when the case was called, it seemed that he had not been overconfident. The Galveston *News* reported: "All the prisoners have proved an alibi, and were put under nominal bonds. It is the opinion of those who heard the evidence that the guilty party is still at large. The party accused had no ill-feeling against the Brassells. Some of them were very intimate with the family. Those who testified against the prisoners were honestly mistaken. They only saw the men that did the killing in the dark, and it was not possible for them to recognize the party." [10]

The old-timers in DeWitt County had expected something like this and did not place much reliance on the local courts. Led by Judge H. Clay Pleasants, they appealed directly to the governor and asked for a detachment of Rangers to come and clean up the accumulated abuses of the last ten years. It took Lieutenant Lee Hall's company some time to pull up stakes and transfer to new territory, but on November 23 Hall wrote to his chief: "I have the honor to report my arrival here [Clinton] with seven men as per order of Capt. McNelly. . . . We were not very warmly recd here by the Shff. . . ."

The fact was that Hall and his men had come in very quietly and camped in Judge Pleasants' pasture lot behind his house, and none of the local peace officers were aware that they had even been sent for. Some of these officers suffered a severe shock when they saw those grim and silent men on the streets of Clinton the morning after the arrival.

Court was about to convene. Criminal cases were to be called on December 18. Hall had nearly three weeks to get ready for action, and he began by taking a thorough inventory of the situation. He reported that "the Shff cannot be trusted to execute writs whenever the Sutton party are interested, and that party or its members are defdts in nearly all the cases of felony on the docket there being thirty one murder cases alone and each defdt has some friend who will assist him, in fact one half of this County is so mixed up in deeds of blood that they cannot afford for any member of the brotherhood to be sent to the penitentiary or prison for fear they may divulge some of their dark secrets. . . . I think it would be well to send eight or ten additional men here by the 18th. . . . The people of this County are completely terrorized and trampled upon by the assassins and cut throats who got their hand in at shedding blood during the Taylor & Sutton troubles, then joined the Vigilance Associations and now kill off witnesses and intimidate the juries by threats of violence till it is impossible to convict one of them, and the great trouble is there is no telling when the end will come." [11]

The Brassell business was his toughest problem. All the witnesses "except three women" had left the country, he reported, "and even they have been notified that if they came before the grand jury that they would be killed and their houses burned. I have a portion of the witnesses now in my camp to protect them against assassination and am in communication with the others who have left the country and think by giving them a guard I can induce them to give in their testimony." [12]

Hall was sure he could break up the feud this time, and he could count on adequate support. Judge Pleasants, the man who had been chiefly responsible for summoning him, was as determined as Hall was to put a stop to the horrors of the past few years. The old judge was a notable character, and though McNelly privately accused him of slackness and timidity, he was about to prove that McNelly was wrong. Nobody in DeWitt County had ever doubted his courage anyway, any more than they doubted his Virginia courtesy and rich Southern accent. He proved it to Hall's Rangers very soon after they arrived. He was driving down the Victoria road with Judge Grimes on his way to court (not many people went out alone in those days) when he saw a man step behind a live oak tree. He drove up within fifty feet of the tree, stopped, trained his shotgun on it, and called out, "I see you, Sah. Come out from behind that tree, Sah." And out stepped a sheepish Ranger who explained that he was laying for somebody and did not wish to be recognized. [13]

The judge could be a lion in his wrath, but he was a

peace-loving man and an earnest Presbyterian. He even brought his minister into the courtroom with him sometimes and opened the session with prayer. DeWitt County was hardly the place where such procedure would have been expected, but there was no place on earth where it was worse needed.

When Lieutenant Hall called on His Honor for instructions, Pleasants told him to go on and do his part—between them they could put an end to the whole bloody business. So Hall laid a trap and executed one of the boldest strokes recorded in the annals of the Ranger companies of Texas.

★

Wedding Bells and Prison Cells

The four Cox brothers had a grown-up sister. Her name was Melissa; she was a personable and lively young lady; and in 1876 she was nineteen years old. Her family was not too happy over an attachment she had formed for Joe Sitterlie, one of the two brothers of that name who had grown up in the precarious atmosphere of DeWitt County and begun to ride with the Sutton faction. Joe was an easy-going boy who loathed hard work, expanded in an environment of bars and poolrooms, and was a handy man with a gun. It was natural for him to join the other handy men of his party and become a peace officer. He was, in fact, a deputy sheriff of the county and a deputy city marshal to boot. The Cox family was a little regretful that Joe was a Catholic while they were not, but 'Liss was determined to marry him, and declared her intention of becoming a Catholic in order to do it right.[1]

The wedding was set for the evening of December 22, 1876, which turned out to be cold and drizzly. The weather did not stop the celebration, however, and a large crowd gathered at Mr. Anderson's big double log house a few miles from Clinton. As usual the women provided plenty of food, and liquid refreshments of all varieties were available to make it a cheerful occasion for Joe and 'Liss and their friends. There was fiddle music for dancing and plenty of partners for the girls. It did not seem to matter much to anyone present that the grand jury two days before had indicted seven of the invited guests, including the bride's brother, for the murder of Dr. Philip Brassell and his son George.[2]

To the Rangers in their cheerless camp at Clinton it mattered a good deal. The indictment was the first step in their campaign, and indictments had not always been easy to get in DeWitt County. They were not surprised when Lieutenant Hall rode out from Clinton after dark and told them to get ready to go on a little scout. "We won't go far," he said. "Don't take any blankets; we'll be back tonight."

Hall had eighteen men with him by now, but two were sick, so only sixteen of them saddled up. As they jogged along he explained the situation to them—seven of the eight men charged with the Brassell murder were to be at the wedding. It was a chance in a million to catch them all together.

The sound of fiddle music and the scraping and stomping of dancing feet filtered out to them from the Anderson house as they pulled up about two hundred yards away. Hall said, "Boys, we are probably going to have a pretty hot fight in a few minutes. Here is something that will maybe help a little." He passed around a bottle of whiskey, and everybody drank. Then they surrounded the place, Hall placing four men with double-barreled shotguns at the ends of the long galleries at each side of the house. He made a final round of his outposts, speaking a cheerful word here and there and instructing them not to shoot unless they had to, but not to let anybody get by, either. Then, carrying his carbine, he walked into the house.

The fiddler stopped as if he had been shot the minute Hall appeared in the door, and the dancers froze in their tracks. For a minute paralysis seemed to grip everybody in the room, and then there was a great roar of screams and shouts and angry questions. Sitterlie, the bridegroom, confronted Hall in the doorway. "Do you want anybody here, Hall?" he demanded.

"I do," answered Hall, so loud that everybody would hear. "I want seven men for murder. I want you, William Meador, Dave Augustine, Jake Ryan, William Cox, Jim Hester, and Frank Heidrichs, all charged with the murder of Dr. Brassell and his son and indicted this day."

At this announcement the surge of angry men from the inside forced Hall out of the doorway and into the space between the two rooms of the double house. A fat man ducked under his arm and charged wildly into the dark, running into Ranger N.A. Jennings, who poked him in the stomach with his carbine, doubled him up, and sent him galloping back into the house as fast as he came out. They found out later that he was the preacher who had just performed the wedding ceremony.

In the midst of the uproar Bill Meador yelled at Hall, "How many men have you got?"

"Seventeen, counting myself."

"Well, we've got over seventy, and we'll fight it out."

"That's the talk! Move out your women and children and be quick about it. I'll give you three minutes to get them out of the way. We don't want to kill them, but we came down here for a fight and we want it."

The audacity of Hall's stand stopped those hardy men where bullets would have whetted their appetite for battle.

"Get ready, men," Hall called out to his Rangers.

"Sweep the porches with those shotguns when I give the word, and shoot to kill. They are going to move out the women and children and then we'll have it."

There were tears in Meador's eyes as he exclaimed, "We don't want to kill you all."

"Then give me that gun—quick!" snapped Hall, and he had Meador's pistol before the words were out of his mouth. The rest was easy. He called in two men to help him and harvested a great heap of guns and pistols without a sign of resistance. In five minutes the entire crowd was disarmed.

It seemed to Joe Sitterlie then that this had gone far enough. "You might let us finish our dance out," he said. "I've just been married."

"All right," Hall agreed. "But if any man tries to get away, we'll kill him. We'll take you to town at daylight."

So the party went on. One of the Calhoun women tried to leave with the excuse that she had a baby at home, but Hall stopped her. "Madam, nobody leaves this house till morning." And nobody did. The Rangers stayed on guard around the house all night, coming in by twos to partake of the wedding supper and the high-nosed hostility of the young ladies. They noticed that these belles danced defiantly and often with the young men accused of murder as if to show that their sympathies were not affected.

At dawn Hall rounded up his seven men and announced to those interested that if there was any attempt at a jail delivery the first people to be shot would be the prisoners. Then he took them into Clinton and jailed them, mounting a guard inside their cell and outside the jail, for there was every possibility that their friends would try to rescue them. The social code almost demanded it. On the second day they were moved to the second floor of the courthouse and were joined there by Charles Heisig (number eight on the list), who had been brought over from Yorktown.[8] The same day

Hall wrote to Captain McNelly, sick at his home in Burton: "The proof is positive and they will likely be ordered elsewhere to jail, in which case I think we will have the Sutton party to fight, in which case I have no doubt but that we will clear them out, but it may cost the lives of good men to do it. The citizens of the country are with me in sympathy alone, and it will be impossible to get them to assist us except a very few. I think though that we have got them fast, that is the fighting portion of the party, and I now have them under guard. If these men can be brought to justice it will end the troubles in this County." [4]

The prisoners had gone to jail in complete confidence that they would be granted bail, as usual, and that they would be tried when and if they pleased. But this time someone else was calling the figures and the tune sounded different. Judge Pleasants heard pleas for habeas corpus for a full week before a courtroom full of clansmen. Once upon a time the fear of the shotguns and six-shooters of those clansmen would have had considerable bearing on the decision, but not now. There were no shotguns and six-shooters. The Rangers removed them from all spectators before allowing them inside the courtroom door.

At last the judge was ready to render his decision and the word went round that he would be shot if he gave the wrong one. The atmosphere was electric as he rose to speak, and it fairly crackled when six Rangers stepped up, three on each side of him, and cocked their carbines. What the old judge said made feuding history in DeWitt County and impressed itself so deeply on the mind of one of the Rangers that he could recite it almost word for word afterward. This is the way N. A. Jennings remembered it:

> The time has arrived for me to announce my decision in this case. I shall do so without fear or favor, solely upon the evidence as it has been presented. This county is and has been for years a reproach to the fair name of the State of Texas.

Over it have roamed bands of lawless men, committing awful
outrages, murdering whom they pleased, shooting down men
from ambush in the most cowardly manner possible. Here in
this very room, listening to me now, are murderers who long
ago should have been hanged. I do not speak of the prisoners
at the bar, but of you who yet are free. You are murderers,
bushwhackers, midnight assassins.

Some of you have dared to threaten me with cowardly
anonymous letters, and I have had to bring State soldiers into
this court of justice. I learn that you have blamed the Sheriff
of this county for calling upon the Rangers to assist in re-
storing order. No, it was not the Sheriff who had the Rangers
sent here; it was I. I called for them and I am going to see
that they remain here in this county until it is as peaceful and
law-abiding as any in the State—as quiet and orderly as any
in the Union. I tell you now, beware! The day of reckoning
is surely coming. It is close at hand. When you deal with the
Texas Rangers, you deal with men who are fearless in the
discharge of their duty and who will surely conquer you.

I shall send these men at the bar to jail to await trial for as
wicked and cowardly a murder as ever disgraced this State.
It is but the beginning. Others will soon follow them. The
reign of the lawless in DeWitt County is at an end! [5]

The old judge's voice rang like a trumpet as he reached
his climax. There were flushed and angry faces before
him, but not a move was made as he paused for a moment
before he spoke his last word.

"Lieutenant Hall," he said, "clear the courtroom, Sah."

The jail that Judge Pleasants picked out for the comfort
and security of his prisoners was the one at Galveston.
Shortly after the judge made his decision known, Captain
McNelly came to Cuero and took charge of delivering
the men to the authorities in that town. The papers he
carried said that the jail in DeWitt County was an "in-
secure prison," which was doubtless, under the circumstances, no more than the truth. On the fifth of January,
1877, McNelly and his charges reached Galveston, but

were allowed to stay only one night, the excuse given being that the jail was full.[6] McNelly thereupon started the first of many journeys from courthouse to jail and back again, which kept those prisoners in circulation for years. This time they paused briefly at Cuero, and finally were shipped on to spend most of the rest of the year in the jail at Austin.[7]

But just because the prisoners were temporarily laid on the shelf did not mean that their friends back home gave up the struggle. At first they seem to have hoped that something might be done by intimidation and there was a crop of anonymous letters. Judge Pleasants got one classical example which he allowed McNelly to send to the adjutant general, the gist of which was as follows:

Clinton, DeWitt, Jan 16, 1877.

Mr. H. Clay Pleasants:

Sir—I now embrace the plasant oppertunity to inform you that you have sent the rong men to prison for the killing of Brassel. It was the Jermans that done it and the reason why they kill them was because the old man and his sons riten a hole lot of blackgard and put it all over the shilow church a bout women, and the Jermans said they intended to have revenge for it, now you know very well that there is two things that has and must be done, and that is that you can send after those men and bring them back and allow them bale, or you, John Worford, old Bob Worford have got to die, and two others, I wont call there names. Just as sure as you three stay on the earth, there is over twenty-five men that have you all five pick out, and they will give you two weeks from the day that this letter is mail to bring them back and alow them bale. . . . I am a going to ack fair with you three; I'll give you your choice to die or bring them back, and Clay I mean ever worde I have put on this paper. if I did not now that thoes boys were inisant then I would not say a word, but they are and I now it, and have told you so in this letter, and father more I am honest with you three, I give you your choice to live or die, and if you think you wont be kill just try us and see. . . . We kill you three if we never do eny thing else as long as we live and then live at home.

The court records of DeWitt County show that a good deal of the deadwood of the feud was got out of the way in June of 1877. Dick Hudson and Kit Hunter were acquitted in the matter of the death of Jim Taylor, for instance, and a couple of months later Martin King was murdered in a saloon in Clinton by unidentified men, undoubtedly because he was blamed for betraying Jim and the men who were killed with him.[8]

That cleared the decks for the big show, which was scheduled for December of 1877, and the curtain went up when Lieutenant Hall brought Augustine, Meador, Cox, Ryan, Hester and Heisig back to Cuero to stand trial. Heisig was granted a severance, given an independent hearing, and turned loose. Hester and Augustine likewise moved for a severance and were tried separately for the murder of George Brassell.

Both sides made every preparation possible. The defendants retained the services of three top-drawer attorneys—E.R. Lane, Rudolph Kleberg, and J.W. Stayton. The prosecution, composed of District Attorney H.L. Browne, County Attorney S.F. Grimes, and W.H. Burges of Seguin, was just as distinguished. The defense tried to establish alibis and emphasized the contradictions in the testimony of witnesses for the prosecution. After ten days of pulling and hauling, on December 29, 1877, a verdict of "not guilty" was handed down, to the great disappointment of all who had been hoping for better days. The defendants were sent back to jail, being still under indictment for the murder of Dr. Brassell, and Judge Pleasants changed the venue of the cases remaining against them and the other prisoners to San Antonio, Bexar County.[9] Lieutenant Hall wrote to Adjutant General Steele that there was "great indignation" over the acquittal.[10]

Meador's case[11] was called in San Antonio in February, 1878. Hall produced a witness named Arnot Jacobs whose testimony was supposed to upset the story of the Cox family that all the defendants had spent the night at the Cox house and never set foot outside during the time the Brassells were being murdered. One of the Cox girls, now Mrs. Jake Ryan, swore she had been in possession of the only key to the house and that the men slept in the upper story from which there was only one exit. She said Jacobs had never been near the place.[12] In the face of this contradictory testimony the jury failed to agree. From then on until 1894 Meador's case continued to appear on the dockets of various counties. He was indicted in DeWitt on March, 8 1880, for the murder of George Brassell—transferred to Guadalupe—and never called to trial. On January 19, 1892, an unsuccessful attempt was made to revive the case in DeWitt County. It was shown that the thing was still pending in Guadalupe County and DeWitt had no jurisdiction. The charges against him in Bexar County were not dismissed until 1894.[13]

Cox, Ryan, and Sitterlie were brought to trial in San Antonio and convicted of murder in the first degree on April 17, 1878. They appealed. The Court of Appeals affirmed the verdict, but there were still the mysterious ways of Providence to fall back upon, and Providence—or something like it—proved to be reliable. The clerk of the Court of Appeals lost the judgment affirming the verdict of the San Antonio Court. It was never found.

The loss of this paper meant a reopening of the whole case. The rehearing was set for March, 1880, and another imposing collection of legal brains appeared before Judge P.J. White to defend the three men. They included J.W. Waelder, J.W. Stayton (later Chief Justice of the Supreme

Court), Congressman Upson, and John Ireland (later governor of the state). Judge White ruled that the trial had not been properly conducted; that the defendants should have been adjudged guilty only in the second degree; and that there had been a fatal flaw in the indictment. The prescribed form for the final words of the indictment are "against the peace and dignity of the State." In this case the words read "against the peace and dignity of the Statute." Nobody knew how the words came to be changed, but there was much comment, especially after Judge White held that the error was fatal and reversed and remanded the case. The story of this strange alteration is still one of the most celebrated in the history and folklore of the law in Texas.[14]

After that reversal the defendants were granted bail and scattered out. Willie Cox drifted out to the Big Bend and later, when so many Texas cattlemen got the New Mexico fever, he went to the Las Cruces region. Jim Hester and Joe Sitterlie joined him there. He became well-to-do and did much to live down his youthful mistakes.

Dave Augustine had the longest siege of any of these men. On December 31, 1891, he was reindicted (along with Cox, Ryan, and Sitterlie) for the murder of Dr. Brassell. On June 21, 1893, he pleaded that he had already been tried and acquitted in this case. In 1893 the venue was changed to Gonzales County, and in 1896 to Hays. He got twenty-five years in spite of the efforts of Attorney Rudolph Kleberg, and the Court of Criminal Appeals upheld the decision. Governor Sayers, however, expressed himself as unwilling to see an old Confederate veteran go to Huntsville, especially when all the rest of the men accused of the same crime were as free as the air and likely to remain so. He pardoned Augustine before he ever set foot in the penitentiary.[15]

The records show that Ryan was admitted to bail on August 23, 1894, and again on January 15, 1895. Hester was admitted to bail on November 7, 1895. Nothing seems to have been done with either case.

The final decision in the case of Dave Augustine was dated October 30, 1899, thirty years after the beginning of the feud and twenty-three years after the killing of which Augustine was accused. It is doubtful if there is another feud on record which covered so much ground, lasted so long, caused so many deaths, or left such a brand on the lives of so many people.

Mart Horrell

Survivors of the Horrell-Higgins Feud

Mr. and Mrs. Tom Horrell

George and Charley Marlow

Pink Higgins (right) and His Men

Judge W. C. Linden
as a Young Man

The Young Texas Ranger—Ira Aten, 1887

Texas Rangers in Camp Near San Saba, 1897:
Ollie Perry
Jack Harrell
Dr. Donnelly
James Bell
Billie McCauley
Dudley Barker
Van Lane
Robert McClure
Captain
Bill McDonald

J. H. Slyfield
and
Capt. John Mitchell

Clem N. Bassett, Sr.

Some Older Jaybirds

Col. P. E. Peareson

Sgt. W. J. L. Sullivan

Volney

Jim

The Gibson Boys

Courtesy Mrs. Lilah Gibson Rice

Guilf

Ned

William Mitchell

Richmond, Texas: Railroad Street in the 8

Two Young
Jaybirds

Courtesy Mrs. Lilah Gibson Rice
and F. M. O. Fenn

The Old Courthouse
at Richmond

Courtesy Ira A

Otis Fenn

Lycurgus Border

Uncle Buck Wall

Walter Reese (right) and Friends

They Fought at Columbus

Ex-Sheriff Lite Townsend (left)

The Terrible Seventies

★

On our own frontier a few decades ago when no recognized government existed, honest men agreed that he who had the strength to maintain order had the duty to do so. A rancher with a dozen straight-shooting cowhands in his employ was a dirty dog if he refused to take an active part, along with his weaker neighbors, in the hard and perilous business of suppressing banditry. The fact that the rancher might not be a peace officer had nothing to do with it. He had the rifles; therefore he could not escape the duty of using them for the common good.

GERALD W. JOHNSON, *American Heroes and Hero Worship*

There is a strange fact about some people, especially a cow thief. He will do most anything for you, help you out of trouble or distress. If he owed you money he would try to pay it, even if he had to steal your cattle to pay it with. So the saying that everybody was honest in the early days does not hold good in all cases.

RUFE O'KEEFE, *Cowboy Life*

DAYS OF WRATH

The sixties were bad, but the seventies were worse. It was the day of the outlaw. Organized gangs of desperadoes did as they pleased; and, to protect themselves, some of the cattle barons kept bands of feudal retainers who were as vicious as the men they were hired to fight.[1] The result was plenty of trouble—fights, lynchings, gang wars, and feuds.

The sorest spots were the frontier districts where there was some sort of boundary for thieves and fugitives to cross. The Red River, between Texas and the Indian Territory, was one such place, and the Texas papers frequently reported bloody broils from that area. The Austin *Statesman* for October 9, 1874, for instance, noted that citizens in the Red River country had been "compelled to organize a vigilance committee" to deal with a gang whose headquarters "are supposed to be on Brushy Creek in the Nation, about sixty miles from Red River Station. . . . The Nation appears to be the resort of the worst characters in the country and Texas has to bear the blame for their acts of robbery and violence."

The Mexican border region in Southeast Texas was another outlaw hangout. In its wild and lonely thickets so many shady characters were concentrated that an honest man almost had to have a pass to get in, as the Englishman R.B. Townshend (*The Tenderfoot in New Mexico*) found out when he tried to buy up a horse herd on the other side of the Nueces.[2] Mexico was the target for many of the raids organized by these people, and some of their stealing was actually defended on the ground that a fair exchange is no robbery. The Galveston *News* for June 14, 1876, ran a long article on "The Western Frontier" quoting this argument. "Their cattle and horses, they say, have been stolen from them by Mexican thieves, and run off into Mexico, and they are justified in making reprisals. It is needless to say that in doing this they are . . . operating on both sides of the river indiscriminately."

The third point where Texas outlaws loved to congregate was in the middle counties west and northwest of San Antonio on the edge of the Indian country. Big herds of cattle and easy access to wild and unsettled spaces offered great temptations to local and imported bad men. They even profited from the danger of attacks by Comanche war parties. Time and again there was every indication that a raid had been pulled off by white desperadoes masquerading as Indians.[3]

The Texas Rangers were reorganized in 1874 to take care of the general lawlessness. Captain McNelly's force was sent to Southern Texas to see what could be done about the Sutton-Taylor feudists and the stealing on the Mexican border. Major John B. Jones was given charge of the Frontier Battalion to attend to the western frontier. To show what these men were up against, it should be enough to mention the "Book of Knaves"[4] which was issued in 1877 to the Ranger captains. It contained the names and descriptions of three thousand men who were wanted—a large proportion of them concentrated in the territory under the supervision of McNelly and Jones.

Conditions could never have been set right without the Rangers, but the force was small, and the parsimony of the law makers, snug and safe in Austin, tended to make it smaller. Working under constant handicaps, the Ranger battalion needed time to get the upper hand, and meanwhile the killing and raiding went on.

So far as the citizens went, there was only one way out —more efficient use of the vigilance committee. Little knots of ranchmen took the trail of thieves with only the unwritten law of self-redress to back them up. Secret societies were organized on the model of the earlier Regulators. And the press of Texas argued pro and con about the morality and necessity of lynching parties.

The larger newspapers were apt to oppose lynch law. "Henderson and Floyd, horse thieves, were hanged at Weatherford by a mob," said the *Weekly Statesman* on June 22, 1876. "The mob too should be hanged." Smaller sheets usually took the opposite view. The Stephenville paper declared in 1877, "The *Mail* can find no reason to repudiate its advocacy of lynch law, and it herewith urges every community in the state to organize its vigilance committee and rid the country of its death-producing tumors."

There were occasional stories of heroic sheriffs who refused to turn over a prisoner to a mob.[5] There were even examples of vigilantes who refused to take extreme measures. "Hill County people," observed the *Weekly Statesman* for June 15, 1876, "deserve great credit. They captured, after desperate resistance, two horse thieves and would not suffer a mob to hang them."

Such things happened, but there was a "strong undercurrent of approbation of mob methods in dealing with crime." Sheriffs and other peace officers time and again were on the side of the mobsmen and even among them. And ordinary citizens said "Amen!"

So the lynching and waylaying went on. No statistics can ever tell the story accurately now, but scores of people were put out of the way every year. The combination of wholesale stealing, weak local authority, and Texas folk law produced a spate of feuding in the seventies which has never been equaled in our history.

As a matter of fact there was so much activity during this period that a single book can hardly tell the whole story. The feud historian, with deep regret, must take up his blue pencil and content himself with bare mention of some important episodes.

One of these would be the Truitt-Mitchell trouble which developed in 1874 in Hood County along the reaches of

the Middle Brazos. Feuding began when two neighboring families fell out over land titles. The Mitchells of Mitchell's Bend were old timers who had befriended the Truitts when they came into the country to settle. Old Cooney Mitchell, the white-bearded patriarch of his clan, had even helped young Jim Truitt to become a Methodist minister. Bad feelings arose, however, and as the men of the two families were on their way home from a trial at Granbury, the guns began to talk. Two of the Truitts were left dead in the road. Cooney Mitchell was hanged for the murder at Granbury on October 9, 1875—his chief accuser being the Reverend James Truitt.

Cooney's son, Bill, would have gone the same way had he not disappeared, leaving behind the threat that Jim Truitt would pay for his deed. It took ten years for Bill to make his threat good, but finally he ran his preacher to earth in the little East Texas town of Timpson. On July 20, 1886, he entered the Truitt house and while Mrs. Truitt looked on, shot Jim through the head.

Bill kept ahead of the law until 1907, dodged the penitentiary until 1912, and vanished for good over the prison walls two years after he began serving his sentence.[6]

A bigger feud was the little war which broke out at Mason in the rich, rolling cattle-and-farming country of central Texas in 1875. It is called the "Hoodoo War" from the name often attached to masked bands of vigilantes. This episode is especially interesting because of a race element, with German and American cattlemen lined up on opposite sides.

Big scale rustling was going on in the county—so big that the citizens organized a posse which soon turned into a lynch mob. Four men were taken out of jail and hanged at the beginning of the trouble, and before long, bushwhacking, forting up, street fighting, and assassination were in full swing. The law was completely paralyzed, and only the intervention of the Rangers under Major John B. Jones could bring the county back to sanity. The Mason County War was over in less than two years, but while it lasted it matched any Texas feud in bitterness and intensity. And even now the old-timers of Mason are careful when they talk about it.[7]

The El Paso Salt War was another major trouble of the seventies which involved a race issue—this time between Mexicans and Americans. It began when Charles H. Howard, a Missouri lawyer and an ex-officer in the Confederate Army, managed to acquire title to some important salt deposits a hundred miles east of El Paso. The Mexican population on both sides of the border asserted bitterly that these deposits were public property under the terms of the treaty of Guadalupe-Hidalgo. Howard was repeatedly mobbed and threatened, and finally became so enraged that on October 10, 1877, he murdered Louis Cardis, an Italian-born politician whom he regarded as the leader of the Mexican faction. A company of Texas Rangers was organized from local volunteers under the leadership of John B. Tays to prevent a general massacre. This company stood a siege at San Elizario, the center of the disturbance, and eventually surrendered—the only Ranger company in history to lay down its arms. Howard and some of his friends, who had taken refuge with Tays' recruits, were shot.[8]

Bloody strife could be expected almost anywhere in Texas in the seventies. But even in the midst of all this terrible trouble, the humorous habit of the American folk mind was at work, as a couple of stories will show. Willie Newbury Lewis tells about the time a Clarendon man was caught rustling, rushed to the nearest tree, and prepared for execution. At the last minute nobody seemed willing to be the one to pull on the rope, so the condemned man said, "Why don't you let the one among you who can honestly say he has never done what I have done hang me?" After exchanging significant looks the men got on their horses and rode away.[9]

Frank Bushick has another tale about the hanging of Green McCullough who killed an innocent bystander in one of his fights and was taken over by a mob. "Damn it, boys," protested McCullough as he stood under a limb with a rope around his neck, "you ain't goin' to hang me, are you?"

"You're as good as hung already," they told him.

At first Green seemed very much taken aback, but pretty soon a happy thought struck him.

"Well," said he, "if I've got to be hung, I'm glad I'm goin' to be hung by my friends." [10]

The seventies were that way.

HOT HEADS AND
HAIR TRIGGERS
The Horrell-Higgins Feud

A little after noon on the nineteenth of January, 1873, State Police Captain Thomas Williams and seven men, including one Negro, rode into Lampasas from the south looking for trouble.

They had come to the right place. In the summer, Lampasas was a resort town where people came from far and near to drink the potent sulphur water from the two big springs; during the rest of the year Lampasas was a dusty little cow village on the edge of the hill country where ranchers came to get their supplies and cowboys whooped it up in the saloons. The wonderful range country round about, with its high, rolling pastures, its limestone-bottomed creeks winding through post oak and mesquite, and its far, hilly horizons was possessed by many an old Texas family brought up to fight the Indians and hate the Yankees. And lately they had been getting into trouble among themselves.

Cattle stealing was at the bottom of it. There were shady characters about and a good deal of stock was being run out of the country. To complicate matters, the town was wide open and the saloonkeepers and gamblers had things their own way. The rough element was growing bold, and there was too much cowboy skylarking to suit the solid citizens.[1]

Five days before the captain rode in, Sheriff Denson had been killed while trying to make an arrest. The men who did it were protected by their pals (including three

brothers named Horrell) and did not even go to jail.[2] When
the news reached Austin, Adjutant General Britton sent a
detachment of his State Police to straighten things out and
disarm the cowboys.

This was a rather risky procedure. To the old-time
Texans in the county the Yankee government was an abom-
ination, and it is said that some of them had sent word to
Governor Davis not to let any of his "nigger police"
show their faces in that country unless he wanted to get
rid of them.[3] That may have been the reason why Captain
Williams took with him six white policemen and only one
colored man, but he made no other peaceful gestures. On
the road that morning he stopped Telford Bean, a freighter
on his way to Austin, to ask how far it was to Lampasas.[4]
Bean noticed that the captain had been drinking, and
heard him remark as he rode off that he was going to
"clean up those damn Horrell boys," whom he seemed to
regard as ringleaders in the Southern party.[5]

The Horrell boys were not the kind that clean up easy.
There were five of them—Mart, Tom, Merritt, Ben and
Sam—who ran cattle in the country along the Little Lucies
Creek and the Lampasas River north and east of town.
They had been there since before the war and had never
been in any trouble, but everybody knew they were
dangerous to fool with. They stood up for their rights, as
they saw them, and took nothing from anybody. They
were dark men with solid powerful bodies and were famous locally for their skill with firearms. Though they
didn't run with the church-going crowd, they were well
liked and agreeable.[6] Even their friends and supporters
admit, however, that some of their associates were not
such desirable citizens, and one of their in-laws, Bill Bowen,
was supposed to be pretty tough.

The Horrell boys were in town the day Captain Williams rode in. They usually congregated in Jerry Scott's
saloon at the northwest corner of the square, where the

Candy Kitchen is now, and on this occasion they had the place practically to themselves, for an important trial was going on somewhere else in town and most of the male population was attending.

As the policemen drew up to the clump of live oaks in front of the saloon, they saw Bill Bowen, wearing a pistol, enter the door. With proper caution the captain sent three of his men to vantage points covering the building, instructed the Negro to watch the horses, and led the rest of his force inside. The place was quiet—it almost seemed as if they were expecting him. He strode up to the bar, ordered drinks for himself and his men, and turned to cast his eye around the room. About fifteen cowmen were standing about in easy attitudes, watching him. Bowen was there, still wearing his six-shooter.

"I see you are wearing a pistol," Williams said to him. "I arrest you."

"You haven't done anything, Bill," said Mart Horrell. "You don't have to be arrested if you don't want to."

There are two stories about what happened next. The Union newspapers reported that Williams grappled with Bowen for the pistol and was fired on by the Horrells. The other story is that as soon as Mart Horrell spoke, Williams drew like a flash and shot Mart, after which the firing became general.

When the smoke lifted, Captain Williams and T.M. Daniels were lying dead on the floor. Wesley Cherry had been shot down just outside the door, and Andrew Melville was drilled as he ran down the street. He got into the Huling Hotel, but he never came out alive. Two of the men who had been stationed outside the saloon managed to dodge the bullets.[7] A third, the Negro in charge of the horses, was never in much danger, for at the first shot he mounted the fastest horse they had and split the wind down the Austin road. One-eyed Tom Horrell, suffering from a shoulder wound, tried to stop him—ran to the corner of the square in order to get a shot and kicked up dust all around the man—but there was no stopping that Negro. They say he went so fast the stake rope tied to the saddle stood straight out behind, and that he ruined a fine horse in his haste to get away from there. When he reported at his Austin headquarters he protested to his commanding officer: "Captain, I thought you said this was a race horse. Why, Captain, he can't run for nothing." [8]

The next day Adjutant General Britton himself came up to arrest the Horrells. His men picked up Allen White-craft, James Grizell, and the wounded Mart Horrell at the home of Mart's mother in Lampasas.[9] Tom Horrell, Bill Bowen, and everybody else were long gone. The three captives were eventually taken to jail at Georgetown, half-way back to Austin, where Mart stayed until he was well enough to leave.

Lampasas now had its first experience with Feudist's Disease, the symptoms being a feverish feeling with sen-sations of panic. On January 30 the County Court met and five justices of the peace expressed their dismay in a letter to the governor. "With humiliation" they confessed that they were powerless, and added: "We respectfully ask that your Excellency give us a police force sufficient to enable our officers to enforce law and order. . . ." [10]

It was no use. Too many people were against the Davis men on general principles, and nobody was surprised to hear, a couple of months later, that Mart Horrell and his friends had been taken out of the Georgetown jail. Mart's wife had been allowed to stay with him as a nurse. When he was able to get on a horse, she notified his brothers. They made up a party, and one night they descended upon Georgetown in force. There was a fight, but the Horrells kept on shooting and soon discouraged the townspeople from interfering while Bill Bowen went at the jail door with a sledge hammer. They all rode back to

Little Lucies Creek together and got ready to leave the country.[11]

The great drift of cattlemen west to New Mexico was already beginning at this early date, and the Horrells had made up their minds to sell out and start life over again four hundred miles west—or even farther. Once back on the home range they began gathering cattle and making preparations to move.

Lampasas County was willing to let them go. They assembled their caravan, sold their cattle to Cooksey and Clayton to be delivered in Coleman County on their way west, and trailed out of the country. They notified the sheriff what day they would be going through Russell Gap so he could do something about it if he so desired. He did not so desire.

They got as far as the country just west of Roswell, New Mexico. Their old friends in Lampasas think they may have planned to go on to California eventually, but it was well into the fall when they reached the Ruidoso, and there they settled down, at least for the winter, near what is now Bonnell's ranch.

They could not have picked a more precarious location. The Murphy and McSween factions, who were shortly to begin exterminating each other in the Lincoln County War with the expert aid of Billy the Kid, were already jockeying for position and accumulating as many good fighting men as they could. The Horrells probably made some capital of this situation. Emerson Hough, who lived nearby and knew the local traditions, says that Major Murphy "staked" the Horrell boys in their ranching venture on the Ruidoso.[12]

In this tense atmosphere quarreling was apt to break out as if by spontaneous combustion. It took only two or three weeks for the Horrell boys to start reaching for their guns again. Undoubtedly race had something to do with it. The

Mexican population of New Mexico never did have much time for the rough-hewn, pugnacious, and often arrogant *Tejanos* who seemed to think they had been specially commissioned by the Almighty to take the country away from an inferior population. On the other hand the *Tejanos* were not fond of the slipperiness, suavity, and superstition of the Mexicans. Often they fought about it, and it is amazing how differently the same set of facts could be recounted by the two sides when the shooting was over.

The exact truth about the "Horrell War" will probably never be known. The Horrell boys did not stay long, and when they were gone there was nobody to tell the story their way. As a result they have always been painted in New Mexico as a bunch of bloodthirsty villains. Without trying to make angels out of a gang of ruthless and efficient fighting men, it is only fair to point out that they had something to say in their own defense. They told their friends back in Texas that the New Mexicans had tried to rob them. They had a good deal of gold coin with them as a result of the sale of their cattle and other goods, and when the Mexicans heard of it they determined to make some easy money. Some of them died when they tried to collect.

The other side says that the trouble started over water rights—that "one of the Horrell crowd shot and killed one of the neighboring Mexicans while the latter was cutting a ditch." [13]

The first pitched battle happened on the streets of Lincoln on December 1, 1873. According to the natives, Ben Horrell and four of his friends came in and "undertook to run the town." When the last shot was fired in the ensuing free-for-all, Constable Juan Martinéz was dead. So were Dave Warner, Jack Gylam, and Ben Horrell of the other side. There are grounds for believing that Gylam and Horrell were shot after they had surrendered and given up their weapons. And that was not all. As the Horrells told it later, Ben had a fine gold ring on one of his fingers. A Mexican deputy wanted it, and when he could not remove it by ordinary means, the finger came off too.

Whether or not this mutilation occurred, Ben's death was hard for Mart and Tom to take. They went to the authorities to demand justice and were told that justice had been done. Ben's slayers were merely policemen doing their duty.

Three days went by and the tide turned the other way. Two of the local Mexicans were found dead in the Horrell's pasture, and it was now the turn of their enemies to demand justice. Sheriff Ham Mills led a posse of forty men to the attack and found the Horrells forted up and ready. When Mills would not or could not guarantee them protection while under arrest, they refused to surrender and started shooting. A detachment of troops from Fort Stanton stood by and observed the light skirmishing which followed but took no action. At the end of a day of fruitless battle troops and posse alike withdrew and went home to supper.

The Horrells would not leave it at that. Two weeks later, on December 20, they came to Lincoln and broke up a wedding celebration. Several Mexicans were wounded and four were killed—Isidro Patron, Isidro Padilla, Mario Balazan, and José Candelaria. No attempt was made to arrest the attackers, who were beginning to seem a little too hot to handle.

By now the citizens had become wildly alarmed and fearful of a massacre. Juan Patron, a son of one of the victims of the fight at the wedding festivities, was sent to Santa Fe to lay the case before the authorities there. Governor Giddings immediately appealed to Washington for help. The answer came back that Federal forces had no authority to interfere in local affairs.

It began to seem that the feud might go on forever, but actually it was almost finished. There was one more skirmish (at San Patricio) and one more murder when Deputy Sheriff Joseph Haskins was dragged from his bed and killed by Edward "Little" Hart (a Horrell man)—supposedly because he had a Mexican wife. Already, however, the Horrells had made up their minds that New Mexico was not for them and they prepared to go back to Texas.

They did not depart unmolested. On their way to Roswell they ran into an ambush and Ben Turner, a brother-in-law, was killed. Bitterly angry, they held a council of war and made up their minds to wipe out Lincoln once and for all. A few miles down the Lincoln road, however, they changed their minds and left New Mexico for good.

Two hundred miles on their way they were attacked again. Part of the gang, composed of Zack Crumpton, Bill Applegate, "Little" Hart, and a man named Still, had detached themselves from the main party and picked up some horses from Aaron O. Willburn of Roswell and Van C. Smith of Seven Rivers. The Willburn brothers organized a posse and hit the trail, catching up with the Horrells near Hueco Tanks, thirty miles east of El Paso. Again there was a pitched battle, and Crumpton and Still were killed —possibly others. At least five Mexicans departed this life at the same time—Seferino Trujillo, Reymundo and Severiano Aguilar, Pablo Romero, and Juan Silva.[14]

When the Horrells got back to Lampasas County, where they arrived during the last week in February, 1874, they told their friends, "We fought them all the way to Fort Davis." Mrs. Tom Horrell, who became Mrs. Mattie Ann Harrison in her later years, used to tell her children how they had an Indian scare on that trip and how she boiled water to throw on the redskins if they got close enough. She remembered that one of their men died while this was going on. They buried him, and built a fire on his grave to keep it from being discovered.[15]

No sooner did their wagons roll back across the Lampasas skyline than they were in fresh trouble. The sheriff was out with a posse after them on the last day of February, before they had had time to catch their breath after the long pull from the Pecos.[16] He took fifty men with him, and since the strength of the Horrells, after the New Mexico subtractions, was estimated at ten men, some idea may be gained of the respect that was felt among those hardy Texans for the fighting prowess of the clan. There were rumors of a bloody battle. Over at Gatesville they heard that "Two members of the Horrell clan were killed. . . . The battle lasted more than six hours. . . . Help had been asked from the neighboring counties of Coryell, Williamson, and Bell." [17] When the facts were finally sifted out, it developed that there had really been a skirmish on the fifth of March with the sheriff and his "Minute Men" on one side and the remaining Horrells (plus Jerry Scott, Bill Bowen, Rufus Overstreet, and a couple more) on the other. Scott got a ball through a lung and was captured, along with Overstreet. A shot meant for the latter took effect in the stomach of one Johnny Green, who happened to be in the house where Overstreet ran for cover. Merritt Horrell was slightly wounded, but got away. Mart and Tom Horrell rode up during the engagement and were fired on, but they turned around and rode off without damage.

The most significant fact of the whole story was tucked away at the end of the newspaper dispatch which described the battle: "The Horrell party didn't fire a shot at the posse during the engagement." [18]

If that means anything, it means that the Horrells came back from New Mexico determined to keep peace, even if they had to go against their natures and run from the enemy.

Apparently the warlike impulses of the sheriff and the Minute Men were exhausted in this encounter, or perhaps they found the sentiment of the county against them. At any rate there is no record of any further attacks on the Horrells during the summer of 1874. In September, on advice of their friends and probably on assurances from the other side that they would be fairly treated, Merritt Horrell and Bill Bowen came in and surrendered to answer to the charge of killing Captain Williams and his State Police the year before.[19] Each was able to raise ten thousand dollars bond, so they must have had some pretty substantial friends. When the case came to trial in October of 1876, they were acquitted.[20]

During all this time the Horrells were back in business as ranchmen, having established themselves about ten miles southeast of Lampasas on the Sulphur Creek just across the line in Burnet County down in the brush. By the time Merritt Horrell was turned loose in the fall of 1876, they were being accused of mishandling stock and were on their way toward more trouble.

What happened to them was what happened too often in the bad old days. They were no longer the carefree, independent, friendly boys of a few years before. They were hunted men, bitterly resentful of the life they had to lead, well aware of the fate they would probably meet, and determined not to be taken advantage of. If anybody got in their way, he was going to get hurt.

The man who accused them of rustling was the leader of a clan just as tough and just as well established as their own. His name was John Pinckney Calhoun Higgins. He was a long, limber-jointed ranchman from northeast of town across the Lampasas River, near the range the Horrell boys had formerly occupied. His people had also been in the country since before the Civil War, and the Horrell and Higgins families are said to have been on the best of terms in the early days. But things were different now.[21]

On Higgins' side were several formidable warriors—especially Bill Wren, a huge, ham-handed, good-natured rancher who later became a very efficient sheriff, and

Pink's brother-in-law Bob Mitchell, not as tall as the six-foot-three-inch Wren, but just as broad, and a terrific fighter. All were married and stood well in the district. Pink is remembered as apt to be fiery and blustery, and the first to get out in front when there was anything to be done. Wren was less apt to fly off the handle, and he and Mitchell usually tried to hold Pink back, but as time went on they lost control. Pink announced that he was going to kill "every goddam one" of the Horrells if they didn't let his cattle alone, and Wren and Mitchell realized that they were close to serious trouble.

Wren used to tell how the three of them were riding through the brush once and met Tom Horrell. Pink immediately goddamned him and said he was going to kill him. Tom replied with characteristic coolness, "Well, it won't be much credit to you—one against three." Bill Wren put in, "Keep your hand off that gun, Pink. We won't have any killing when it's three against one." The Horrells did not forget this when things went against them later.[22]

January 22, 1877, was the day which both sides have wished ever since they could forget. It was a Monday, and cold. Merritt Horrell rode into town and went to his

accustomed haunt at Jerry Scott's saloon. A fire was blazing at the back end of the place, and there he went to
warm himself. Later Higgins and Mitchell rode in and
likewise came into the saloon. One story makes it appear
that Higgins came on purpose to have an accounting with
Horrell. The old men say he came in at the back door,
approached Merritt from the rear, and shot him dead. The
newspapers said that he entered the front door with his
Winchester, called Merritt by name, and shot him in the
body. "Horrell arose and crossed in front of the fireplace
and leaned on the shoulder of Ervin, when he received a
second shot, from which he fell to the floor, after which
he was twice more shot. . . . Horrell was dead in a few
seconds. Any of the four shots would have killed him.
Litigation and angry feeling have existed between the parties for several months, Higgins charging Horrell with
tampering with his cattle. . . ." [23]

Mart and Tom Horrell joined a posse which brought in
four of Higgins's men next day, but Pink himself was not
to be found, though sixteen of Captain Sparks's Rangers
went out after him.[24] The old timers say now that Pink
never left the county and did pretty much as he pleased,
staying most of the time at the home of one of his friends.

In the midst of all this, on March 26, court opened in
Lampasas under that model of all frontier judges, W.A.
Blackburn. On the same day Captain Sparks of the Rangers rode in with his company, and the first thing he heard
was news of a heroic action at a little creek four miles east
of town which has ever since been called Battle Branch.

Tom and Mart Horrell, for some reason, had to appear
at court that morning. On their way in they had reached
the creek just mentioned and were letting their mounts
drink when a party of ambushers cut loose at them from
behind the creek bank. Tom was seriously hit in the hip
(the man who shot him was an old Confederate veteran

who had learned that the saddle is the steadiest part of a man-horse combination).[25] He fell heavily and lay in the road. Mart's mount tried to bolt, and most men would have been more than willing to let him run; but Mart was not made of that kind of stuff. As soon as he could pull his horse down, he rode back, dismounted, stood there in the road under fire, and ran off the entire bunch of ambushers singlehanded with one Winchester and one ton of cold courage.[26]

He had a bad wound in the fleshy part of the neck himself, but he half-carried Tom to the home of Mr. Tinnins half a mile away. Then he rode into town and reported to Captain Sparks what had happened.

Sparks and his Rangers immediately got ready to go in pursuit and asked Sheriff Sweet for some help. To their surprise Sweet said he couldn't do a thing. Court was in session and all his men were busy. Sparks turned to Horrell and asked if he would show them the place of attack. Horrell would. And the chase was on.

As a result of considerable trailing and deducing, Bill Tinker was arrested. The Horrells identified him as one of the attackers, but he "proved" an alibi and got out of it. Papers were got out for Bill Wren too, but he hid out for a while, and when he came in at last nothing seems to have been done to him.[27]

Probably nothing could have been done to him without serious consequences. Judge Blackburn wrote to Major Jones on March 30 about the "hazardous condition" in the county. "I believe," he said, "that the most violent and bloody scenes would have been enacted here during this week, but for the presence of Capt. Sparks & his company." The only bright spot was the surrender of Pink Higgins and Bob Mitchell to Captain Sparks in the latter part of April. Sparks wrote to a friend in Austin reporting that Higgins and Mitchell "are now in my camp" and "have been allowed bail, in the sum of ten thousand dollars each. It is hoped and we naturally expect better times in the future." [28]

The feeling of hope seems to have been general. The *Dispatch* remarked with rueful pleasantry, "we are all civil now, nobody having been killed in a week or more. By the time the summer visitors make their appearance, we will all be on our good behavior." [29]

The confidence of Captain Sparks and the Lampasas *Dispatch* was misplaced. Trouble was only just beginning. On Monday night, June 11, somebody jimmied the door of the courthouse, got into the district court room, and carried off every paper on file relating to the suits which were pending. Every scrap was gone next morning.[30]

On June fourteenth, as if to provide new material for the paper files, there was a big fight.

This battle was something of an accident. All through this year both factions had been wary of each other. When the Horrells came to town there were no Higgins supporters in sight ordinarily, but the minute the Horrells left, Mitchell or Wren or somebody else would drift in casually and ride off after a while in the direction which the other side had taken—just keeping an eye open. On the fourteenth this system of keeping just out of each other's way seems to have broken down somehow and both factions found themselves in town at the same time. It was about ten o'clock in the morning that seven Horrells and four Higginses ran into each other and started shooting. Bill Wren and Bob Mitchell were riding in together when the bullets began to whistle. They left their horses and ran in opposite directions, Wren heading for the wagon yard a long block north of the square. He reached the yard safely and tried to return the fire directed at him, but found that Mrs. Gracey, an Amazon who ran the hotel across from his refuge, was standing in her doorway completely indifferent to the fact that she was directly in his line of fire. In a little while he walked back to where he had left his horse, and about that time somebody shot him in the region described in the news stories as "the base of the spine." He was badly hurt, but dragged himself up a flight of stairs to the second story of an office building and managed to get in a shot now and then.

The firing was kept up for some time. About noon Pink Higgins managed to slip out of town and rode hard to get reinforcements. Before long he returned with more men and the fight was renewed "with great ferocity," but by this time some of the citizens had recovered themselves enough to act as go-betweens, and about one o'clock they persuaded the factions to cease firing and get out of town. It was discovered then that Bill Wren was not the only one hurt. Frank Mitchell, a younger brother of Bob, had been shot down and killed on one of the side streets. He had never been active in the feud, was busy unloading flour from a wagon at the time, and would undoubtedly have arranged to be somewhere else if he had known that powder would be burned. There was a rumor that one of the Horrell party was dead also, but it was probably only a rumor. It is certain, however, that when the fighting stopped, the Horrells "left the country" for some little time, which probably means that they kept to themselves in the brush down on the Sulphur, waiting to see what would happen next.[31]

What happened next was a visit from Major Jones, chief of the Frontier Battalion of Texas Rangers.[32] His presence, with fifteen men, was reported on June 28, and on July 10 he expressed his opinion of the situation to Adjutant General Steele as follows: "The Horrells, who left this county before I started to Austin, returned last Saturday and the people here are in constant dread of another collision between them and the Higgins-Mitchell party. This trouble is one of the most perplexing to me that I have yet had to contend with. Putting the parties under bonds for their appearance at court will not prevent them from fighting if they meet. That has already been tried and failed—So I am taking the responsibility in the interest of peace and quiet, rather than in accordance with the dictates of law, to intercede and endeavor to reconcile the difficulty and thus terminate this long continued feud. I am on good terms with both parties and hope to effect something towards the desired object in a few days."

As an afterthought the major added to this letter a request that he be sent "three Springfield Carbines and belts and three pistols with belts and scabbards." Apparently he had a feeling that he and his men might see some action.[33]

The first half of his plan for "reconciling the difficulty" was carried out by Sergeant Reynolds (later Captain Reynolds, "the intrepid") who succeeded in rounding up the Horrell boys. On the night of July 27 Reynolds set out with a detachment of his men for the Horrell stronghold on the Sulphur. His guide was none other than Bill Wren, who was able by now to sit in his saddle and knew the country, even in the dark, as well as he knew the back of his hand.

The story of the arrest, as told by James B. Gillett in *Six Years with the Texas Rangers*, has become one of the famous exploits of Ranger history. According to his account the detachment came within a mile of the house in which the Horrells were spending the night, at which point the guide halted and said, "There is where the Horrell boys live. I am going back to town." He added, when they told him he was welcome to come along, "No, not for a million dollars!"

The Rangers quietly surrounded the house; waited until it was almost daylight; then moved in. Gillett continues: "Sergeant Reynolds and his men tiptoed right into the room in which the Horrells were sleeping. Some of the men were on pallets on the floor, while others slept in beds in the one big room. Each Ranger pointed a cocked Winchester at the head of a sleeper. Reynolds then spoke to Mart Horrell. At the sound of his voice every man sat up in bed and found himself looking into the muzzle of a gun. The sergeant quickly explained that he was a Ranger and had come to arrest them. Mart replied that they could not surrender, and Tom Horrell said it would be better to die fighting than to be mobbed.

"This gave Reynolds his cue. He warned the outlaws that if anything was started there would be a dozen dead men in that house in one minute and advised them to listen to what he had to say. He then guaranteed the Horrells upon his honor that he would not turn them over to the sheriff to be put in jail and mobbed, but promised he would guard them in his camp until they could secure a preliminary examination and give bond.

" 'Boys, this seems reasonable,' said Mart Horrell, rising to his feet. 'I believe these Rangers can be relied on to protect us. Besides this fight has been thrust upon us. If we can get a hearing we can give bond.'

"They all agreed to this proposition of Sergeant Reynolds and laid down their arms, mounted their horses and under guard of the Rangers were marched into the town of Lampasas." [34]

The Wren family say that Gillett got some of his facts wrong. As they tell it, Bill Wren did not turn back a mile from the house, but went on in with the Rangers. When the Horrell boys woke up, they were willing to surrender because they saw Bill Wren, whom they trusted, among the strangers, and insisted that they be put in his charge.[35] Whichever way it happened the prisoners were taken to town and guarded day and night in the courthouse by a very alert and grim-looking bunch of officers. Would-be lynchers, if there were any, took one look at them and changed their minds about organizing a necktie party.

Meanwhile Major Jones was busy with the second half of his plan, which was the arrest of the Higgins faction. He did it without fanfare and merely reported to the adjutant general on July 31 that he had in custody "twelve prisoners—five of the Horrell party, three of the Higgins party and four others."

"The cases of the parties to the feud in this county," he said, "have been undergoing investigation before the county Judge yesterday and to-day, and will probably be protracted through several days to come. So far, the Horrels have been held to bail in two cases each, and two cases are still pending against them.

"Higgins, Mitchell, Wren of the other party have given bond in one case and there are two cases pending against them." [36]

The major's plan was working out very well. He had arrested most of the responsible parties on both sides and put them under bond. His next step was, to get them to agree to a suspension of warfare. He knew it would do no good to bring them together to talk things over, for they would probably start shooting at once. So he went back and forth between them and collected signatures to a couple of remarkable documents. The first reads as follows:

Lampasas Texas
July 30th 1877

Messrs Pink Higgins Robert Mitchell and William Wren. Gentlemen:—

From this standpoint, looking back over the past with its terrible experiences both to ourselves and to you, and to the suffering which has been entailed upon both of our families and our friends by the quarrel in which we have been involved with its repeated fatal consequences, and looking to a termination of the same, and a peaceful, honorable and happy adjustment of our difficulties which shall leave both ourselves and you, all our self respect and sense of unimpaired honor, we have determined to take the initiatory in a move for reconciliation. Therefore we present this paper in which we hold ourselves in honor bound to lay down our arms and to end the strife in which we have been engaged against you and exert our utmost efforts to entirely eradicate all enmity from the minds of our friends who have taken sides with us in the feud hereinbefore alluded to.

And we promise furthermore to abstain from insulting or injuring you and your friends, to bury the bitter past forever, and join with you as good citizens in undoing the evil which has resulted from our quarrel, and to leave nothing undone which we can effect to bring about a complete consummation of the purpose to which we have herein committed ourselves.

PROVIDED:—

That you shall on your part take upon yourselves a similar obligation as respects our friends and us, and shall address a paper to us with your signatures thereon, such a paper as this which we freely offer you. Hoping that this may bring about the happy result which it aims at we remain

Yours Respectfully,
Thos. L. Horrell
S.W. Horrell
C.M. Horrell

Witness
Jno. B. Jones
Maj. Frontier Battalion

The Higgins forces were given this letter for consideration. They took several days to make up their minds, but eventually sent this answer:

Lampasas Texas
Aug 2nd 1877

Messrs Mart. Tom and Sam Horrell
Gentlemen

Your favor dated the 30th ult was handed to us by Maj. Jones. We have carefully noted its contents and approve most sincerely the spirit of the communication. It would be difficult for us to express in words the mental disturbance to ourselves which the said quarrel with its fatal consequences, alluded to in your letter occasioned. And now with passions cooled we look back with you sorrowfully to the past, and promise with you to commence at once and instantly the task of repairing the injuries resulting from the difficulty as far as our power extends to do. Certainly we will make every effort to restore good feeling with those who armed themselves in our quarrel, and on our part we lay down our weapons with the honest purpose to regard the feud which has existed between you and us as a by gone thing to be remembered only to bewail. Furthermore as you say we will abstain from offering insult or injury to you or yours and will seek to bring all of our friends to a complete conformity with the agreement herein expressed by us.

As we hope for future peace and happiness for ourselves and for those who look to us for guidance and protection and as we desire to take position as good law abiding citizens and preservers of peace and order we subscribe ourselves

Respectfully &c
J.P. Higgins
R.A. Mitchell
W.R. Wren

Witness
Jno B. Jones
Maj. Frontier Battalion[37]

These documents were signed just in time. The Lampasas Fair was scheduled for August 21, 22, and 23. There were to be speeches by Governor Hubbard and others, trotting races, premiums, and even a balloon ascension. Everybody was glad that the feud was not going to be allowed to interfere with business.

Many a peace treaty has been signed by weary feudists in Texas, but the one between the Horrells and the Higginses is the only one on record so far which has amounted to more than a very brief breathing spell. The feud was over from this time on. It should not be supposed, however, that former enemies now fell on each other's necks and staged a feast of love and good will. The very next spring they were bristling at each other again.[38] Sergeant Collins of Company C rode into Austin on his way to Huntsville with some prisoners on April 9 and reported that the parties were aroused again. "There was a fear of collision before he left, both parties being in town and armed for fight. The Horrells were there to attend court, they having removed from the county after Major Jones made peace between the two parties last year. . . ."

There may have been some skirmishes, even after the second generation had taken over. When Mart Horrell's son J.S. Horrell, an El Paso dentist, died in Juarez in 1928, his friends recalled that he "was credited with slaying four persons at Lampasas, Texas, in his youth during a land feud," and gave the details as follows: "One night four men attacked him at his farm gate and shot him down. His wife hurried from the house and gave him a gun and he killed all four assailants." [39]

For the remaining Horrell boys there was not much time left to renew the feud. In 1878 Mart and Tom were to meet at the hands of a mob the terrible death they had always tried to avoid.

All the details of the story cannot be dug out at this late date, but it starts with an old bachelor storekeeper named J.F. Vaughan who lived at Rock School House on Hog Creek thirty miles west of Waco. He was supposed to be moderately rich himself, and had a habit of keeping other people's money in the safe in his store. On the night of May 28, 1878, a gang of robbers paid him a call.

They got him to open his store so they could get some tobacco and shot him down as soon as he had unlocked the door. His nephew, Mr. Cantell, and some of the neighbors heard the shooting and came up just as the gang was riding off. They managed to wound one horse, but the rider promptly got up behind one of his pals and all of them disappeared in the darkness, unharmed and unrecognized. When Mr. Vaughan's safe was examined, it was discovered that three thousand dollars was missing of which seventeen hundred belonged to Bosque County and a good share of the rest to Mr. Vaughan's friends. Thus a good many people were affected by the murder.[40]

Several men immediately went to work to track down the criminals—among them Deputy United States Marshal John Stull of Coryell County. It happened that Stull was on bad terms with a powerful and dangerous man named Bill Babb, who was absolute ruler of that little section of Texas. J.B. Cranfill, who was friendly with Babb, describes him as "one of the most picturesque characters that West Texas ever knew. . . . His store at Babbville was one of the largest general stores west of Waco. Not only that, but he had extensive cattle and land interests, and the men who companioned him were accounted the most courageous and daring denizens of the western plains. . . . He was feared by all of Hamilton and Coryell Counties, and even as far down as Waco. When he was sober, he was of amiable temper, but when on one of his sprees, he was a dare-devil. . . . It was as much as a man's life was worth to openly oppose him. . . ." [41]

This was the man on whom John Stull tried to pin the Vaughan murder. One day in the middle of June he swore out a warrant and brought Bill Babb, his son Bill Ike, Dave Ware, Clark Ware, and John Mayfield to Meridian under arrest. How Stull did it has never been revealed, but his deed was certainly a minor miracle. Babb was hustled off so fast that he was not able to pick up any money and had to ask Captain Cureton of Meridian for a loan in order to feed his men. Cureton gave him a twenty-dollar gold piece and the men were able to eat while Judge Childress was making up his mind that there was enough evidence to hold them for the grand jury.[42]

They were all furious. Long John Mayfield stood

around with his hand on his six-shooter, first on one foot and then on the other, and if Bill Babb had just pointed a finger, John would have made it hot for somebody. In view of this state of affairs, it was no surprise to anybody when Stull was murdered outside his blazing house in the early morning of December 8, 1878, by unknown assassins.[43]

Meanwhile another detective, Captain W.H. Glenn of Waco, had traced down the wounded horse and the one which carried double as the robbers were leaving Vaughan's store. Glenn is supposed to have followed the trail to Mart Horrell's place.[44] On August 24 he arrived at Meridian with one of Horrell's men in custody—a twenty-five-year-old McLennan-County boy named Bill Crabtree.

Crabtree was described as "an accomplished desperado," but when his guns were taken away from him he promptly folded up and turned state's evidence. As a result of his testimony Mart and Tom Horrell were arrested on September 8 and brought before Judge Childress for examination. The hearing lasted two weeks. At the end they were refused bail and locked up. Bill Crabtree was the star witness against them, and after it was over he and his conscience hurried to get out of town. Before he reached the outskirts of Meridian, however, he was shot off his horse and left lying under an oak tree by persons who remain officially unknown.[45]

Mart and Tom Horrell were in a very bad spot, and they knew it. They saw a gleam of hope when Judge Blackburn, conducting the October term of District Court back in Lampasas, asked to have them brought back to answer "charges pending against them in Lampasas County," but Judge Childress refused to let them go. He remarked, with unconscious irony, that "They would be in danger from a mob if taken from the jail here." [46]

And so, about eight-thirty on the evening of December 15, 1878, while the good people of Meridian were at church listening to a sermon by the Reverend Mr. Weir, a band of masked men rode into town and surrounded the jail. One of them knocked on the jail door and said he was Deputy Sheriff Whitworth. Mr. Crandell, the jailer, believed him and opened the door to find himself looking into the muzzles of half a dozen pistols. He made no resistance.

Inside, the mob found the door to the cell block fastened securely and guarded by two men. For half an hour they argued and threatened. Then they began to discuss the possibility of soaking the building with kerosene and burning it down. Under this treatment the guards weakened and "opened the door to them, whereupon they proceeded to the cell in which the Horrells were confined and, forcing another prisoner to hold the light, shot both of the Horrells dead in their cages, literally riddling their bodies with bullets.

"Then they emerged in the streets, and, after firing several volleys, they rode out of town, shouting triumphantly and shooting as they went." [47]

Between one and three hundred men were in the mob. About fifty did the work in the jail, and the rest kept firing off their guns outside to discourage interference. It is said that at the first shot Mr. Weir found himself alone in his church talking to empty pews.

Ed Nichols, who lived near Meridian, was in town when it happened. He saw the bodies of the Horrells as they lay on the floor of the blood-spattered cell, and heard how they met their death. Tom weakened some and tried to dodge around the walls while they were shooting at him, but Mart took hold of the bars of the cell door and cursed the mob for the cowards and murderers they were. They pumped five or six shots into him, but he hung onto the bars and cursed them some more, saying that if he had any kind of gun he would run them all off singlehanded. They fired another volley at him and he fell dead, but he didn't need to be ashamed of his exit.[48]

One more thing ought to be said. The old men at Lampasas are certain that Mart and Tom Horrell were not in on the Vaughan murder. "If Mart and Tom had been there," says Gus Coffey, "there wouldn't have been any killing."

That is about all of the story. Someday a good book will be written about Pink Higgins and the history he made after the feud was over.[49] The same could be done for Bill Babb, who was unsuccessfully tried for the assassination of John Stull and finally moved out to the trans-Pecos region near Langtry, where he often used to play poker with Judge Roy Bean, "The Law West of the Pecos." [50]

Of the Horrells only Sam was left. He reared two beautiful daughters and lived peaceably for the rest of his life. Mart's son Sammy, after serving in various city and county offices in Lampasas, went to school and became Dr. J.S. Horrell of El Paso. Pink Higgins's two boys became distinguished lawyers. As usual the second generation showed that the times more than the people are responsible for the breaking out of feuds.

JUSTICE AFTER DARK

The Shackleford
Vigilance Committee

This story begins about the time the first pangs of civilization began to be felt in the neighborhood of Old Fort Griffin, a hundred and some odd miles west of Fort Worth, and known far and wide as the Babylon of the Border. There is not much left of the old place now—a deep cistern, the powder magazine, the old bakery (minus its roof), and a wall or two of one of the officers' quarters, all overgrown with brush and tall grass and infested with rattlesnakes. Below the hill on which the fort was built, in the valley of the Clear Fork of the Brazos, are more extensive relics of the town of Griffin where three or four hundred permanent inhabitants once went about their legitimate business, and a large floating population operated less legitimately. It was a wicked town which "had its man for breakfast" many a morning, but it was exciting and alive, and the men and women of Albany have tried to recapture a little of its vigor and gusto in an annual "fandangle" held on the site of the old fort.

The post was established in 1867 for frontier protection against wild Indians whose depredations were a constant menace until the middle seventies. For the first few years of its existence the military authority was the only law in the region and things went pretty well. Then in 1874 the county of Shackleford was organized; control passed to the civil authorities; and a wave of immigration brought in a mob of gamblers, gunmen, bad women, thieves and crooks of every description. Griffin was a

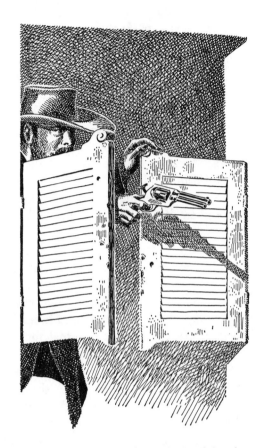

headquarters for the long-haired buffalo hunters; the Dodge City cattle trail passed by it and wild cowboys yipped and yelled in its dozen-odd saloons and honky-tonks every night. There was constant movement of frontier characters in and out, and vice and murder flourished.[1]

Soon after the organization, the town of Albany, now the county seat, was laid out and a mushroom village of canvas and shacks sprang up. The only hotel in town was a big tent with cots scattered about inside and an eating tent off to one side. For a long time the ladies did their shopping at Griffin, fifteen miles north, breathing deep sighs of relief when they got home, but gradually the population grew. In 1881 Judge Clark persuaded the railroad to go through the town by giving them some right of way and a block for the depot, and after that it was just a matter of waiting for the place to grow up.[2] There were growing pains, however.

Being pretty far out toward the arid plains, this part of Texas was not considered good farming country in those days. Mrs. Matthews in her book, *Interwoven*, says the residents of Griffin did not even try to raise gardens because the rainfall was too uncertain. Nevertheless a good many farmers and small ranchers took up land in the bottoms. At old Camp Cooper near Griffin there was one nest of them known as "the grangers," originally from Grimes County, who were heard from when the feuding started.[3]

The thing that brought the trouble on was an organized ring of stock thieves who ran off both cows and horses to the Indian Territory, defying pursuit and killing anybody who tried to interfere with them. As usual they had confederates among the settlers. By 1876 things were so bad they could hardly have been any worse. The *Frontier Echo* over at Jacksboro remarked that "the stealing of horses has become so frequent that the losers could not purchase fresh stock fast enough to satisfy the demand of the horse thief" and suggested that "no medicine will reach the case but blue whistlers or hemp." [4]

This state of affairs called for a strong, determined character to set things right, and the man who seemed to be anointed for the emergency was John M. Larn.

Dark-eyed, athletic, fine-featured, and graceful, he was probably the best-looking cowboy that ever came to Shackleford County, but he had more than good looks to offer, for he was pretty well educated, ambitious, brave, a fine shot, and a natural leader who made friends anywhere he went. Nobody knows much about his background, but one contemporary account says he came from Colorado, and others mention Dodge City, Kansas, as his home. Shortly after his arrival he made friends with one of the best families in the county, became their ranch foreman, fell in love with one of their lovely young daughters, and married her in spite of the uneasiness of her parents. They were both very young (Larn was not much more than twenty-one) but it could have been a perfect marriage. Mary Larn undoubtedly worshiped her husband and never wavered in her belief in him. On his side there was an unfailing devotion to her and their two children. She was heard to say that he never had spoken a cross word to her in his life. They prospered in the cattle business and built a fine, two-story rock ranch house on the site of abandoned Camp Cooper near Griffin on the Clear Fork. Larn was ambitious to make the most of what he had, and nobody foresaw anything but happiness for them.[5]

Larn had a great reputation for courage and audacity, and lived through some hair-raising scrapes in Indian-fighting days. In March of 1874 he was the subject of a story in the Dallas *Herald* about an escape from a band of raiders: "Mr. John Larn, who lives about six miles from the post on Clear Fork of Brazos, was out horse hunting last Wednesday. When in the vicinity of Flat Top Mountain he found his horses. He heard men talking and soon saw horsemen approaching him rapidly, and supposing it to be Lieut. Jones' scout, he continued on toward them, when they suddenly divided so as to encircle him. He then discovered that it was Indians. Riding a fleet animal, he did some expert riding for five or six miles, closely pursued by 12 or 15 savage fiends yelling and shooting. He got in about dark. Following Larn nearly to his home, the Indians obliqued to the right, going through the Matthews' field, taking his horses, then crossed the river, getting G.R. Carter's, John Newcomb's and John Selman's horses, getting, in all, nearly twenty head. They then turned down the Clear Fork, and were followed by citizens to near Brownin's ranch. On hearing this intelligence,

General Buell dispatched, last night at about 8 P.M., Captain Lee and a scout of 20 men and four Tonks, with seven days rations." [6]

They decided to make Larn sheriff. Jacobs, the old sheriff, was not making much progress, and the solid citizens thought some new and young blood might make a difference. The Commissioners' Minutes of Shackleford County show that Larn was sworn in on April 18, 1876. He was only twenty-five years old at this time.

One of his first acts in his new office was to appoint as his deputy a man who had been his neighbor and business associate for some time. John Selman was the man's name. He was a dark, angular, uncommunicative fellow, an all-around gambler, horse trader, and gun toter who twenty years later became famous for killing John Wesley Hardin in an El Paso saloon. He must have had a good deal of intelligence, for the Rangers spoke of him later as a hard one to catch.[7]

Larn and Selman started out strong. According to Edgar Rye, who came to Shackleford County a few weeks before the events he describes, one of their first assignments was to arrest a tough cowboy named Shorty Collins, a desperate fellow with a long record. Larn told him he was under arrest, and when he reached for his gun Selman laid him out as cold as a "Texas norther." [8]

Of course the real reason Larn was put into office was to break up the thieves' ring which was stealing the cattlemen blind. Edgar Rye calls it the McBride-English-Townsend gang, but it seems that one Henderson was the real leader, or at least the worst villain of the band. After a bad robbery and murder in Jones County, the first county west of Shackleford, Larn was given a warrant for Henderson's arrest and disappeared in pursuit. On April 27, Marshal Gilson got a telegram from Larn saying that he had arrested Bill Henderson in Dodge City, Kansas, and was bringing him back. About the first of June he did bring him back along with another member of the gang named Floyd.[9] The responsible citizens rubbed their hands and congratulated themselves. This was the sort of man they needed to run the sheriff's office in that county.

Earlier, however, a vigilance committee had been organized on the best secret-society model. Nobody was supposed to know who the members actually were, but lists of the membership (possibly conjectural) are in existence, and some very important names appear on the rolls. Don Biggers in his reliable *Shackleford County Sketches*, says Larn was "a long time chief in the vigilance committee."

They went right to work. The *Frontier Echo* for April 14, 1876, recorded their first successful foray: "The gang of horse and cattle thieves which have infested Shackleford County for some time past has received a death blow at the hands of the cow men of that section. Joe Watson, the supposed leader of the gang, Charles McBride, 'Reddy' and Dan— were hunted down and killed, McBride was hung near Griffin, Watson, Dan— and Reddy[10] were shot, captured and hung. Much rejoicing among the good citizens at Griffin and this place over the affair as the men were notorious desperadoes and the country is better off without them."

On April 20 they accounted for Houston Faught. He had been caught in the act of stealing a horse, was wounded, captured, and put in the military hospital at the fort. About eleven o'clock on the night of his death a party (composed of "some of the best citizens of the place"), escorted Faught to the river bottoms where there was a good selection of trees, and hanged him thoroughly. On his clothes they pinned a card which read: "Horse thief No. 5., that killed and scalped that boy for Indian sign. Shall horse thieves rule the country? He will have company soon." [11]

Public sentiment was undoubtedly behind the vigilance committee. When the McKinney *Enquirer* suggested whipping, branding, and hanging, in that order, for first, second, and third offenses in the matter of horse stealing, the *Frontier Echo* laughed derisively: "Get out with your nonsense; what's the use of all that bother. Hang 'em first, then if they persist in their innocent amusement, cremate them. If that does not put the kibosh on 'em we don't know what will." [12]

The higher-ups naturally could not see it this way. The governor issued a statement blaming the local officers for mob activity, and the *Echo* for May 19 quoted him: "I have never heard of a sheriff or a jailer being hurt, or one of them hurting any of the assailants; nor have I ever known a *bona fide*, resolute resistance made by a sheriff or a jailer to the demands of a mob, fail to be successful." Judge Fleming in his charge to the grand jury at Jacksboro, June term of 1876, sounded off in the same key: "The Courts, the Juries, and the County officials, gentlemen, are responsible for these infractions of the law." [13]

The vigilantes paid no attention to the protests of governors and judges but went right on hanging. Their next job was done at Albany, the new county seat town. It had no jail as yet—would not have one for some time to come—and when prisoners needed to be secured, the officers had to do some improvising. True, there was one building devoted to public affairs—the courthouse, a primitive edifice of "picket" construction which resembled a barn in size and general effect. There Sheriff Larn's prisoners, Henderson and Floyd, were confined after their unwilling trip from Dodge City in his custody. On June 2 they were still there, but not for long. About eleven o'clock the prisoners were asleep. Their guards, who were named Wilhelm and Berner, had settled down to the job of lasting out the night, when Wilhelm heard a noise outside. Whether he was expecting to hear a noise or not, the record does not say. At any rate he stepped to the door where he was confronted by something like fifty men afoot and twenty more on horseback who "rushed toward him with the command to 'put down that gun.'" [14] Wilhelm gave up meekly and so did Berner. The vigilantes took charge and hustled the prisoners into their clothes. Then they all disappeared into the night with the exception of four men who stayed as a guard over Berner and Wilhelm. In the morning the trail was followed for a quarter of a mile and the two bodies were found hanging to a tree. A local correspondent for the *Frontier Echo*, who recounted these events the day after they happened, remarked with mingled sadness and pride: "It is at best a deplorable state of affairs when Judge Lynch is called to preside, but so far, call them what you may, vigilantes, tall tin hat fellows, or what you please, they have made no mistakes. There is nothing like knowing your man."

Some months went by before there was another necktie party, but the next hanging was big enough to make up for six months neglect. Not many details found their way into print, but in bare outline the facts are startling enough: "Eleven horse thieves just captured and hung 7 miles west of the Fort. Had 27 head of stolen stock. 4 more of the band taken just this side of Ft. Sill." [15]

It was some time during the next year that John Larn got his contract for supplying beef to the army post. Through the fall of '77 and the early winter of '78 he supplied from one to three beeves per day to the quartermaster, and the peculiar thing about it was that his own herd did not seem to get any smaller. But other people's herds did, and that reminded the suspicious ones of something that had happened in 1874. A man named Bryan who was running stock with Larn, was killed by one of Larn's men, and Larn "kept the cattle without administration." The grangers near his home complained that their fat stock was disappearing regularly, while the thin stuff always came home on schedule. Apparently some brand blotting was going on, too. There was some kind of showdown between Larn and the cattlemen early in the game, but everything was kept carefully under cover. One account, published shortly after the feud was over, says that his father-in-law interceded and the stockmen "were temporarily pacified," adding that "everyone was afraid to appear as a witness against these men for fear of being bushwhacked." [16]

Either because he was too busy with his butchering, or because of resentment over the feeling that was growing up against him, Larn had resigned his position as sheriff in the spring of 1877 after about a year in office. Edgar Rye, who was not on Larn's side by any means, states that "during the first six months of his term Larn did more to quell lawlessness than any man who served the people as sheriff before or since this time." [17]

The center of infection as the trouble developed was Larn's home ranch, where some very queer things were said to have happened. The first was the disappearance of Wilks and Jones, two stone masons who had constructed a mile of stone fence on the ranch, the price being set at five hundred dollars. They collected a hundred dollars, demanded the rest when the job was done, and then suddenly disappeared—at least Larn's enemies said they did. When two bodies, so badly decomposed that they could not be positively identified, were found in the river later on, the finger of suspicion pointed sharply at Larn and Selman. In justice to them it should be said that the identification of the bodies was doubtful, that the coroner was not convinced that the dead men had met with foul play and refused to call it murder, and that there was talk of one of the "corpses" having been seen alive later on.[18]

By now the new sheriff, whose name was Bill Cruger, had been stirred up sufficiently to get out a search warrant. Armed with this, a detachment of Rangers invaded the Larn ranch to see what they could find. They must have had a hot tip of some kind, for they immediately started dragging a deep water hole in the Clear Fork close to Larn's slaughter pens and dredged up a number of hides which had been weighted and sunk. Some of the brands could be made out, and it appeared that the neighboring ranchers and grangers had contributed to the collection. It looked like a clear case, but even yet the law could not cope with Larn and Selman. The account already quoted (Galveston *News*, July 13, 1878) stated as a fact that "Larn and Selman defied the Rangers and refused to be disarmed or arrested. They repaired to the magistrate's court armed, and forcibly took away the principal witness from the court, and he soon left the country. For the want of this witness's evidence, no information was filed. The hides were at the court to be examined, but from fear of the parties accused and witness gone the prosecution was abandoned."

The reports of Lieutenant G.W. Campbell of the Rangers throw only a little more light on the situation. On February 26, 1878, he wrote to Major Jones from his camp in Throckmorton County, not far from Griffin, that there was "a big excitement in the settlements over making arrests on Jno. M. Laren and Jno. Sillman, charged with stealing cattle and selling them for beef, they have been furnishing the town of Griffin for some time, the citizens swore out a search warrant and I served it, and found six beef hides in the bed of Clear Fork, not in their own brands (Laren and Sillman's)—taken them to Fort Griffin and turned them over to the officer, a compromise was made and the parties were released. . . ."

Later accounts have stated that two hundred hides bearing brands of all the nearby stock owners, were found in the water hole.[19] Lieutenant Campbell's report, indicating that there were only a few hides and that the brands appeared to have been blotted, makes the evidence against Larn sound much less impressive.[20] At the time the hides were found, he himself swore that the whole thing was a frameup.

This, at any rate, was the start of a feud situation. Larn's neighbors, the grangers, began to go in groups and stay home after dark. They found their horses shot on the prairie, wantonly killed. And they told stories of armed bands of men calling at their houses at night trying to get them to come to the door, of attempts at bushwhacking, and of daylight pursuits of one or another of their number. About the first of February a granger out hunting his calves disappeared and did not come back. Another named Lancaster, who was supposed to have given information which led to the first arrest of Larn and Selman, likewise disappeared one day and was found by a deputy sheriff, who had been sent for, hiding in the brush along the river. He swore that Larn and Selman had chased him, fired at him, wounded him, and would have killed him if they could.[21]

It was said, while all this was going on, that the grangers were so terrified "that they ceased to work their crops, kept close in their houses, and would not even go to their cowpens to milk; sending their wives out to transact all their business that was attended to. But few of them undressed themselves at night for two weeks for fear of an attempt to mob. They were trying to sell their places, improved river valley land, with the growing crops, for a pittance to get away on."

How tense the situation was is best revealed in two letters written to Major Jones. The first was written on June 15, by Sergeant J.E. Van Riper. He reported: "Through a sense of duty and justice to this country I am induced to report to you, though it will be but a feeble endeavor to portray a just and true state of affairs in this section of the country, which are in a terrible stage—armed parties of men are continually riding the country—riding at midnight into the door yards of peaceable citizens and discharging their fire arms frightening women and children, citizens are being run out of the country, leaving their property. Mr. Treadwell and others living in the neighborhood of Jno. M. Lauren and Jno. H. Sellman are continually finding their horses and cattle shot down on the prairies. Milch cows and calves are shot down on the premises after night fall. They have recently lost several hundred dollars worth of stock in this manner, they have now taken up arms in defense of their lives and property, as a last resort, having received no redress nor encouragement by law, both parties going in squads, serious trouble is hourly expected. . . ."

Van Riper was sure the lives of many, including his own, were in danger, that his reports were being tampered with in the post office, and that if something were not done about it very soon the whole country would be "the scene of blackening crimes horrible to think of."

Lieutenant Campbell, on his way to another station after his company had been discharged, sent off a letter to Major Jones the following day (June 16) from Fort Griffin. He recounted killings and disappearances, which had gone before, and described the situation at the moment: "There are about 16 men in the Lauren and Sellman party," he said, "armed with shot guns and improved cartridge guns, the Grangers, as they are called, have taken up arms in self defense for the protection of lives and property. . . . I could give you some names of parties and prove to you that they are into things that is not right in this country, that would make you almost shudder at the thought of such in the standing that they are of being in such business. I only keep back names for self protection but will put you on the track. . . . There was no bill against those parties that killed all of those cattle. WHY? because the majority of the officers in the County who is and has been into a secret organization who was sworn to stand up to whatever was done by any of his party, and there was at one time about eighty of them. . . ."

The only good thing about the Shackleford County feud was the fact that it did not last long. Seven days after Lieutenant Campbell wrote his letter, it was all over in a burst of gunsmoke.

On Saturday night, June 22, Sheriff Cruger got together a posse of eight men and went out to arrest Larn. It was a ticklish assignment for him. Larn was a dead shot and as fearless as a man can be made. Furthermore he was bitter and resentful about what he considered the persecution he had been enduring, and they knew he was bound to make a fight. The sheriff and his posse were mighty thoughtful as they rode out of town, and pretty sure that a number of them were likely not to come back.

But luck was with them this time. They surrounded Larn's house that night. It would have been useless to approach it in the daytime, for he had a lookout post in a cupola on top and they would have been detected long before their arrival.

About daybreak Larn himself came out to do the morning milking. Leaving the rest of his posse out of sight, Sheriff Cruger took Ben Reynolds and Dave Barker with him into the corral and made the arrest as easily as saying, "Good morning!"

Some say it was so simple because Larn had left his gun in the house for the first time in history. Others think he had unbuckled his belt and hung it on the fence out of reach. Ben Reynolds used to say[22] that Larn simply turned over his pistol when Cruger said he had a warrant for him. When he saw that the warrant was from Albany he did say he wished he hadn't surrendered, and that may be the basis for the tale which says he offered Cruger five hundred dollars to give him a gun and let him fight it out. It was also rumored that he asked if he might go back to the house for a minute and remarked, when his request was refused, that he would have killed every one of them if it had been granted. These stories sound a little too lurid to be true.[23]

Old people at Albany remember that he was afraid of being mobbed on the way to town and insisted that his wife and child accompany him, so Mrs. Larn and their boy Will came along in a buggy. They passed through Griffin and arrived safely in Albany where Larn was shackled, with several other prisoners, to a staple in the wall over the fireplace of a private house which was being used as a jail. Meanwhile Mary Larn had picked up a lawyer—as if a lawyer would do any good in a case like that. According to his own story, Edgar Rye, justice of the peace for that precinct, was approached by Mrs. Larn and her lawyer, John W. Wray, in an attempt to get a hearing and have bail granted. They even offered to post a bond of twelve hundred dollars if he would let them guard the prisoner in the hotel. Rye refused. He says a member of the vigilance committee was listening at a crack in the wall and later told him he would have been killed if he had done anything for the protection of the prisoner. He goes on to tell a romantic tale of a race between two bands of men—Larn's friends under Selman, and the vigilantes—the vigilantes arriving first.[24]

John Poe, the town marshal at Griffin, was on guard. Poe went west shortly after this episode, settling in Roswell where he served as a peace officer and became a successful banker. He was with Pat Garrett at the time Billy the Kid was killed and wrote a little book about that happy event.[25] In Albany he was called on often to help the sheriff, as on this particular evening. At twelve o'clock, when he was about to go off guard, the vigilantes seized him, took his weapons, and captured the makeshift jail.

Larn stood up when they came in and looked at them

out of his fierce, dark eyes. The other prisoners rolled over on their stomachs and hid their faces so they would not recognize anybody.

There was very little conversation. The leader of the vigilantes told Larn why they had come and asked if he had anything to say.

"Not to your bunch of cowardly murderers," he replied. "But if you'll turn me loose and give me a forty-five, I'll fight your whole outfit." Seeing that this sort of talk was getting him nowhere, he looked them in the eye and said, "Go ahead. I'll take my medicine."

Eleven men lined up and fired a volley which killed him instantly.

His wife, waiting up in the hotel for what she was afraid might happen, heard the shots and realized that she was a widow.

According to the Rye account, Selman's men were reconnoitering for their own assault when the guns went off. Realizing that it was all over, Selman skipped out and kept ahead of the sheriff until the posse gave out.[26] He headed for Fort Sumner and the wilds of New Mexico where he lay low for a while. In May of 1880, he was back in circulation again, turning up in the neighborhood of Fort Davis with the Jesse Evans gang.

On June 14, Sergeant L.B. Caruthers wrote to Major Jones from Fort Davis: "I find that the band numbered some twenty men last year, and that they have their agents here and in Stockton, their agent here is Capt. Tyson, his real name is John Selman. . . . I think from what I can learn that he is chief of the gang and as he was getting very scarey I had him appointed Dept. Sheriff and Jailor as the jailor had just resigned." On June 22, Caruthers telegraphed that he had arrested Selman, who had offered to give his gang away, and did turn over a list of men in the Shackleford County mob.[27]

Selman's arrest was a considerable embarrassment to the

men of Shackleford. The Rangers wanted to bring him back, but Sheriff Cruger wanted to keep him away as far as possible. He wrote to Major Jones that he could not answer for Selman's life if he returned, and surmised that "the indictments are probably found in order to keep him out of the County as he is such a great thief and scoundrel and withal so sharp that he can not be caught in his rascality." A conviction, he feared, would be hard to get, and if the charges were not sustained there might be "a renewal of the times we have passed through." [28]

The Rangers nevertheless brought Selman back, holding him in jail at Comanche until court time.[29] What happened next is not a matter of record, but Mr. Henry C. Herron of Albany used to tell about it. Selman was lodged in the Albany jail with nine indictments against him. One day the sheriff said he was going to take him over to Griffin to see if he could raise bail. Deputy Herron asked, "Do you want me to take him?"

"No," said Sheriff Cruger. "I want you to go out to Fort Phantom Hill with some papers."

Herron saw what was going on and made no further suggestions. A man named Shailes was deputized specially, and rode over to Griffin with Selman. They went into one of the Griffin stores. Pretty soon Selman asked to go outside, and he and Shailes stepped out behind. In the back yard Shailes fired off his gun a few times and Selman disappeared. "Escaped" is hardly the word for it.[30] He dropped out of sight for a few years but turned up in El Paso in the nineties, old enough to be "Uncle John" Selman to boys like Owen White but still man enough to shoot John Wesley Hardin when they got into an argument. His own turn came very soon after that.[31]

Long before Selman went over the horizon for the last time, the feud was dead. Lieutenant Arrington wrote to Major Jones on August 31, 1878: "I have conversed with quite a number of the good citizens and find everything quiet and from what I can glean I am satisfied that at *one* time nearly everybody belonged to the mob—but the good men are now satisfied that law and order can be maintained without lynch law and the extremists, the smart young men *like it,* from so much experience in the business—and they want to hold on to the substantial men as backers.

"However I think by a mild course, first gaining the confidence of the masses, everything will work well."

It did. But when Mary Larn died in 1947, she was still unreconciled. A year before her end she wrote back to Albany to have her husband's grave furbished up.[32] Through all those years she blamed some of her own closest relatives for what had happened, and she never once admitted that Larn deserved what he got.

One wonders sometimes if she may not have been more than half right.

FOUR ON A LIMB
The McDade Hangings

The old Houston road leaves Austin in a leisurely, winding fashion and takes its time through the cotton fields and brushy pastures—the sweet potato patches and watermelon plots—the mesquite and prickly pear and occasional post oaks which keep this land so shaggy and green. The little towns, dusty and friendly, scatter themselves casually along the highway—Manor and Elgin and McDade, historic places which history has never condescended to celebrate.

McDade, for instance, is hardly more than a wide place in the road today, a run-down-looking little country town of less than five hundred population. There is a single block of one-story business buildings on the south side of the highway, a wooden station beside the tracks across the way, a few stores and residences north of the tracks, a large stock pen at the eastern edge of town. Only that and not much more. Iron gaspipe posts hold up an awning over the low concrete gallery in front of the block of stores, and the sociable proprietors have put out chairs and benches to promote relaxation and gossip. On these chairs and benches the men of McDade have been telling, for the last eighty years, about the terrible hanging feud which raged in that region long ago. They can still show you which of the buildings was the old Rock Saloon, where Billingsley kept his store, the exact spot where Jack and Az Beatty lay dead in the street on Christmas morning, and the place a mile north of town where three men were lynched on Christmas Eve. Of course that is all over now, and McDade is just as sleepy as it looks, but don't let that fool you.

Out north and east of town on the Yegua and the Blue Branch are little inland communities which have changed little if at all in half a century. They still prefer a Winchester to a lawyer in those towns. The difference is that nowadays they don't have to use the Winchester quite so often.

And don't be fooled, either, by the politeness and gentleness of the men you talk to. Of all places in Texas where the old stock have kept their roots in the soil, the McDade region probably ranks first. The vigilantes and feudists never did move out and they all had large families who remained to multiply in their turn. So that anybody you talk to probably has feuding blood in him. But they are all good people—there are no better in Texas, which means there are no better in the world. Like their grandfathers they would never take the law into their own hands if they could get justice any other way.

From the very earliest times, this country was no place for a timid man to fool around in. The Indians infested its thickets and lurked along its highways for many years, and by the time they had been cut down to normal size, there was an adequate supply of tough white men to take over the thieving and killing. The western part of Bastrop County is good farm land but the post oaks and tangled thickets of the Yegua and its branches off to the east gave refuge much too often to all sorts of hard citizens, and even among the respectable settlers life could be pretty primitive.

A center of infection in the early days was the district known as "the Knobs" because of three good-sized hills which show up as little green bulges on the northeast horizon as one leaves Elgin for McDade, ten miles away. In the shadow of the Knobs was the Blue or Blue Branch community where terrible deeds were done in the seventies, and where a man could probably still arrange for a fight if he wanted one.

The Civil War had not been over many months when an

unpleasant odor began to arise from the log houses and lonely woodland roads of this part of Texas. In 1868 stories were getting around about horse thieves and desperadoes in the cedar brakes of Bastrop County, among whom "it may be unsafe for horsemen to travel without being well armed." [1] Good citizens, not yet convinced that the law could not help them, were offering their services to the sheriff.

When the Central Railroad established its railhead at McDade in the fall of 1871, boom-town life on a small scale was added to the ordinary perils of existence.[2] A gang of thugs began preying on anybody who had money. Men who had picked up a few dollars at the gambling tables in the back room of the Rock Saloon were apt to be relieved of their winnings on the way home. Settlers who brought in their cotton to be shipped sometimes suffered the same fate. And as for stock stealing—well, that went on all the time and it appeared sometimes as if everybody was doing it on a reciprocal, round-robin basis. The big cattlemen kept bands of tough cowboys who didn't much care what brands were on the hides of the steers they drove off. And the little ranchers got even by taking toll of the big herds whenever they got a chance. This, of course, was just casual, friendly stealing. The really important rustling was done by "the gang."

Peace officers could not do much about it. The gang members, whoever they were, protected each other as devotedly as if they had been brothers in a righteous cause —lied, perjured themselves, intimidated witnesses, and murdered people who got in their way. By the middle seventies a counterorganization had begun to take shape; at least there was some vigilante work going on. On May 4, 1874, a Negro was lynched near McDade for killing a white man.[3] Early in January of the next year two men named Land and Waddell were finished off by the stranglers and found hanging from a tree one Sunday morning.

It was supposed that they were "dangerous characters and desperadoes." [4]

The gang held up its end successfully and made life extremely uncertain for the opposition. First Old Man Horace Alsup, coming home from Lexington on horseback, was bushwhacked (he knew too much about something);[5] and then they got Pea Eye.

Pea Eye was the nickname of Bill Craddock, an old man with a pair of very small eyes. He was a good citizen—in fact too good, for he had seen the gang stealing cattle, recognized some of them, and appeared in court against them. So they waited until he took a load of cans to the syrup mill in his ox wagon one Monday morning in September of 1875. As he was coming back from town they slipped up behind him and left him dead in the bottom of his own wagon with twelve buckshot in his body, one in the heart. Mrs. Craddock found him there when the oxen, long overdue, jogged into the yard.[6]

This was a particularly scandalous murder, for Craddock was "an old harmless citizen" respected by everybody. People began to ask, "Shall this man's blood cry to heaven for vengeance in vain?" [7]

Apparently the answer was "No," for immediately the lynching business increased its tempo. A mob over on the Yegua hanged a "hereditary horse thief" named Cordell in November,[8] and during the spring of '76 the Turner and Crow affair came up, making a small separate feud all by itself.

At its northern extremity Bastrop County comes to a point and plants a spearhead in the flank of Williamson County. North of this point lived the Olive brothers, Jay, John, Prentice, and Jim, a powerful clan of ranchers, farmers, and peace officers who seem to have been pretty well able to take care of themselves and their own stock.[9] Not everybody had a high opinion of their methods as stock raisers but they had many friends and supporters who

backed them up when they announced, after putting up with constant losses for a long time, that they "would kill anyone they found skinning their cattle or riding their horses." [10] A possible result of this declaration was the death of Turk Turner and James H. Crow on the high prairie in Lee County not far from McDade on March 22, 1876, under peculiar circumstances.

A detailed account of this episode was given by the Austin *Weekly Statesman* for March 30: "Two beeves had been killed and skinned and in the absence of the parties who did it, the carcasses were discovered, and watch kept to see who would return to carry away the beef and hides. Finally the above parties returned with a wagon, and after having loaded up and started away, they were fired upon by unknown parties and both killed. The bodies were found by a son of old man Crow, who had been sent out to look for his father after he had returned from school in the evening. The remains were found several hundred yards apart, and the team tied to a tree near which the beeves had been killed. The marks and brands on the hides showed that the animals were not the property of the men who were hauling away the beef and the hides. Turner had long been regarded as a lawless, dishonest character and desperado, but old man Crow, though he had a son in the penitentiary, was not so regarded. The gentleman who furnished us this information says that in the last three or four months twelve persons, all thieves and desperadoes, have been killed in that country within a radius of about twenty-five miles, and that the gang has not yet been entirely wiped out."

What the *Statesman* did not know or did not choose to mention was the odd way in which the killers had disposed of their victims. Turner and Crow had been wrapped in the green hides they had just removed, and left there—a neat way of reminding those interested of the nature of their offense.[11]

The gang bided their time and did not strike back until August, but when they did strike they cut to the bone. Again the *Statesman* printed the details:

"A letter received in this city Thursday from Post Oak

Island says that on the night of August 1, a party of fifteen or twenty men attacked the Olive brothers on their ranch. Besides the three brothers there were three white men and two negroes. Jay Olive was shot in the body in twenty-two places, and it is thought he will die. Prince Olive was shot in the hip; and a man named Butler several times in the leg and hip. Bill Wells, one of the negroes, was shot twice in the head. The Raiders got $750 from the house, and then forced one of the negroes to burn it. The trouble is said to have grown out of the Crow and Turner tragedy, which occurred in that neighborhood some six months since. . . . Crow and a suspicious character named Turner were killed in the woods near McDade while skinning a beef with the Olive brand. Crow had a son who had served one or more terms in the penitentiary and he accused the Olives of killing his father, and threatened to revenge his death. Since that time it is said he has been at the head of a band of roughs and desperadoes, and this crowd is suspected of committing the horrible tragedy . . . of August 1." [12]

This early flareup of the Bastrop County troubles seems to have fizzled out in September of 1876. The Olives went on trial at Georgetown for murder. Their friends camped out on one side of town; the friends of Turner and Crow took up positions on the other; and for a while the air was full of sulphur. A startled traveler passed through town at the time and ran onto the two bands, one of about sixty men and the other of about forty. He asked the people in Georgetown what was going on, and nobody would say a word. Down the road a little way he found people less reticent and learned that the two parties "were awaiting the verdict of the jury in the case, and if it were against the Olive boys, they would sally into town and take them from the officers of the law; that the company of sixty men were organized to prevent these results, and to see that the law was vigorously executed. The men, however, in each company stated that they were all law-abiding citizens, and were organized for no bad purpose, but simply to see that the law was vindicated." [13]

The records show that the Olives were acquitted, and apparently both parties accepted the verdict, since no report of hostilities came to the outside world.

Meanwhile other dead men were turning up. Two of them had been found hanging by their own stake ropes near the Williamson County line on May 22 of that same year—1876. They were strangers who had plenty of money on their persons, and nobody could tell why they had been left hanging there. Later in the summer, another murdered man was left naked, except for a hickory shirt and a blanket, in the woods near Taylor in Williamson County, and there were conjectures that there was a connection between this episode and the "Post Oak Island tragedy," meaning the Turner-Crow business.[14]

The good people of Bastrop County were becoming desperate. One of them who functioned as correspondent for the Galveston *News* wailed in print: "Crime is holding high carnival in this state. Here in Bastrop County, under the very shadow of the capitol, there have been ten persons killed in the last few months. Who is to blame for this terrible increase of crime throughout the land? . . . There have been more men killed in Texas in the last year than she lost during the late war." [15] The editor of the *Statesman* suggested a remedy: "Instead of hanging, have horse thieves and robbers surgically rendered incapable of crime and of the procreation of knavery." He figured it would cost about ten dollars a case.[16]

The inevitable answer to these outrages in the seventies was a secret organization of rope workers, and the new abuses caused a reorganization of the vigilantes or at least an intensification of their activity. The editor of the *Western Chronicle* at Sutherland Springs passed on to his readers a report that, "In Caldwell and Bastrop Counties societies have been formed to protect citizens from being stolen out by horse thieves. An initiation fee is charged and the money used in sending a delegation after thieves who steal horses from any member of the society." [17] If there was such an organization, its constitution and by-laws have never been published. The old residents, how-ever, have no doubt of its existence, and the great hanging of 1877 is pretty good proof.

Five men were wanted by the vigilance committee and a way was found to round them all up together. At this time a famous local character named Pat Earhart was living out at Blue just under the Knobs. He may have seemed a little out of place in this frontier community for he had better clothes and better manners than his neighbors, and some extra education too. In addition to managing his farm he ran a singing school and did a little preaching on the side. Also he was a fine fiddler and gave frequent dances in his house.[18] Of course everybody went to those dances, and it was practically a certainty that the five men would be on hand whenever the fiddles began to squeak.

On June 27, 1877, Pat gave the dance which made history. It was a gay affair with refreshments presided over by Pat's Negro cook, Aunt Rose Carpenter, while Steve Hawkins (a Negro fiddler) helped with the music. Sure enough the five showed up and practically took over the party, including the refreshments.[19] In the midst of the festivities, however, members of the vigilante organiza-tion appeared at front and back doors and had Pat Earhart call out the names of the men they wanted. Four of them responded. Their names were Wade Alsup, John Kuyken-dall, Young Floyd, and Beck Scott. The fifth one, whose name was Scales, somehow had managed to be somewhere else, and there are those who say he hasn't stopped running yet.

John Kuykendall had enough arms in the lean-to at the back of the house to fight off an army, but not one of those four young men thought about putting up a fight. It may have been that they did not realize the seriousness of their predicament until it was too late. Beck Scott, who was dancing with Fanny Alsup when his name was called, borrowed her fan (it was a hot night), remarking, "It will be hot as hell before we get to Giddings." Wade Alsup caught on faster; he knew they were not going to jail at Giddings. "You won't need no fan where we're going," he said.[20]

It was about two o'clock in the morning when this happened. The masked men took their prisoners off into the darkness, and four or five hundred yards from the house they hanged them to a tree—four on a limb.[21]

The horrible and sudden death of these four young men threw a bad scare into many people, some of whom had unstained records. Jim Floyd, brother of the Young Floyd who was lynched, left the country and became a preacher, and others may have had their lives as violently wrenched into new patterns. But mostly the sinful continued to sin and the good people continued to lose their lives and their money. By 1883 the time was ripe for another explosion.

There is no positive evidence to fall back upon, but ancient gossip reports a split in the band of outlaws by this time. Bitter hatreds had grown up within the group itself; a few of the disgruntled may possibly have joined the vigilantes and may even have taken care of some of the executions decreed against their former friends.[22]

In any case conditions had to get worse before they could get better. A few examples will illustrate what sort of things were going on in Bastrop County, Texas, in the year of our Lord 1883. On August 23, a man named Bob Young got into a quarrel with storekeeper George Milton in McDade and tried unsuccessfully to shoot him with a shotgun. The next morning he lay in wait for Milton and tried again, but George was hard to get and wounded

Young, probably fatally, at the same time scaring an unsuspecting drummer half to death and puncturing the trousers of a couple of bystanders, not necessarily innocent.[23]

The Keuffel affair came next. Old Mr. Keuffel was a country storekeeper and postmaster living some nine miles from McDade at the little settlement of Fedor. On the night of November 22, 1883, when Keuffel and his clerk were closing up, a young fellow entered the store, seized the proprietor by the shoulder, and told him he wanted his money. Keuffel quietly unlocked his cash drawer, whereupon the robber shot him in the mouth at such close range that the flash burned the poor old man's face. The bandit then turned to the clerk. "Pull the drawer open," he ordered. The frightened clerk did as he was told and was promptly shot through the head. The man got fifteen dollars in money out of the drawer.[24] Two men were arrested for this deed, but the next robbery was more mysterious.

It happened to Allen Wynn, a citizen of McDade who had been a partner of George Milton's in the store and saloon business and who was at this time cotton farming out near the Knobs. In November of 1883 he had left town with some cotton money in his pocket and had crossed the heavily wooded Yegua bottoms when two men slipped out of hiding, climbed in at the back end of his wagon, beat him in the face, and robbed him. He lost sixty-five dollars of a neighbor's money and fifty of his own. He recognized the men but did not dare make open complaint.[25] The vigilance committee, however, noted down all the facts.

It took one more shooting to get out the night riders once more. This time it was Deputy Sheriff Heffington of Lee County who had to die. He had been very active in hunting the murderers of Keuffel and his clerk. On the first of December he came into McDade looking for somebody, and about nine-thirty that night he approached a dark figure standing beside a tree, asked who he was, and got a bullet in the breast instead of an answer. The man slipped away in the darkness.[26]

That was more than enough. Seven days later two hundred citizens assembled openly at the wooden church in the east end of McDade (the only one) to talk about a little righteous hanging. Even now nobody will tell who was there, though all the old-timers could mention some names. And a wise man doesn't try very hard to find out. What good would it do to know? It is said, however, that they went very thoroughly into the list of men who would have to go before there would be peace and order in the county, and at least one of those present heard the name of a near relative called out and confirmed while he sat tight, unable to do a thing about it.[27]

There was nothing secret about the meeting except the names of those in attendance and of the men they proposed to liquidate. The Galveston *News* carried a story about it the day after it happened: "Today 200 citizens from this and adjoining counties met here in church. Their object was to assist the officers of the law to use every effort to suppress lawlessness. The people in this section are thoroughly aroused, and appear to be determined to stop the frequent killings and robberies which have recently occurred in this vicinity. The very best citizens are interesting themselves in this matter." [28]

On Christmas Eve the meeting bore fruit.

The town was crowded with last minute shoppers and people getting a start on their Christmas celebration. A noisy bunch of men had accumulated in the Nash brothers' Rock Saloon—among them several members of the Notch Cutters, as the old gang, or at least one wing of it, had come to be called.

About seven-thirty the noise came to a sudden stop when a group of masked men quietly entered the front door. There were more of them outside, somewhere between

forty and eighty, as the story has been handed down.
They never said a word, but each one had a Winchester in
the crook of his left arm and they nudged three men out
of the saloon with those gun barrels. The three were Thad
McLemore, Wright McLemore, and Henry Pfeiffer. Thad
had been arrested earlier in the evening on a charge of theft
preferred by S.G. Walker of McDade. Just how he came to
be spending a pleasant evening in the saloon when he was
supposed to be under arrest, the record does not state.
Pfeiffer and Wright McLemore are said to have been under
bonds for cattle theft, but that does not mean they were
guilty. Old residents say Pfeiffer was not wanted at all,
though he had been running with the bunch. They took
him because he recognized one of the masked men, called
him by name, and asked him what he was up to. He might
as well have cut his own throat.[29]

The two McLemores were older men—Thad was over
forty; Wright was past fifty and crippled up with rheu-
matism. Wright's wife wrote in the bitterness of her
heart a few days after the lynching that he "had only been
in the county six months, was almost an entire stranger. . . . He felt his life was nearly over, and came here to
spend his remaining days near his brothers." [30]

The Heffington murder probably gave the mob its mo-
tive. Felix McLemore, a brother of the dead men, told a
reporter for the St. Louis *Globe-Democrat* on the twenty-
ninth that "The Regulators probably thought my brothers
killed him. This was not true." He went on to tell how
Heffington had come to town looking for two boys suspected of robbing a post office—that the McLemores were
at home eating supper when the killing took place—and
that two men named Fitzpatrick and Goodman were the
killers. Thad, said Felix, afterward had a conversation with
these men. "Fitzpatrick and Goodman were out by a
tree in the dark, when Heffington came along and peered
closely into their faces as though looking for some one. He

was so disguised that neither of them recognized him. As he started on Fitzpatrick caught him by the arm, drew a revolver and shot him, thinking it was Joe Nash. I have no doubt but Fitzpatrick killed Heffington. Fitzpatrick skipped out and has not been heard from since. This led to the organization of the vigilance committee some weeks ago." [31]

In the saloon playing pool that night was a young man fresh from Georgia—one of the curious who had come to see for himself if the West was as wicked as he had been led to believe. When the three men were herded together and shoved outside, he got his hat and joined them, thinking they were going to walk to the Knobs where there was a Christmas party and dance going on. One of the vigilantes finally motioned him away and he came back into the building complaining about this lack of hospitality and exclaiming about how queer it was. Nobody would say a word to him about it or answer a question. In fact all conversation in that building was over for the evening. He did not hear until the next afternoon that the three men had been taken a mile north of town into the brush and hanged to a blackjack tree. When he finally realized what he had tried to join, he got so sick he had to go to bed. [32]

Jeptha Billingsley was a young man then. He went out with Deputy Sheriff Sid Jenkins to get the bodies and helped to cut them down. Sixty years later he was still haunted by what he saw. "I knew all three of these men pretty well," he once said, "and the sight of them with their twisted faces and the nooses hanging at different angles about the victims' necks was about the most gruesome thing I have ever witnessed. I don't ever want to see anything like that again." [33]

Meanwhile Christmas morning had come, and the rumors had begun to spread through the neighborhood. Nobody knew yet what had happened to the three men, or if anything had happened at all. But people began to gather to ask questions and speculate, and some of the businessmen made sure their weapons were handy. It was well within the bounds of the possible that the friends of the McLemores might come in to take the matter up.

Two who seemed to have special reason for being alert were George Milton and Tom Bishop. Milton was the owner of the principal store in McDade. The St. Louis reporter described him as "quite wealthy and well liked: quiet, dignified deportment; medium size." He wore a goatee and seems to have lived up to it. Bishop had a saloon and was not so much the old-school gentleman as Milton, but he seemed just as quiet and inoffensive. The man from St. Louis said he was "small, light-haired, modest, boyish and insignificant in appearance.[34] His friends remember that he had extremely small feet which he shod in the shiniest of cowboy boots. In spite of all this he was probably the most efficient fighter in town and had come out on top in several shooting scrapes. Neither he nor Milton were the kind who argue very long when a fight is brewing, and they seem to have made common cause against the Notch Cutters.

About nine o'clock the two of them came downtown and sat with some friends on the gallery in front of Milton's store for a while. They saw a band of six men ride in from the north, cross the tracks, and go into the Rock Saloon. Somebody asked, "I wonder what brings those men to town so early?" Bishop said, "Well, it's Christmas, isn't it?"

It seems that it was really Christmas which had brought the six men to town. They were Charley Goodman, Byrd Hasley, Robert Stevens, and three of the Beatty boys—Jack, Heywood, and Az (for Asbury). They were all related somehow, Stevens being a brother-in-law of the Beatty boys. They lived out in the Post Oak district—Stevens on the Yegua; the Beattys north of McDade about seven miles toward the Knobs. They were friends of the

McLemores and there was bad blood between all of them and the men in town. Only the Saturday before, the Beattys had quarreled with Tom Bishop and there had almost been a shooting. Men who once lived with and worked for the Beatty family say that they were not much to look at—just ordinary unrefined frontier Americans.[35] Dr. G.T. King, now of Elgin, insists that they always paid their bills and didn't have to be asked for the money, either. Old Walt Beatty, the father, wasn't anybody to fool around with, and his wife would fight you as quick as any of the rest of them if she thought you needed a whipping. Az was something of a fist-fighter, but Jack was inoffensive and peaceable. They were fairly well-to-do— at least not poor—and lived in a big log house with room for four boys and a daughter or two.[36]

The story the Beatty boys told was that they had not come to town looking for trouble. Not all of them were armed, and Heywood Beatty had only four cartridges in his six-shooter. As he spoke for himself, this is how it happened: "I . . . went to the town of McDade on the morning of December 25, 1883. I went to get some money I had at Mr. Milton's—thirty-five dollars. I carried my pistol with me, so as to get some cartridges to fit it. I did not have but four cartridges in my pistol. I wanted to kill some hogs in a few days; they were running in the woods." Stevens said he went because he wanted to buy some medicine for one of his children and exchange some boots at Billingsley's store.

As soon as they entered the saloon some obliging bystander wanted to know if they had heard of the mob the night before. No, they hadn't. Another contributed the information that Heywood Beatty's name had been called. This stirred the Beatty boys up considerably and they began talking loudly and profanely. Jack declared that there were a lot of so-and-sos around there accusing boys of doing things they were innocent of. He remarked to

Horace Nash, one of the proprietors of the saloon (as Nash testified under oath) that "Bishop and Milton had accused Heywood Beatty of helping Fitzpatrick to kill Heffington and robbing Winn, and that I, or we, intended to kill both Milton and Bishop." While they were in this angry state of mind somebody suggested that they go down and see Milton. So they went.

From here on it looks as if the brothers and their friends were hunting for trouble. Goodman went off to get some more cartridges, but had bad luck. In Bassist's store they told him that all their forty-five pistol cartridges were gone. So he bought fifty forty-four Winchester cartridges, which could be used, but were not very accurate. There might have been more bloodshed that day if he had been able to get ammunition. Jack Beatty had entered Milton's store and gone back to engage Mr. Milton in conversation. He wanted to talk about the lies that were being spread implicating Heywood in the Heffington murder. "I haven't heard anyone accuse him of it," replied Milton, "but I have heard it reported around that he carried Jeff Fitzpatrick out of town behind him on his horse after the killing."

"That's a damned lie too!" Jack exploded. "And now I hear there have been three men taken out of this town last night. . . ." At that moment the shooting started.

Az Beatty had come up to Tom Bishop, who was still sitting on the gallery talking to Dr. Vermilion, cursed him, and told him he would have to get out of town. Bishop replied in the same key, pulled his six-shooter, reached around Dr. Vermilion (who was scurrying for cover inside the store), and shot Az in the thigh. He said he thought Az was reaching for his own pistol at the time. Az closed with him, pushed him off the gallery, and wrestled with him in the street for possession of the gun.

At the first shot Milton, inside the store, got up and ran for the door. Jack Beatty tried to stop him, but Milton threatened him with a pistol which he carried until he reached his shotgun near the entrance. Byrd Hasley and Charley Goodman were at the door, apparently trying to keep him from coming out and joining in the fight. He fired his shotgun to scare them off and in a minute everybody was outside.

By now the scuffle for the pistol was over. Bishop had got in another shot and Az was dead or dying, so they turned on the other Beatty boys. At least one other person was firing from across the tracks by now and the air was full of lead. Jack Beatty dropped, shot in the head and body. A bullet struck Goodman's pistol in his holster and wounded him. Stevens ran for the stockyards. Nineteen-year-old Heywood Beatty was the only one left in the fight, but he was game. A young man named Willie Griffin dashed out of Nash's saloon at this moment with a pistol in his hand and yelled for everybody to leave town. Heywood shot him through the head.

This is how Heywood described what happened: ". . . I went out to where the boys were. I said, 'Tommie, what is the row about?' and he said, 'What are you coming out here for with your pistol out?' I then threw up my hands and said, 'I ain't got it out.' About that time Milton came to the door with a double barreled shotgun and said, 'Get away from there, everybody.' I then started to run in the direction of Bassist's store and the shooting commenced. Both of my brothers were shot down. I was off about thirty steps when Milton shot me twice with a shot gun. I was running; when he shot me the last time I pulled out my pistol and shot at him twice. I do not recollect seeing Griffin during the fight. If I shot Griffin I did it accidentally. I and Griffin, and Bishop and Milton had always been good friends and on good terms. After I was shot I went below town, crossed the railroad, and through Milton's pasture home, afoot." [37]

Milton told a friend one time that Heywood Beatty was the gamest man he ever knew. After the first exchange of shots Heywood turned his back and walked away, reloading as he walked. When he had the chambers full, he turned around and shot some more. They say he was marked by bullets in no less than seventeen places, but he walked home and didn't come anywhere near dying.[38]

In spite of conflicting testimony, it seems that Jack Beatty and Stevens were unarmed, and Charlie Goodman did not draw his pistol. A bullet fired at him struck his gun and wounded him slightly, practically proving that his pistol was in the holster at the time.

An episode like that is over in a few minutes, but not the consequences. Telegrams were sent off for the sheriff at Bastrop. He came up as fast as he could, located and cut down the bodies of the men who were lynched, picked up the Beatty brothers off the street, where they had been left lying in their own blood and brains, and proceeded to make arrests. Milton and Bishop were placed under bonds of fifteen hundred dollars, and Heywood Beatty, Stevens, and Goodman, were arrested and taken to Bastrop. The governor got excited and ordered the Brenham Grays to proceed to the scene of the crimes. They proceeded, and immediately turned around and went back, seeing that there was nothing for them to do.[39]

Heywood and his friends were let out under heavy bonds. Heywood himself was prosecuted in May for the death of Willie Griffin, but the jury hung. On November 1, 1884, it was announced that the cases against him and the rest were *nol prosequied*.

There was a reason for it. Another (unpublicized) mass meeting is said to have been held at McDade about this time. A list of people was made up, a spokesman (a local doctor) was selected, and he made the rounds telling the chosen ones that they had ten days to wind up their affairs.[40]

With or without benefit of warnings, Heywood Beatty left the country, settled near Mineral Wells, and did not come back for many years. There is a story that he was

pursued by one of his enemies but reached home before his
pursuer could catch him, got his gun, and put in the first
shot. An old McDade boy, now living at Bastrop, saw him
once at a Woodman's convention at Mineral Wells and
recognized him, but did not introduce himself. The story
is told that years later, when everything had quieted down,
he wrote to Milton saying that he had harbored bitterness
in his heart for many years, but it was all gone now; that he
had some business to settle up and would like to come
back to McDade if there would be no trouble. Milton told
him to come on but not to linger after he had finished what
he came to do. So he came back for a few days and sold
some of the old Beatty property. After he had finished, he
and a friend or two got on their horses to ride to McDade,
but when they reached the outskirts he stopped his horse.
"Boys," he said, "I'm out of trouble and I want to stay out.
I won't go in there." And he didn't.[41]

One man looked him up in later years and quizzed him
about the feud. This was Dean T.U. Taylor of the University of Texas, an indefatigable collector of out-of-the-way
bits of Texas history. In 1939 he published an account of
an interview with Heywood, then seventy-six years old.
The story differed in many respects from the one he told at
the examining trial in 1884, but he still felt that he had been
in the right.[42]

Trouble was not yet over in Bastrop County, though
the feud was, when the Notch Cutters broke up. In June,
1884, Pete Allen was shot by unknown assassins near
Blue,[43] and in 1886 Frank Renault was hanged out in the
woods somewhere and left there "until the buzzards flew."
This was the last hanging, and the stealing petered out
after that.[44]

The Pete Allen killing is sometimes used by the older
generation as an example of the danger of bringing these
sins to light again when once they have been forgotten.
Pete was found dead in the road and somebody had left

the print of a boot heel in his face. Twenty years afterward some of his friends or kinsfolk started speculating about who did it and made up their minds that they could fix the blame. The next step was to try to get even. One night somebody roped at the man they suspected and nearly got him—the rope bounced off his shoulder. Before they could try again, another man, on his deathbed, confessed that he was the one who had stomped Pete Allen's face.[45]

Too much talk, they say, could still cause trouble.

The Subsiding Eighties

★

. . . the scene was changing in Texas so rapidly as to defy description. The cowmen had within five years following 1877 covered the Western Plains, taken the Panhandle, and the arid and broken spaces that are drained by the Pecos. Behind the cowmen came the farmers to fence the water holes and turn the prairie sod. . . . Civilization had overtaken the Rangers. . . .

WALTER PRESCOTT WEBB, *The Texas Rangers*

The people of both factions, especially the mob element, were antagonistic to us when we first went to San Saba, and our lives were in danger. When we four boys pitched our tent at Hannah's Crossing, we shook hands with each other and made a solemn pledge that we would stay there and do our duty if we all had to die together. We vowed that we would arrest anybody of either faction whom we caught disobeying the law, and that we would die working the lever of our guns before we would give up our prisoners, no matter how many men we had to fight.

SERGEANT W. J. L. SULLIVAN, *Twelve Years in the Saddle*

BETTER DAYS

The really bad times in Texas were over by the mid-eighties.[1] Not that mobs, lynchings, vigilantes, difficulties, pistol duels, ambushings, factional quarrels and all the other elements of feuding were a thing of the past—but the turning point had been reached. Texas was becoming civilized.

Two obvious reasons for the changed conditions were the westward movement of the frontier and the ministrations of the Texas Rangers.

The frontier moved with a tidal wave of cattlemen who overflowed the arid regions of West Texas, inundated the Panhandle, and sloshed over into New Mexico. In 1881 the railroad reached El Paso and the last great Indian fight in Texas occurred. At least some of the dangers and uncertainties which helped to produce frontier justice were now a part of history.

As for the Rangers, that indomitable band of men so insignificant in numbers and so mighty in achievement—the Rangers had broken the back of organized lawlessness in the state. Captain Oglesby wrote to Adjutant General King from San Diego, Duval County, on March 3, 1882: "After an experience of four years in the Southwest I feel safe in saying that law and order prevails now to a greater extent and the country is in better condition than I have known it during the time of my service."

It was that way all over Texas. The anguished and hopeless wails of the seventies, when no force seemed able to cope with the universal wickedness, were raised less often in the eighties. The Rangers could prevent some of the killing; could stop it if it got started; and could bring the guilty to punishment at the very least. Justice could be had.

The feuds which started in the eighties were few in number and, with three exceptions, not very big. The running battle between the Marlows and the mob at Graham in 1888, the mob trouble in San Saba County (which did not reach its climax until 1896), and the Jaybird-Woodpecker War at Richmond, in 1889, are the best the eighties have to offer. There were, of course, a hundred—maybe a thousand—family squabbles and fusses between neighbors which might be spoken of as feuds, but they are too small to bother with here.

Strangely enough the two great bones of contention during this decade—the trouble over barbed wire and the feeling between cowmen and sheepmen—did not produce any major feuds. The fence cutting, which came to a head in 1883, made a terrific amount of trouble and cost many a man his life, but it was a sort of state-wide guerrilla warfare and never did attain the focus necessary for a real, man-sized, long-drawn-out feud situation. The same is true of sheep trouble. There were fights and killings galore, but no big feuds. This will surprise many people, including some historians, who have always believed that sheep and barbed wire were the major causes of feuds in the early days. It just goes to prove the dangers of too much early reading of the novels of Zane Grey.[2]

A FAMILY
NAMED MARLOW

There were five Marlow brothers, all brave men. Their names were Charley, Alf, Ellie (or Epp—for Llewellyn), George and Boone. They lived in clan fashion, sticking together through good times and bad, ready to fight for each other if and when the need arose.

They never had much, but they got along. They might have done better if they had stayed in one place long enough to accumulate property, but they were nomads of the American frontier, always on the move. Their father was a rover out of Nashville, Tennessee, who raised horses and practiced medicine (his professional training was probably sketchy) until his death in 1885. His restless nature drove him always onward—to Missouri, California, Texas, the Indian Territory, Mexico, Colorado, New Mexico, Oklahoma, and Texas again. His family had small opportunity to form strong ties with outsiders, though the boys did manage to pick up wives as they went along. Their loyalty to each other, however, was unshakable.[1]

They were just ordinary frontiersmen to look at—short, wiry, roughly dressed men with blond hair and blue eyes. They were mild mannered, soft talking, and inoffensive.[2] Boone Marlow, the one who came to be best known, was described in 1888 as twenty-three years old, five feet seven inches tall, 145 pounds in weight, slightly bowed in the legs, with a very small light mustache and a missing forefinger on his right hand.[3] Neither he nor any of his brothers looked the part they had to play.

They worked at any job that came along but their real business was farming and stock raising. At the time of their trouble their enemies described them as "a family of five noted thieves and cutthroats," [4] but there is no evidence that their business included rustling or that they themselves were desperadoes. They regarded themselves as victims of the big cattleman's perennial urge to drive his small competitors off the range.

It is true that they lived in the Indian Territory, where shady characters often took refuge, and that they had many friends among the Comanche and Kiowa Indians, but these facts prove nothing about the Marlows and their record. About all we can say of them for certain is that they were hard-working boys who lived in wild country and fought hard when they had to fight.

They had their first brush with trouble in 1886, when they were living in Wilbarger County on the Texas side of the Red River. They had a few cows, but they were actually working out a grading contract for the Denver and Fort Worth Railroad. The country round about was still short on law and order. Four years before their arrival the Texas Rangers had been called in to break up a mob (which included the sheriff) organized to hang cattle thieves.[5] In such an environment almost anything could happen at almost any time.

By now Elizabeth Marlow had married and settled near her mother and brothers. Boone got on his horse one day and rode over to see her. As he approached her house, a man named James Holdson (or Holstein) started shooting at him.[6]

It would seem that there must have been some build-up to such procedure, but the Marlows always said that Boone didn't know the man at all, never exchanged a word with him, and had no idea why he was being attacked. They deduced that Holdson must have been drunk and that he mistook Boone for somebody else. In any case, he had picked the wrong man to shoot at. Boone got off his horse, took his Winchester out of the scabbard, and shot Holdson dead.[7]

The authorities at Vernon seem to have done nothing

about the killing at the time, but Boone did not wait around for developments. He left at once, and the family soon followed him. They lived in Colorado for a while and eventually moved back to their old haunts in the Indian Territory. For something like six years they raised horses and corn and made no news.[8]

Then in the early fall of 1888, their names came to the attention of Deputy United States Marshal E.W. (Ed) Johnson down in Young County, Texas. Graham, the county seat, was also the seat of the United States Court which exercised jurisdiction over a large section of the Indian Territory, including the part where the Marlows lived. It was eighty-five miles northwest of Fort Worth and a long day's ride south of the Red-River boundary between Texas and the No Man's Land to the north.

Johnson, a tough peace officer in spite of the fact that he had only one hand, was beginning a campaign against rustlers at the request of an anti-thief organization which had been set up by the big cattlemen of the region. He turned his attention to the Marlows when a telegram arrived in 1888 reading as follows:

> Look out for the five Marlow brothers, who are endeavoring to get away with forty head of horses stolen from this place.

It was from Sheriff Doc Burns of Trinidad, Colorado. The Marlows say that a short time later Johnson received a letter from Burns retracting the telegram: "I find that I was mistaken in regard to the forty head of horses. The parties owning them have since found them. They were only estrayed." [9]

The Marlow story says that Johnson paid no attention to the letter, kept its existence from the knowledge of his deputies, and set out to hunt the Marlow boys down, though he knew they were innocent. He was afraid that the cattle

barons "would lose confidence in his ability unless he arrested someone once in a while." [10]

Johnson's posse picked up all five of the boys without difficulty. Old Mrs. Marlow, completely unsuspecting, directed the officers to the corn field where Boone was working. The rest were rounded up in other places. Only George was wanted, but Johnson thought he had better bring in all the Marlows he could.

The Graham *Leader* reported that the men were "charged with horse stealing in the Territory and Trinidad, Colorado. Boone Marlow is also wanted in Wilbarger County for the murder of Holdson in 1886." [11] In the issue of October 11, the editor commented approvingly: "Mr. Johnson has been quite successful in bringing to justice the evil doers from the Territory as well as elsewhere. . . . We learn that Bill Murphy, who is a nephew to the Marlow brothers, has agreed to testify in behalf of the government against the others."

The women followed their men to Graham,[12] frantic over what had happened and unable for some time to find a way out of their difficulty. The jail was filthy; the guards were brutal; the magistrates were deaf to their pleas. They had no money, and they knew nobody who would go bail for the boys. Eventually they brought some cattle down from the Territory to use as security, and with the help of a few friendly ranchmen, particularly Mr. O.G. Denson, bail was arranged. It took three months to arrange it, however, and by that time the brothers were bitterly resentful of the treatment they had received, especially from Tom Collier, the deputy sheriff. Toward Sheriff Marion D. Wallace, who was a very popular official, they apparently had no hard feelings.

On Saturday, December 15, 1888, Boone was finally released. The rest had been turned loose earlier and had found places to live in the county. George and Ellie had moved into a log cabin on Mr. Denson's place about eight miles from town. Charley and Alf with their mother were occupying another seven miles farther out.[13] On the day following Boone's release, the whole family gathered at the house on Denson's place for dinner and a reunion. It turned out to be a sad meeting for all of them.

By this time the authorities at Vernon had learned the whereabouts of Boone Marlow and had issued a capias for him in the matter of the death of James Holdson. It may be that Ed Johnson had suggested that they do so. The Marlows say he did. By now the charge of horse stealing was breaking down, as they tell it. The old Indian Bar-Sin-Da-Bar, who was supposed to have lost 130 head, had been heard to say that he never had owned that many horses in his life, and hadn't lost any of those he had. He added that if he felt he had to watch any white man it would be Sheriff Johnson, not the Marlows.[14] Under the circumstances, Johnson may have thought that he had better not depend on the horse-stealing accusation.

The Marlow family was at dinner when Sheriff Wallace and Deputy Collier rode up to serve the warrant. Wallace went around to the rear to tie his horse. Collier walked his mount to a front window and looked through at the Marlows seated around the table. In spite of the hard feelings generated by his three months in jail, Boone felt obliged to be hospitable.

"Hello, Tom. Come in and have some dinner."

"I'm not hungry."

"Come in anyway."

Collier got down, tied up his horse, and walked into the house. As he came through the door he said, "Boone Marlow, I'm after you." What happened after that is a matter for argument.

As Collier told it, Boone reached for his Winchester and fired at him the moment he spoke, the bullet just missing one of the deputy's eyes and carrying away a slice of his hat brim. The Marlows say that Collier fired first without regard for the women and children.[15]

By this time Sheriff Wallace had come around from the back and was approaching the door. Boone's second bullet went through him just above the hips, damaging both kidneys. Apparently the shot went through the casing of the door and caught the sheriff before Boone even saw him.

Collier fired one shot, which went astray as Wallace fell against him. Then he turned and ran. He said later that Wallace urged him to retreat since it was one against three and he had no chance.[16]

He did not get far. Boone was out on the porch by now and had a bead on him. Collier came back when Boone told him to. The Marlow account pictures him as crouching down behind Charley, who was holding Wallace's head in his lap, and begging for protection when Boone declared his intention of shooting him. Charley told Boone to put down his gun and sent riders off for a doctor and for the neighbors.[17]

The country was terribly aroused when the news was brought to Graham. George Marlow, who brought it, was promptly jailed. As soon as might be, his three brothers were put in jail with him, and half a dozen parties of men from Young and Jack counties went looking for Boone, who had succeeded in disappearing completely. On the day before Christmas Wallace died, and the cry against the Marlows grew louder, for the sheriff was much respected and beloved. A reward of fifteen hundred dollars was offered by the citizens for Boone's arrest, and Governor Ross added two hundred more if the man were delivered to the sheriff "inside the jail door of said county" within six months.[18]

Tom Collier took Wallace's place as sheriff. He appointed one of Wallace's nephews as his deputy and they immediately gave their full attention to the Marlow case. The day after Christmas they arrested Mr. Denson, on whose place the Marlows had found refuge, and saw to it that he was bound over for the grand jury on five hundred dollars bail.[19] The four brothers were given their preliminary trial on January 4, 1889, and they found themselves charged with complicity in the killing. "It is the theory of the State that they were present, aiding and abetting in the offense, if not actual participants," said the *Leader*.[20]

Considering the excited state of the county, it is not surprising that they were all held for the grand jury and that their bail was set at one thousand dollars apiece. They were unable to raise it, of course, and had to go back to the primitive jail they had just left. It looked to them like a clear case of persecution, and they resolved not to put up with it.

On Monday, January 14, they escaped by sawing their way out of the iron cage in which they were confined. A fellow prisoner named Speer passed them a pocket knife on the end of a broomstick and they took turns sawing every night, concealing the debris under their beds. It took them a week to do the job, and then they slipped out through the hole as dusk was coming on, made a rope out of strips of blanket, and slid down to the ground. If they had waited an hour longer, they might have got away, but instead of marking time until the sheriff came back to the jail and turned in for the night, they and a prisoner named Cummings walked out while he was still away. Shortly after they left, Collier returned, discovered what had happened, and went in pursuit.

He did not bother to follow their trail. He didn't have to. They were without food, weapons, or adequate clothing, and he was sure they would head for home first. When they came within sight of the Marlow house next morning, just about the time breakfast was on the stove, Collier and his posse picked them up and marched them back to jail. Their women were busy preparing a meal and never knew the men were close by. When they got back to the jail, they were shackled together two and two, Charley and Alf, George and Ellie, and put under heavy and hostile guard.[21]

One reason the Marlows were so anxious to escape was their fear of being mobbed. They knew that the big cattlemen could be ruthless, and they thought they knew the men who were taking care of the big cattlemen's interests. Later on, when they were being tried, they named the men, and those names included prominent peace officers, county officials, and the sons and nephews of the most influential men in the county. How right the Marlows were in being alarmed was proved on the night of January 17, when the mob came to the jail to lynch them. It was about three A.M. when some forty masked men surrounded the building. The sheriff and Constable Sam Waggoner were out of town, but there were plenty of guards. Eugene

Logan and Dick Cook were there, and so was John Leavel, the turnkey. The Marlows included all three of these men in their list of mobsmen later on.

The lynchers seem to have had no difficulty getting into the jail. "The first warning the guards had of their presence," said the *Leader*, "was the opening of the door and the pointing of a dozen or more guns at their heads, with a demand to surrender—a demand with which they readily complied. Then the mob made them go up and open the cages and call all the prisoners out except the Marlows." [22]

It really should not have been much of a job for forty armed men, secure behind their masks, to finish off four shackled and unarmed cowpunchers, but the cowpunchers were Marlows, and that made a difference. Ellie, or somebody else, unscrewed a section of the water pipe in the cell and handed it to Alf, who was the strongest. Alf took up his post at the door.

"Come out!" said the leader of the mob.

"Come and get us if you want us," replied the Marlows.

Bob Hill tried to come through the door to get at them and caught a straight left to the chin from Charley Marlow. He struck his head against the stone wall as he fell and was permanently out of the combat. Nobody else was willing to try it, and finally, after much shouting and threatening, the mob slunk away.

People wondered at the time, and have wondered ever since, why they didn't shoot the men and be done with it. Texas mobs were fond of shooting prisoners in jail and had done so time and again. Perhaps they were afraid of raising an alarm. Perhaps they were just not proud of what they were doing, and a determined stand was enough to turn them back. They took the deputies and the turnkey with them when they left and turned them loose at the graveyard. As might have been expected, "the guard failed to recognize any of them."

Unfortunately the courage which saved the brothers' lives on Friday was not enough to keep away trouble on Saturday. The news of the attempted lynching was telegraphed to United States Marshal Cabell in Dallas, and he telephoned Ed Johnson to take the prisoners to Weatherford for safekeeping. Ed did as he was told, assembled a guard, and told the Marlows to get ready to march. The Marlows took one look at the guard and swore it was just plain murder; these men were part of the very mob that had tried to take them out of jail the night before. Nevertheless, about nine in the evening, the procession started. Six prisoners, the Marlows and two men named Clift and Burkhardt, were driven off in a light wagon followed by Johnson and the guard in another hack and a buggy. The prisoners were chained to each other but not restrained otherwise.

The moon was just coming up as the procession moved leisurely out of town. One mile—two miles they traveled. Then they came to the bed of Dry Creek with a narrow, mesquite-lined road rising on the other side. As they paused briefly in the creek bed, Johnson called out loudly to the prisoners, "Let's have a drink, boys!"

"That's a signal," Charley whispered to Alf.

As the horses settled into their collars for the pull up the west bank, the mob rose up out of the brush and opened fire. This is the official story of the fight as it was told in Graham next day:

"The first shot hit Deputy Marshal Johnson in his only hand, thus disabling him. As soon as the firing commenced the Marlows rolled out of the hack and got to Mr. Johnson's hack, where they got hold of some arms and fired into the mob. It is thought the prisoners did more shooting than the guard. The mob became demoralized and the prisoners held the field.

"Alf and Epp. Marlow, prisoners, Sam Creswell, guard, Bruce Wheeler and Frank Harmison, of the mob, were all

instantly killed; Deputy Marshal Johnson shot in the hand—
a painful but not dangerous wound; Charley Marlow seriously shot in the breast and jaw; George Marlow shot in the
hand; Clift, another prisoner, shot in the thigh, and Eugene Logan, Constable Belknap Precinct, and one of the
mob, shot in the breast and arm, which may prove fatal.
. . . It is thought that others of the mob were hurt, but
none of them have yet reported. It is reported that there
were only twelve of the mob." [23]

The Marlows had probably made up their minds what to
do when and if they were attacked. Shackled as they were,
they had run under fire to their guards, wrenched weapons from them, and run the mob off again. George Marlow
later said that as the masked men retreated, he and Charley
called them cowards and invited them to come back and
fight. One of them—Frank Harmison—couldn't take that
and came back to "see it out." He and George faced each
other in a finish fight and kept on shooting until Harmison
fell with a bullet between his eyes.[24]

What happened next is hard to believe, even of the
Marlows. There they were, Charley and George, wounded
but alive and each chained to a dead brother. There was
only one thing to do: "They got hold of a knife—it is
thought one of the other prisoners took it out of Creswell's
pocket—and unjointed their dead brothers' ankles so that
they could slip the shackles off, and, with Clift and Burkhardt, drove off in the hack, cursing the mob. They drove
to Finis, where they got an axe and cut their shackles off,
and then drove to the Denson farm, where their families
are." [25]

There Sheriff Collier and a posse found them, and found
them still full of fight. They allowed Dr. Price to come
inside and patch them up, but said they could still shoot in
spite of their wounds and would surrender only to Marshal
Cabell or Chief Deputy Morton.

Collier was all for digging them out, but responsible

men in his posse thought that enough blood had been shed and persuaded him not to try it. There must have been some suppressed admiration even in that crowd for the cold courage which the Marlows had shown for the second time. They telephoned Marshal Cabell and he sent Deputy W.H. Morton with a posse which drove all night from Weatherford and arrived at the Marlow place about daylight Wednesday morning—two days after the fight. The boys gave themselves up at once, and the party started for Dallas.

Nobody thought that Charley would live to reach the city. He was so full of buckshot that he actually coughed two of them up as he sat in the wagon, but he never complained. Morton told a reporter when he finally arrived: "The prisoners have plenty of grit. They bore their wounds in silence throughout the whole journey." [26]

In all this blood and gunsmoke Boone Marlow had no part. He had escaped the posse in the first place by hiding in a straw stack near his own house while fifty or sixty men combed the country for him. After three weeks of this game of cat and mouse, the Marlow women got a horse for him and he slipped away to his old haunts in the Indian Territory. On January 28, 1889, three men from the Chickasaw Nation brought his dead body to Graham and demanded the reward. Their names were Martin Beavers, G.E. Harboldt, and J.E. Direkson. Justice Starrett held an inquest and the three men testified that they had tried to arrest their man on Hell Creek, twenty miles east of Fort Sill, had not been able to persuade him to give up peaceably, and had been forced to kill him. They got the reward money, but they must have stayed around too long and talked too much, for late in February a posse went out and arrested them for the murder of Boone Marlow. The rumor was that they had poisoned him. They were released on bail and apparently not prosecuted any further.[27]

Many prominent citizens were summoned to answer before a federal grand jury in Dallas for the work of the mob. P.A. Martin, Marion Wallace, John Leavell, Eugene Logan, and Dick Cook, all peace officers or county officials, were charged with obstructing a deputy United States Marshal in the performance of his duty. Half a dozen others were jerked up for murder or conspiracy to murder. "If the court listens to the testimony of the Marlows," remarked the *Leader*, "they will have every officer in the County, who has had anything to do with them, arrested." [28]

It took months and even years for after-effects of the trouble to disappear. "Mob" and "Anti-Mob" factions were active in local elections for a time, and prominent citizens were in and out of custody several times a year as the mob cases progressed through the courts. Tom Collier died in jail before he could come to trial. Johnson had to have his remaining hand amputated. There were a few jail sentences and fines, but actually not much was done to the accused. Too many important people were involved, and too much conflicting testimony was brought forward. It was best to let the whole thing die as soon as possible. [29]

The Marlows were put under light bond to insure their reappearance as witnesses, but they paid off the bondsmen and left the state, eventually settling in the spectacular mountain country of Colorado just north of Ouray. They could not remain out of it, however, and made repeated trips back to Texas to testify in the mob cases.

When at last they could be left in peace, they concentrated on raising their families, making friends, and earning a living. Charley moved to California, where he died at the age of seventy-seven. George continued as a citizen of Colorado until his death in 1945. "Uncle George" was a lively, friendly little man who loved everybody and was much loved in return. He was particularly close to his son-in-law C.V. Hallenbeck, a Grand Junction contractor,

who cherishes the old man's memory fondly. Mr. Hallenbeck remembers that Mr. Marlow had one young friend
who became a fighter pilot in the South Pacific and used
to send letters home. Once he wrote: "When I see them
coming, I just imagine you sitting beside me and I have no
fear."

"Uncle George" carried that letter under the sweat
band of his hat for a long time. He couldn't read it himself,
because it made him cry and he couldn't see the words,
but he liked to have other people read it to him.[30]

THE FEUD OF THE PIOUS ASSASSINS
The San Saba Mob

There was a time in Central Texas, not so long ago, when a group of church people used to gather at the Buzzard's Water Hole[1] to plot murder—when as many as two hundred citizens from one small district were frightened from their homes under threat of death—when a remark dropped by a child at school was enough to cause the death of the child's father—when it seemed that all law but mob law was about to vanish from that part of the earth—and when a fighting district attorney and a few Rangers were all that stood between the people and chaos. All this actually happened in the hilly pastures of San Saba County in the eighties and nineties, the last case being dismissed in Austin by Judge Morris in 1903. The story is not an easy one to tell, partly because people connected with it are still alive and partly because so much of it was dark and mysterious, full of secret fears, midnight plottings, and unknown figures moving behind the scenes.

Sixty and seventy years ago there was a good deal of this sort of thing in the region which included Llano, Lampasas, San Saba, Mills, and adjoining counties. Horse thieves and cattle rustlers moved in and out, aided by many a confederate who posed as a respectable rancher or farmer. To combat this situation a number of "mobs" came into being. A mob was a secret organization of regulators or vigilantes who specialized in running undesirables out of the country or hanging them if they would not run. They kept no records; they were ready to swear that they knew nothing about their own mob; and they carried on their business with impenetrable secrecy. The penalty for "talking" was death, whether the talker belonged to the group or not. Consequently it was almost impossible and always dangerous to find out much about them in days gone by, and even now there is a memory in the blood of many an old Texan which makes him keep his lip firmly buttoned up when these matters are discussed. Much of what is told about the mobs is certainly folklore, but a few general statements will probably hold water.[2]

There may have been a great many mobs. Dr. J.B. Cranfill, in his *Chronicle* of his career as doctor, publisher, and Baptist leader, tells a good deal about the mob he had to contend with in Coryell County. Uncle Ed Nichols of Meridian told me tales of the mob which existed in his part of Texas, and what Ed Nichols said can be trusted. I have heard old-time peace officers talk about the Llano Mob and the Lampasas River Mob, but on the other hand I have heard others deny that such mobs existed. More than once I have picked up stories indicating that some of the mobs co-operated, like farmers trading work or preachers exchanging pulpits for a Sunday's preaching. As it usually worked out, the local boys would send off to another mob when somebody in their town had to be attended to, and a few nights later a band of masked riders would canter in, hang, shoot, or whip somebody, and ride out again. They usually favored hanging.

In only one case that I have heard of—the San Saba Mob—is there any evidence of a formal organization with a ritual, but there may have been others.

And finally there were "good people" in every mob, at least in the beginning. It was a case of the old pattern working itself out anew: frontier conditions called for an application of frontier justice; and frontier justice, according to rule, got out of hand when its dispensers developed delusions of grandeur and undertook to substitute for God

Almighty in meting out the Lord's vengeance. The good people were soon pushed aside and the only way to stop the thing, after it was well started, was to root it out by force and fear.

Geography had something to do with it. San Saba is a cowman's country and in those days it was mostly held by big owners. In the creek and river bottoms, however, there was fertile land which tempted many a "hoe man" to set up his farm among the giant pecans and cottonwoods. In the northern and western part of the county, near the Colorado bottoms, was an area of sandy soil and scrubby timber sometimes known as "the post oaks." The Locker community, in the heart of this district, was the center of mob activity, though it spread out all through the countryside and spilled across the Colorado River into Mills and Brown Counties. Settlement here was begun early— in the sixties and seventies—by men with the ancient English names which are heard so often in the history of Texas and its feuds.

Newspaper paragraphs in the middle seventies show how ruthless and skillful those men could be in taking the law into their own hands: "The San Saba *News* gives an account of two men who were discovered dead at the Henderson water hole; one was shot in the neck severing the spine; the other through the body. They were supposed to be horse thieves." [3]

And again: "A man named Kelley, accused, it is thought unjustly, of horse stealing, was pursued, captured and hung by unknown men last week, near San Saba." [4]

In 1878 there was so much feeling over local option that the Rangers under Lieutenant Arrington were sent in. The adjutant general was afraid there might be a feud brewing in the county and remarked in his annual report that there were "strong indications of mob law." [5]

In June of 1879 the caldron bubbled again. A member of the Brown clan came from the Post Oaks down to San Saba to remonstrate with the district attorney about something and got himself killed. T.G.T. Kendall, who was charged with the killing, was to be tried in September but forfeited his bond and did not appear. On February 6, 1879, he wrote to Major Jones of the Rangers: "Now then I will here state that I am perfectly willing to go, and am anxious to be tried and have the matter disposed of but I am not willing to go or to start there and be butchered on the road. You are aware of the facts that there is in and around San Saba an organized mob, who would not hesitate to take my life regardless of consequences if they get an opportunity, and would have done so last summer had it not been for the interference of a company of your rangers. . . ." [6]

The "mob" of which Kendall spoke was not the San

Saba Mob with which we are concerned but the organization that called the San Saba Mob into existence. It was a
gang of rustlers who specialized in running off bunches
of stock from the big ranches but took what they could
pick up from other people as well. They were powerful
and well organized and loyal to each other. Their most effective instrument was a group of professional witnesses
which could be produced at sessions of court anywhere
they might be needed to swear out alibis, serve as character witnesses, or otherwise prevent the law from taking its
course. Lieutenant Nevill, who was sent to San Saba in
March of 1880 to keep an eye on Kendall's trial, wrote to
Major Jones that the outlaws had "about twenty strikers
here and in vicinity." [7]

So a countermob was organized—the real San Saba
Mob. It is said that seven rich cattlemen got together in the
first place and made up their minds to appeal to Judge
Lynch since other judges would not or could not help
them. Who these seven men were I have never heard, and
I am not particularly anxious to know. Small farmers and
little ranchers came to their support and for a short while
they had hopes of bringing the situation under control,
but as time went by they found out what all mob organiz-
ers eventually find out—that they could no longer manage what they had created. Men as bad as the thieves had
got into the organization and were running the show, ordering inoffensive people out of the county and killing
off their personal enemies. Their trademark was an early-
morning ambush by three men who always put nine ex-
pertly placed shots into the head and body of each victim.
The seven good men had a bear by the tail and could not
turn it loose.[8]

Of course nobody can say now when or how the Mob
was organized, but it must have been in the middle eighties. Its first move was an expedition across the river into

Brown County for the purpose of regulating a man accused of playing in with the thieves' ring. A young schoolteacher named Ellis asked to go along out of curiosity and was allowed to do so. Still curious, he violated orders by creeping up close to the house in which the accused was supposed to have taken refuge. Something scared him when he came near, however, and he broke for the brush where his friends were hiding. They saw somebody get up and run, supposed it to be the man they were after, and shot the poor schoolteacher dead. He was the first casualty in the feud. The Mob dropped his body off in front of the house of Jap (or Jep) Snelling, a queer fellow who lived in the Locker community; but nobody ever thought he did the killing, for the condition of the body showed that it had been thrown across a saddle and brought from some distance.

Later two men who had taken part in this episode got drunk in a saloon in Lampasas and had a good public laugh about how the horse had pitched when they laid Ellis' body across the saddle. A few days later they were shot down by unknown assassins, showing that a member of the Mob had to keep his mouth shut if he hoped to live.[9]

These early episodes have to be learned about mostly from oral tradition, but by 1888 conditions were so bad that the newspapers had to take notice. In the issue of August 17 the San Saba *News* reported that "C.W. Smith, who lives some 12 or 15 miles north of town, was shot Tuesday evening late, near his home. There were ten shots fired at him, but only one struck him. That has been extracted and no serious results are anticipated. It is supposed that this is another result of the feud which has existed in that section for some months, and which has already resulted in the loss of several citizens to this county, Brown, McCulloch and Mills County." In the same issue appeared the laconic announcement that "J.Y. Criswell was shot from his wagon and instantly killed on Thursday of last week near his home in McCulloch County. It is not known who did the shooting."

Many San Saba people believe that the Mob got Charley Smith on the second try. He disappeared a short time after he was shot and no trace of him was ever found, but his rifle was discovered in a cave along the Colorado and everybody supposed that his body had been placed there and washed out by high water.[10]

About this time, supposedly late in 1888, Ase Brown was lynched. Ase was a brother of the Brown who was killed in a row with the district attorney in 1879 and also of Jim Brown, once sheriff of Lee County, a famous gambler and race horse man in the early days, who was killed at a Chicago race track. It was supposed that Ase was a leader of the gang the Mob was trying to regulate, and one night a band called at his house two or three miles east of the Buzzard's Water Hole, took him out, and hanged him.[11]

This killing had some unlooked-for consequences. A good, respectable ranchman named Leroy Beck happened along just when the Brown hanging was being successfully completed. According to Mob ethics there was nothing to do but take him into custody, try him, and sentence him to hang, all of which was done within ten minutes. Beck put up a good talk, however, and promised that if they would let him go he would sell his livestock, dispose of his ranch, and be out of the country in four days. They agreed, but on the afternoon of the fourth day he was shot out of his wagon by two men. His granddaughter was riding with him and said she thought he was killed by a couple of Negroes. From this it was deduced that the assassins wore black masks.[12]

There were a good many other episodes in the early days of the feud which people still mention occasionally—for instance the shooting of Willis Johnson at Jones Valley in

Mills County in '86 or '87.[13] At first the Mob encountered plenty of opposition and some of the dead were undoubtedly their own men, though it is hard now to tell which side the victims were on. By 1888, however, they were running things pretty much their own way. Evidence introduced in court when the whole matter was aired ten years later shows that they killed Sam Williams some time during that year, bushwhacked Bob Davenport as he rode up to his house on January 1, 1889, and ran Joe Murphy off in a cloud of dust a little later with fifteen or twenty men shooting at him. Joe became a deputy sheriff in Stephens County, many miles away, but was brought back to give testimony when the Mob cases came into court.[14]

He was one of several intended victims who managed to get away. Squeaky Evans was another. Squeaky lived near Cottonwood Pond four miles north of Richland Springs. When it came his turn to be regulated, the Mob ran him through the water hole but didn't catch him and he left the country. In the brief interval before his departure a friend asked him what was wrong. He replied, "I guess I seed too much." [15]

The worst murder of all was pulled off in July of 1889. Up in the Locker community lived a little old man named Turner with one lame leg who kept the post office, ran a farm as a side line, and spoke his mind when he felt like it. He had a wife, a married daughter (Mrs. Alice Roberts), a girl in her teens (Louise), and two boys, one of whom was the victim of a drowning accident a week before Turner himself was killed. A mile away lived Mat Ford, a cousin of Mrs. Turner's, still remembered as a "bellerin' Methodist" devoted to piety and good works. He had difficulty with his reading and writing and was not much to look at, being a large, weather-beaten specimen with very stooped shoulders, but he seemed the soul of kindness. When the little Turner boy was drowned, he came over and helped make the coffin, and had even paid Turner's taxes not long before the murder.[16]

Other neighbors included the Reverend W.P. Smith, an old fire-and-brimstone Baptist preacher who is said to have been one of Quantrill's raiders in his youth, and Aaron Meek, sometimes known as Parson Meek, who was the local justice of the peace and coroner. They were all praying men in that neighborhood, it seemed, though later events made it appear that they had their weaknesses like everybody else, the greatest being a conspicuous shortage of respect for the sixth commandment. Smith had come to the county in 1870; Ford in 1874; and their neighbors not much later. There had been time enough for the seeds of discord to sprout.

Westward, on Wilbarger Creek, lived J.F. Dougherty, who set off the fireworks in the Turner affair. Turner mentioned to him one day that he did not like the way the Mob was killing people and running them out of the district. He added that he thought Mat Ford was a member. Dougherty promptly relayed this opinion to Ford himself and thereby made plenty of trouble.

Immediately a number of people took a strong dislike to Turner. Dougherty testified, when the case finally came to trial in 1897, that the people around Locker thought the old man was going through the letters in his post office and "giving information to one Murphy, Louis Davenport and others who had been run out of the country . . ."

In other words Turner was anti-Mob and had to be disposed of.

One Friday night about the middle of April after Mr. Turner was in bed, a gang of fifteen men rode up to the house and helloed. His daughter and son were in the post-office room writing. The boy went out into the yard to see what it was all about. "Is your father at home?" they asked him. Being wise for his age he answered no. "Well," said one of them, "you tell him that if he don't get out within three days, we will shoot hell out of him."

On the Sunday following Mrs. Turner heard a disturbance among her chickens some time after dark and, looking out, saw three men with guns lurking in her chicken yard. She recognized one of them, she thought, but didn't say anything about it until much later.

Turner knew he was up against it, but somehow he postponed the end for three months. Then on the morning of July 19, 1889, they caught him in his field plowing cotton and riddled him with bullets. Mrs. Turner was in her kitchen when she heard the shots. "There, they have killed Father!" she exclaimed and got out of the house as fast as she could. Both she and her daughter Alice, who was on the porch, saw two men running off from the field and recognized them, though it was contended later that at a distance of 350 yards it was impossible to recognize anybody for certain. When they reached Mr. Turner, he was stone dead. The assassins had made sure of him after he was down by shooting him again at such close range that his shirt had been set afire.[17]

Mrs. Turner's cousin, Mat Ford, sent over to see what he could do as soon as he heard of the murder and put his son Jim to work finishing the cotton that Mr. Turner had been working on.

At the inquest presided over by "Parson" Meek there was some excitement. Alice Roberts maintained that she could identify at least one of the killers so the inquest was continued until the next day. While Alice was watching her father's body being lowered into the grave, she was taken into custody by a newly appointed constable and brought before Justice Meek a second time. Her mother and some family friends had by now been able to persuade Alice that "she and all the family would be killed" if she said anything. So she changed her testimony and the case was apparently closed.

It must have seemed to the Mob at this stage that they were all but invincible. In fact, after more than twenty killings and uncounted enforced departures from the county, they had everybody so scared that it was not necessary for them to do much regulating for some time. Only one man was rubbed out during the next year (1890). This was Ed Hartman, who lived on the Colorado River and had somehow antagonized a few of his neighbors. At the time of his murder Rangers W.J.L. Sullivan, Red Murphy, and Tom Platt were in town to keep things in line at the fall term of District Court, and when Hartman's brother Nat asked them for help, they got on the trail at once. They found Ed's body near the house of a Mr. Campbell, a deputy sheriff. They arrested him, his sons Meck and Dave, and five other men in the neighborhood. Dave and his father were indicted, and eventually the old man did some time, but he was tried sixteen times in eight years before he was convicted. To show what times were like in those days, it might be mentioned that on the evening Ed Hartman was murdered he went out of the house after sundown for the first time in nine years.[18]

Everybody knew that there was a dark brotherhood of some sort behind the killing. W.W. Martin, the district attorney, wrote to Adjutant General King: "The developments . . . put it beyond question that there is an organization here, other than those of the Brown party, of a very dangerous character, and by this party or organization young Hartman was murdered. Young Hartman belonged to no party." [19]

But what could the authorities do? It was slackness in administering the law that had led to the formation of the mob in the first place, and now the thing was working underground, leaving them more helpless than ever. Everybody expected worse things to happen—but nothing further occurred. Gradually the shudders subsided. Good men began to wonder if there were really any Mob at all; maybe it was just talk. For three years they continued to wonder. And then, in 1893, the killing started up again.

Some four miles north of San Saba town was a peculiar outcropping in the level plain known as China Knob—a steep hill about 300 yards long and 125 feet high with shiny vitreous outcroppings which gave it a name. Not far away was a rural schoolhouse which served as a church and social center for the country round about, and there in August of 1893 the Reverend Mr. Mathias began a series of revival meetings. Everybody went, of course. A protracted meeting was a great social occasion there, as in other parts of the South and West, but in this case society was by no means the chief attraction. Elders and deacons were the backbone of the Mob, and there were pious people on the other side as well. The China Knob revival was well and enthusiastically attended.

More than once in Texas, however, a religious meeting

has given a feuding faction the chance it needed to even a score with its enemies. The one who was to suffer in this case was a young man named Jim Brown—a son of the Ase Brown who had been hanged by Mob sympathizers in 1888. Jim was a noisy fellow who was probably not as bad as he wished to be considered, but he had convinced the leaders of the Mob that he was up to no good (they thought he was tampering with other people's cows), and they determined to get rid of him. The China Knob meeting gave them their opportunity.

By an ironic chance Jim had practically married the Mob. His wife was a McCarty, the daughter of a man who was supposed to be one of the inner circle, and his sister had married Bill Ogle, a jovial Irishman who had become a pliant tool in the hands of the leaders. The McCarty relationship helps to explain some arrangements that were made on the night of August 24, 1893.

The meeting was over. The preacher had shaken hands with everybody. The women had torn themselves reluctantly from the last morsels of neighborhood gossip. The horses had been brought up, and it was time to ride. Jim McCarty, Jim Brown's brother-in-law, took particular pains about arranging his little party. He and his sister rode off first, leaving Brown and Will Ledbetter to bring up the rear. What happened was described by the *News* editor the following week: "On crossing a little ravine about three-quarters of a mile beyond China, Brown was fired upon from ambush. The weapon used was a shotgun loaded with buckshot. About fifteen shot entered his right side, one or two passing out on the left side, the others lodging about the heart and lungs. When he was shot, he clinched his horse and dashed up beside his wife who, with her companion, was at that time a short distance in front. Then a second shot was fired. This shot missed Brown, but some two or three shots hit Mrs. Brown, inflicting painful wounds. About this time Brown fell from his horse, the distance from where he was shot to where he fell was 75 steps. There is as yet no clue as to the guilty parties." [20]

One reason for the apparent absence of clues, came out four years later when Captain Bill McDonald was looking into the case. "Another one of the mob has unfolded to me," he wrote to Adjutant General Mabry, "and made affidavit to it, of the signs, pass words, etc. . . . He says he joined them in the sheriff's office & the sheriff his deputy and other prominent men gave him the obligation instructions etc. Hudson was the sheriff at the time." [21]

It is said that at one time the sheriffs of both San Saba and Mills counties were members of the Mob,[22] and the old men at San Saba agree that the thing was organized like a lodge with signs, oaths, and all the rest of it.

After the Brown killing there was another considerable interval before the murdering started up again. One bushwhacking seemed to have the effect of scaring the good people into keeping quiet and the bad ones into leaving or mending their ways. Nobody now can say how much went on beneath the surface in 1894 and 1895, but no further violence was done until the early part of 1896. In June of that year there were two Mob killings.

The first was the shooting from ambush of T.A. Henderson up in the post oaks as he was cutting cord wood. His wife wrote to Captain McDonald on November 13, 1897, telling how it happened. "Some time in August 1894," she said, "my husband was without cause ordered to leave the country within three days, which he did, going to Brownwood where he remained until the grand jury met, when he returned to San Saba and swore positively to several of the men who were in the crowd that ordered him away. They were Billed and in November 1895 one of them was put on trial and acquitted, the other cases being thrown out of court.

"These men then went before the Grand Jury and obtained a Bill against my husband for perjury and he was afterward hunted down, brought back to San Saba and given bond and while awaiting trial was, on the 22nd day of June, 1896, cruelly murdered while at work trying to make a living for his family." [23]

Mrs. Henderson might have mentioned that her husband, his brother Fayette, and one of his boys were cutting wood for a neighbor two miles north of Richland Springs when they were fired on from ambush. Fayette was shot through the shoulder but returned the fire and managed to get away to Richland Springs, taking the boy with him. They did not dare to make a move till night—did not even dare to tell about the dead man lying out there in the brush. When it was dark the boy went home to break the news and Fayette did a complete and successful job of disappearing.[24]

A week after the murder of Henderson, William James was killed. He was living near the Hannah Crossing on the Colorado in the heart of the feuding district but had never been involved in any trouble. His crime was discussing the killing in his home. His children quoted him on the playground at school, and the word got around that he had "talked." On July 28 he went to the crossing after water and had just come out of the river with his load when he was fired on and killed. Neighbors heard the shooting, went to investigate, and met the wagon with blood on the wheel where he had fallen over it. They found the man himself lying in the road with the usual nine Winchester balls in his head and body. Dave Chadwick stayed with him for seven or eight hours keeping the hogs and blow-flies off while the rest went for help.[25]

James left a wife and a "house full of children," and this fact, along with the cruelty of the killing, finally aroused the responsible people of the county. The day after it happened, District Judge W.M. Allison wrote to the adjutant general asking for a permanent Ranger camp in the vicinity. "The quiet good people of the neighborhood are terrorized," he declared, "and feel should they take any active part, or even become a witness against these murderers that their lives would pay the forfeit. This lawless element dominates along the Colorado river & includes portions of Mills and Brown Counties." A week later he wrote again: "The law abiding people of the locality mentioned cannot remain there unless something is done promptly—I understand some have left—and many others are preparing to leave. . . ." [26]

Outside the county the report spread that there was a reign of terror in San Saba and that the place was "a veritable hell." Editor U.M. Sanderson of the San Saba *News* was cut to the quick by all this bad publicity and defended his community strenuously, but finally broke down and admitted that "this mob work is a disgrace to the county." [27]

Immediately he was reproved. "You have gone too far," warned one correspondent after another. This made the editor furious, and beginning in the issue of August 14, 1896, he attacked the Mob tooth and nail—made a crusade of it and defied them to do their worst. This was really a heroic action for which he might well have paid with his life, but he had two things on his side. One was the growing indignation in the county over the Mob killings; the other was a detachment of Texas Rangers who moved in on August 13. These included Edgar Neal and A.R. Maddox from Captain Brooks's company at Alice, and Sergeant W.J.L. Sullivan and Dudley Barker of Captain McDonald's company at Amarillo. [28] Editor Sanderson was not exactly alone.

These developments had the effect of forcing a definite alignment in the county. Mob sympathizers began to defend the cause and Mob enemies gathered courage to attack. The people around Locker were much agitated. One of the "praying men," a pulpit-thumping old Methodist preacher named C.S. Baird, snorted scornfully in the columns of the *News* that when he tried to get some of the indignant citizens to tell him who was in the Mob, "not a name could I get." [29] On the other side were people like P.C. Jackson of Lometa, who wrote to the adjutant general that "the mob in San Saba county have murdered in the last ten years more people than was ever murdered by the Indians in the same area. The work of this mob is just awful—fully 50 men have been murdered up there in the last 10 years saying nothing about those run out of the county." [30] Another correspondent of the *News* calculated that a hundred children had been left fatherless by the Mob, and the editor himself estimated conservatively that twenty-five men had been killed in ten years because of the feud.[31]

By now the elections were getting close, and the Mob issue was a major one. The key position was the sheriff's office, with two strong candidates in the contest. A.J. Hawkins was running on the Free Silver ticket; John F. Campbell was a Democrat. Another strong character who was up for office was a young lawyer from Llano named W.C. Linden. With the blessing of Mr. Sanderson, who described his record as "bright and lustrous as the star which glows in the morning light," he began campaigning for the office of district attorney.

By the end of summer the political fever had reached such a height that the anti-Mob faction had to blow off steam. They called a mass meeting at the courthouse on August 19, Judge W.M. Allison presiding, "for the purpose of expressing our condemnation of lawlessness, our determination to assist . . . in its suppression." [32]

The men in the Post Oaks retaliated by holding a meeting of their own with the Reverend C.S. Baird as chairman to give the lie to the "wholesale slanders passed on the good citizens of the northern part of our county." [33]

Meanwhile the Ranger detachment was doing its best to get the right answer to the question: "Who are the Mob?"

It was hard and dangerous going at first. All four of the boys camped at the Hannah Crossing had shaken hands over a pledge to stay and die together if they had to. Nobody would talk to them at first—"on account of fear," said Sergeant Sullivan, and then added, "Preachers and religion is mixed up with this mob affair." [34]

Sergeant Sullivan is still remembered with mixed feelings by many old-timers in San Saba County as a result of his campaign against the Mob. He was a lean, rawboned, powerful man who made a good deal of fuss over what he did, sported a heavy beard (most of the Rangers were not much more than boys and were well content with a mustache), and seems to have been a strange combination of egotism and bravery. Captain McDonald thought he was too ambitious, and eventually he was discharged. It nearly broke his heart, for he would rather have been a Ranger than President of the United States. He found some employment as a special ranger, and eventually settled down to a small job in the State Capital. His four months in San Saba County were the high point of his career, but they were full of trouble.

He and his men made what progress they could by pursuing a rigidly neutral course. They ate dinner with either faction when they were invited and accumulated as many allies as they could. When the election came off in November, they made friends with W.C. Linden, the new district attorney, and A.J. Hawkins, the new sheriff. Linden wrote to Mabry: "Sullivan is preeminently the man of all men to handle this matter. . . . His work is intelligent, thorough, and courageous." Hawkins also wrote to Mabry, "I cannot speak too highly" of Sullivan. [35]

This condition of peace and unity continued until Sullivan began getting some really sensational information, after which he and Hawkins fell out. Hawkins was a pretty good man personally, but was not regarded as an officer of much force and determination. The votes of the

Mob had put him in office for exactly that reason. They figured they could do more with him than with Campbell, his opponent. Linden said of him that he was "willing and earnest," but with "absolutely no experience in the duties of the office," and that furthermore he "was elected by almost the unanimous support of that element in the county."

Linden and the Rangers concentrated first on getting information about the Turner murder of 1889. They re-examined witnesses, brought back people who had left the county years before, and gradually built up a case. On October 16 Sullivan brought his detachment into town from their camp on the Colorado, turned over a great sheaf of testimony neatly written up by Ranger Neal, and was ready to appear in court when the Mob cases were called on the twenty-third. Sullivan himself was badly smashed up when his horse fell with him as he was pursuing a horse thief who had walked out of the courtroom, but he was still full of fight. He wrote to Mabry on November 3, "We have got all the witnesses I think, & will do something if they will only try. We have got them bothered. I think they are scared pretty bad."

Sullivan did "do something." As a result of his efforts the Grand Jury indicted two men from the Locker neighborhood for the murder of Turner. One was an undistinguished farmer named George W. Trowbridge. The other was, of all people, Mrs. Turner's cousin, pious, kindly, stoop-shouldered old Mat Ford. The Rangers were prepared to prove that Ford was the real leader of the Mob and that he had been one of its most reliable hatchet men for a long time. The idea seemed ridiculous to many people, and half a dozen preachers made a great to-do about it. District Attorney Linden took no chances. He asked for a change of venue and the cases were scheduled for trial in the district court at Austin where, presumably, the long arm of the Mob could not reach.

Immediately Sullivan felt a change in the atmosphere.[36] "As long as an officer don't bother that class of people," he wrote, "he is all right with them. But just as soon as he begins to catch them & jail them, he is all wrong in their estimation." Mob sympathizers did their best to persuade the governor and General Mabry that he ought to move the Rangers out, and the letter-writing was fast and furious for a while. But the Rangers stayed.

On February 22, 1897, Ford and Trowbridge were tried at Austin. The cases aroused state-wide interest. Some of the best lawyers in the region, including Judge James H. Robertson, appeared for the defense, and the prosecution was led by District Attorney Burleson of Austin (later a member of Woodrow Wilson's cabinet) and District Attorney Linden. They put on a show with plenty of fireworks.

The case really turned on the possibility that Mrs. Turner and her daughter could positively identify at 350 yards the men who did the killing. Witness after witness swore it could not be done. Attorney Linden took Sheriff White over to the window of the courtroom and pointed out several men coming down the steps of the Capitol, 500 yards away, and White called their names without hesitation. Still the defense insisted that the identification could not be positive. "How could they help identifying Mat Ford with that buffalo hump on his back?" asked one of the attorneys. "Nobody could be sure," the defense replied. The jury was out for a week, eleven for conviction and one for acquittal. Finally the judge discharged them and ordered a new trial. There is a good deal of storytelling, perhaps not all folklore, about the sturdy soul who hung that jury.[37]

The new trial was set for June, and Ford and Trowbridge were released on bond. They went home considerably chastened. As soon as he could arrange it, Attorney Linden went out to the old Turner home with a number of observers to see whether that 350 yards was really a barrier to positive identification as the defense had maintained. He found that it was easy to identify an acquaintance at that distance, though he had no use for the knowledge at that moment.

Meanwhile Sergeant Sullivan was having hard sledding back in San Saba. Linden thought the Mob had put Hawkins up to fighting with him, "coaching and grooming him for a row." They fell out over a prisoner named R.L. Wright, who had been brought back from New Mexico a short time before to stand trial. Hawkins allowed him to go about with considerable freedom, let him keep his pistol, and otherwise showed him special consideration. Sullivan was indignant and said so. In May, 1897, the two men came together in the corridor of the courthouse. Linden had advised Sullivan not to let anything get started and for once in his life he took a conciliatory tone, but Hawkins would have none of it. He "began boasting that he was not afraid of Sullivan," as Linden told the story, "and finally threw his hand back for his pistol and said, 'Don't you jump on me.' Sullivan quietly replied, 'I don't want to jump on you but don't draw your pistol,' and as he said this he leveled his pistol on Hawkins while the latter was still fumbling about his coat tails." This blew over, but early in July Sullivan resigned at the request of his superior officer.[38]

The Ford-Trowbridge case came up again in Austin on June 14 with more witnesses and fanfare than before. Trowbridge was tried this time. Again the jury stayed out day after day while two jurors blocked a conviction; and again, after ten days had gone by, they were discharged.[39]

About this time the Jim Brown murder case began to break. Bill Ogle, Brown's brother-in-law, was arrested during the last week in August and indicted in December, only to be let out on bond in January of 1898.[40] By this time Captain Bill McDonald himself had taken over at San

Saba and was quizzing witnesses, protecting them in his camp, and showing the Mob that if he couldn't hang them he could at least worry them to death. As he dug deeper into the mare's nest, he grew more and more horrified at what he found. This, he wrote to Mabry, "is the worst and biggest thing on earth made so by the prominence of many of their number. The Comanches were never so bad according to my notion nor nothing else I ever heard of." [41]

Sheriff Hawkins was not turning out to be worth much as a supporter of law and order. McDonald said frankly that "the main leaders of the mob are the best friends of the sheriff & they are busy all the time trying to head us off . . . how such a big thing has been concealed & suppressed so long I can't imagine, only that the officials have stood in with the murderers." [42]

In spite of opposition McDonald made his case, and the grand jury in December of 1897 got out a number of indictments. A.K. Bailey and W.J. Burnett were charged, as Bill Ogle had been, with the murder of Jim Brown. John Haas, Bill Kimmons, Little Jim Ford (son of Mat), and Nelson Smith (son of Preacher Smith) were accused of doing away with W.A. James in 1896. Ogle was tried at Llano in May of 1898 and was sent up for life. Later he was pardoned out through the efforts of Linden, who thought he had been more weak than criminal, and a tool in the hands of others.[43] The rest of the men were brought up for trial at San Saba in April and their cases were continued.

It was during this session of court that the San Saba Mob trouble threatened for the last time to end in a general slaughter. Its back was finally broken by the courage and audacity of one man—District Attorney Linden.

Emmett Vaughn and J.C. Skelton were on trial for assaulting Lou Shelton and wounding him as he was coming home from a brush-arbor revival of some sort. They were getting even for something he was supposed to have said

about a sister of one of them—the affair had no real connection with the Mob business, but Vaughn and Skelton
had friends in the Mob. One of the men had just been
acquitted and the trial of the other had begun. Eleven of
the men who had sat on the first jury were in the box for
the second case, and Little Jim Ford (so called to distin-
guish him from Big Jim Ford, Mat's brother) was on the
witness stand.

"Your name is James Ford?" asked Linden.

"Yes."

"Better known as Little Jim Ford?"

"Yes."

"Mr. Ford, is it not true that you are now under indictment in this court?"

Little Jim turned a fiery red, but admitted that he was.

"Is the defendant in this case a witness for you?"

Again Jim had to answer yes.

"In other words you and he are just trading off."

Linden then turned to the jury and made a speech that
burned their ears. The judge had known ahead of time
what he planned to do and had asked him not to do it—
had warned him that he would be stopped, and that trouble might break out in the courtroom. Linden went ahead
anyway. He said he knew he could not expect a conviction from them. They had just turned one man loose, and
he knew this one was going to get off too. He also knew
why. They were too cowardly to convict a man who had
the Mob behind him, especially when the leaders of the
gang were sitting down there looking at them. "You know
who they are," he said, "and so do I." And he proceeded
to point them out and name them one by one, concluding
with a reverend gentleman leaning over the rail at the
back. "And there is their chaplain," he finished, "who is
praying to God at this moment to strike me dead for what
I am saying."

The room was as quiet as death throughout this terrible

speech. The defense attorneys were too startled to make any objection. Once when Linden made a quick turn in front of the jury box, his Prince Albert coat swung open to reveal a pearl-handled six-shooter on his hip and somebody in the audience gasped audibly. "Yes, I carry a gun," he told them. "I carry it for just such occasions as this, and you all know I can use it." Then he sat down. The defense, sure of an acquittal, had nothing further to say, and the case went to the jury.

It was getting along toward evening when Linden left the courtroom, alone, and started west from the square toward the Dofflemeyer Hotel. The main building had been burned some time before, but the Dofflemeyers still served meals in their house and put up visiting lawyers in a shack out behind. Halfway to the hotel Linden saw that he was running into trouble. Little Jim Ford met him, carrying a knife in his hand. Sitting around on the steps and curbings nearby were his friends and relatives, all with their coats on. They had been in their shirt sleeves in the courtroom.

"Mr. Linden," said Little Jim, "do you know why I was indicted?"

"Yes," replied Linden. "I'm not a fool. I know why you were indicted." Then he pulled his pistol and, turning to Mat Ford, said, "Why don't you carry out your plot?"

Mat was very angry. Like Little Jim and the rest of his crowd he felt that Linden was persecuting and hounding him, and he answered sneeringly, "If you know so much about it, maybe you can tell us what the plot is."

"You're right I can. You put Jim up to start an argument so you could kill me and call it self-defense. Every one of you has a six-shooter under that coat. I can also tell you why you won't carry your plot out—because you've got so used to murdering men from ambush you don't dare kill anybody who is looking at you. If there were two logs and some brush between here and that corner, you'd be lying behind them shooting at me right now. And besides you don't know which one of you I'll kill while you're killing me. But I know. And I think I can get three of you before you get me. Now you turn around and walk away from here, and I'll shoot the first man that stops or turns around."

They marched off. Linden went on to the hotel. And a few minutes later a friend came to tell him that the impossible had happened—the jury had brought in a verdict of guilty.[44]

That just about finished the Mob in San Saba. There were no more convictions, but Linden found another way to make sure there would be no further outbreaks. He had hardly enough evidence to hope for convictions in the James case but he had enough to give the defendants a hot time. So he had them brought into court, their bondsmen released, and the cases put on the retired list. He told the men that he would give them six months to sell their property in the county, move out, and buy holdings elsewhere. If at the end of the specified time he had assurance that they had separated and settled in other counties, he would let things stand as they were. But if they failed to do as he said, he would change the venue of the cases and run them all over Texas. If he couldn't put them behind the bars, he could at least bankrupt them. At the end of six months they were all gone and had settled for good in other places.[45]

That left only the Ford and Trowbridge matter. It was continued several times, and at last, on May 16, 1903, Judge Morris dismissed both cases on motion of District Attorney Warren Moore who decided that "the state cannot produce sufficient testimony to authorize a conviction." [46]

After that the war in the Post Oaks was over and the two factions buried the hatchet. Edgar Neal gave up his job with the Rangers to take over the sheriff's office and proved very efficient. The feudists stopped hating each

other. W.J.L. Sullivan said when he wrote his reminiscences: "The last time I was with them they were going to
church and visiting each other, and all signs of former
strife and bad feeling had faded away." [47]

There are men still alive, however, who think the whole
campaign against the Mob was unnecessary. "We didn't
need the Rangers," they will tell you. "The Mob was made
up of the best people and they were only trying to make
the county fit for decent folks to live in. If they had let us
alone we would have handled everything without outside
help. We were doing all right."

Then they will caution you: "If you tell anybody I said
this I'll say you are a liar."

So you don't tell anybody.

OLD SOUTHERN STYLE
The Jaybird-Woodpecker Feud

Groups under emotional tension, like individuals under strain, act in conformity to local attitudes and practices. And throughout a vast part of the United States, these community attitudes readily encourage the formation of mobs. That almost no lynchers have ever been punished by the local courts further suggests the degree to which the mob's characteristic discharge of reckless violence is locally accepted.

Arthur F. Raper, *The Tragedy of Lynching*

"Trot out your brave Woodpeckers. The cowardly Jaybirds are coming!"

H.H. Frost

★

Prelude to Trouble

At the time the feud was brewing in 1889 one of Richmond's best-known, if not best-loved, citizens was Carry Nation. She was not yet famous as Carry the Crusader, and her performances with a hatchet in the barrooms of Kansas were still far in the future, but she was getting ready. The wickedness of Richmond was continually on her mind, and she saw twice as much of it as anybody else because of her dual position as postmistress and operator of the National Hotel. Carry often held forth on this subject when she met her Sunday-school class in the hotel dining room after wearing out her welcome in two churches.[1]

Richmond was just an ordinary little town to look at in the eighties. It was not any too clean. The streets were sandy in dry weather and muddy when it rained. The single track of the railroad crowned a weed-grown embankment in the middle of Railroad Street and on either side was a solid row of the stores and saloons of the period— flimsy porches, false second stories, fly-specked show windows, hitching posts out in front, and all the rest of it. A man who couldn't find his social level in that collection of grog shops on Railroad Street would have been an odd one. A single example may be mentioned—the Brick Saloon, run by Alexander McNabb. He and his sickly wife boarded at the National Hotel with Mrs. McNabb's aggressive mother, Mrs. Carry Nation. There were many thorns in Carry's tender flesh at this time, but a saloonkeeper son-in-law was undoubtedly the sharpest of all. Mr. McNabb may have done more than anyone has yet surmised to add vigor to his mother-in-law's hatchet arm.

South of Railroad Street lay, and still lies, the main part of town. Morton (or Main) Street ran parallel a block away, terminating in the Brazos bottom on the east and in the flat, shaggy prairie on the west. A block from the river stood H.H. Frost's Brahma Bull and Red Hot Bar, where the Jaybirds gathered. Westward were banks, stores, and the National Hotel. At the terminus of this business district was the courthouse, a fine new structure with plenty of decoration and an iron picket fence in front. The Woodpeckers (who had been secure in office for twenty years) made this their headquarters.

All sorts of people spoke of Richmond as their town. From the rich red lands of the Brazos bottom came well-to-do planters. From the ranches to the west came the cattlemen. From everywhere, particularly on Saturdays, came a dark river of Negroes which overflowed the town.

It flooded Railroad Street so deep that trains had to hoot themselves hoarse in order to get a clear track. The colored folks outnumbered the whites approximately four to one in those days.[2] Furthermore they could and did vote and were the deciding force in local elections. That was why there was a feud. The Woodpeckers controlled the Negroes and ran the county. The Jaybirds (who included the majority of the white people) waited and hoped and damned the Woodpeckers until they could stand it no longer, after which the shooting started.

It would be enough to say of those white residents that they were Southerners. They belonged to old and aristocratic families, many of them tracing their ancestry back to Stephen F. Austin's "Old Three Hundred," to the first families of Virginia, and even to William the Conqueror. They prized military distinction and produced captains and colonels in profusion; they cherished their honor above all else except the purity of womanhood; and they would never have thought of working with their hands. Add to this the fact that everybody carried a pistol, and that everybody in town was related to everybody else, and you have the groundwork for the feud.

Fifty years or so before, the grandfathers of these men had invaded the enormously fertile bottom lands, burned the canebrakes over the backs of the astonished rattlesnakes, and established the social standards of the Deep South. Their big plantations were organized like feudal states. Their scale of living, if not princely, was at least baronial. The war changed all that, of course, reducing many a rich family to poverty; and then came the Reconstruction, which broke numerous planters who had managed to survive the war years. It took two decades more for the people who had founded and built the country to get it back under control.[3]

The most humiliating thing of all to these people was the fact that some of the Southerners sold out. Not many carpetbaggers came to Fort Bend County, but a handful of them, plus the local politicians who controlled the Negro vote, built up a machine which for a long time was unbeatable. By 1888 Fort Bend was one of the few counties in Texas where the Negro vote, controlled by a few white men, swung the big stick.[4]

To an ignorant cotton-field Negro the idea of holding office was, of course, hypnotic. The difficulty was that to keep one of these offices a man had to post a very large bond. As the system worked here and elsewhere, a Negro would get himself elected and a white man, or group of white men, would back him. Then the Negro would appoint a white deputy who was the real incumbent.

In Fort Bend County in 1888 the office holders included a Negro assessor, a Negro district clerk, a Negro treasurer, and three Negro commissioners. In nearly every precinct there was a Negro justice of the peace and a Negro constable. And that was not all. Walter Burton had served as sheriff and had spent twelve years as state senator. He is still remembered around Richmond as a "right plausible nigger"—quiet, self-possessed, well spoken. The white men of the county thought so much of him that they presented him with a gold-headed cane as a gesture of respect.[5] In their minds the principle of the thing was unchanged, however: Even the most plausible nigger had no business in the State Senate.

There was probably a good deal of graft. Precinct voting was the rule. No poll tax receipts were required. Managed elections were not merely possible—they were easy. Always the Woodpeckers kept the reins in their own hands, as was shown in 1885 when T.M. Blakely resigned the sheriff's office. Three of the four county commissioners who assembled to appoint his successor were Woodpeckers, and they steam-rollered tall, positive, pugnacious Jim Garvey into the job.[6] With the help of the colored voters Garvey was returned to office at the next election, and another county post was in the hands of the Ring for two more years.

The assessor's office was the real key to the graft. Valuations were fixed with one eye on a man's political views and the other on his ability to pay through the nose. It was bad enough, the Jaybirds thought, to be underdogs, but to pay extra for the privilege was definitely a hardship. Where the money went nobody knew—but everyone was aware that county finances were in shameful condition. All payments were in scrip, which was worth from twenty-five to sixty cents on the dollar. When the village blacksmith did twenty dollars worth of work for the county, he put in a bill for eighty to make sure he got what was coming.[7]

The Jaybirds couldn't seem to do anything about it. They tried getting together in 1888 in the Rosebud Club, which pretended to be a literary society but wasn't.[8] It met in rooms over Frost's saloon and listened to speeches, but did the Woodpeckers no perceptible damage.

How the two parties got their odd names has caused a good deal of speculation and comment. Apparently they came from the Negroes. An old darky named Bob Chappel used to say that anything particularly uppity was "like a jaybird," and he had a song about a jaybird and a woodpecker, the first stanza of which, somewhat expurgated, ran as follows:

> The jaybird flew to the woodpecker's hole.
> The woodpecker said, "Doggone your soul."
> The jaybird said, "Oh you needn't for to cuss,
> For I didn't come here for to kick up any fuss."
> The woodpecker cried, "I've got my doubt."
> Then the jaybird said, "You'd better walk about."

The second stanza told how the jaybird chased the woodpecker from his hole, and used some four-letter words which made it unsuitable for introduction into polite society. Whether this song was suggested by the rival organizations, or the names of the organizations were suggested by the song, is anybody's guess. We know, however, that long before 1889 the members of the Ring were describing their enemies as Jaybirds, and the enemies were retaliating with the term Peckerwood, or Woodpecker. Either word could be a jeer or a battle cry, depending on who was using it.[9]

The division was based on a race issue, and consequently it went very deep. To a Jaybird anyone who associated on any terms with the Negroes had put himself outside the bounds of decent society. The Woodpeckers understood and even shared this feeling, which did not make their bitterness any less. The result was a rift in the social life of the town. Parties were apt to be either Jaybird or Woodpecker. David Nation wrote a column called "Richmond Rustlings" for the Houston *Post,* noting all the social functions he could get any information about, and he showed clearly enough what was going on. Once he described a "delightful reception" at which Miss Jovita Boyd was elected Queen of the Jaybirds and "received her subjects with queenly grace." [10]

The Jaybirds did not thank David for noticing them. He was probably the only white man in the county who could have been suspected of being a Republican, and in Richmond one had to be a Democrat or nothing. Even the Woodpeckers called themselves Democrats—"Independent Democrats" was the phrase they used. The Jaybirds were "Straight Democrats."

In numbers and wealth the Jaybirds were far ahead of the Woodpeckers, and their best men were salt of the earth. There was Colonel P.E. Peareson, for instance— Confederate soldier, brilliant lawyer, polished speaker. There were John Fenn, the planter from Duke's Station down the Brazos; J.H.B. House, owner of a big cotton plantation; William Darst, the cattleman; Isaac McFarlane, who "stood mighty well" in the town; Judge Davis, John M. Moore, and other honorable gentlemen. And there was Clem Bassett, tall, dignified, unassuming, but high-principled as Moses. He was a good enough Baptist to preach to the darkies of a Sunday afternoon.[11]

These men were not troublemakers, but they found themselves trapped in a blind alley from which they could not escape. It was not they who wanted to settle the issue by violence. Rather it was their sons and nephews— the young bucks of Richmond—the high-spirited, often pugnacious young men who knew there would have to be a fight and wanted to get it over with.

Their leader was not of their generation. He was a middle-aged business man who ran a general store and saloon—the latter known as the Brahma Bull and Red Hot Bar. His name was H.H. Frost, but they called him Red Hot Frost. His pictures show him as a vigorous, full-faced man with thinning hair and a compensatory Kentucky-colonel goatee. Undoubtedly he was a natural leader, cool, aggressive, courageous, magnetic. About his other qualities there is much division of opinion. On one side are his admirers who call him "the knightly Frost." On the other are his detractors who tell you that he was second-rate socially; a drunkard who would shoot the lights out of his own house; an encourager of the wastrels of the town. At this distant time, how can one tell which is the truth?

Perhaps Carry Nation can help a little. She says that when she was conducting her Sunday school in the hotel dining room "one poor saloon keeper named Frost came several times and always gave a dollar." [12]

The Woodpeckers were fewer, but not without distinction. Perhaps the best of them all was Jake Blakely, sheriff in the early eighties, a strong and intelligent man. He was the one who dared to ask his successor Sheriff Garvey "what he meant" by getting drunk and causing a disturbance; and he was the one who took Carry Nation aside and told her that her friends "were becoming very uneasy about the state of her mind, that they were afraid she was thinking too much on religious subjects." Equal to him in importance was C.W. Parker, a perennial office holder, and in 1888 a member of the State Legislature. He was slender, wiry, and tough, with black hair and brilliant eyes. Even his enemies admitted that he was "not afraid of the devil," and that he was the driving force of his party. Finally there was Jim Garvey, sheriff at the time of the big fight. He too was courageous, but it is charged against him that he was quarrelsome in his cups. "He was brave," said Colonel Peareson on the witness stand, "but a cruel and dangerous man." [13]

So they lined up: cousin against cousin; uncle against nephew; friend against friend. For years their dislikes and suspicions piled up, like water behind a dam, without any open outbreaks, but on the second of July, 1888, the dam began to crumble.

It was a bright Monday morning, and the town was getting ready for a busy day. Wagons and carriages were coming in. Children's eyes were glued in fascination to the gorgeous uniforms visible here and there as the Peareson Guards, best-dressed drill company in the state, began to turn out. There were a few solemn faces, but it was a happy occasion for most—this was organization day: The Young Men's Democratic Club of Fort Bend County was being born. The Jaybirds were at last closing their ranks and mustering for battle.

About the middle of the morning they marched forth to parade. A long train of wagons and buggies rolled down the main street and came to a halt before the residence of Miss Adeline Booth. At the gate they were met by Miss Charlie Woodall of Huntsville carrying a beautiful silk banner, made by her own hands, and emblazoned with the words *Young Men's Democratic Club of Fort Bend County*. As the Richmond *Democrat* reported the event, Mr. Jeff D. Bryant made the acceptance speech, which concluded: "And should it be the fate of any of us to fall under this banner, may the hand that bedecks our grave be as pure and lovely as the hand that painted these emblems of truth."

Mr. Bryant had no serious notion at the moment of falling heroically under this or any other banner, but a little more than a year later he was facing a charge of murder for his activities in the cause.

In the South in those days one speech was just an appetizer. There was more oratory at the club rooms over Frost's saloon where the constitution of the new political organization was read to thunderous applause.

The object of the club, read the secretary, was "to secure a wise, impartial, economical and unselfish administration of the affairs of our county"; to give all taxpayers a voice in "supervision over appropriations and expenditures"; and to loosen the grip of the "arbitrary and selfish minority that has so long disregarded the consent of the governed."

There were 225 signatures beneath the document on the front page of next Saturday's *Democrat*. There would have been more, but the space ran out.

Even now the spirit of democracy was not exhausted. At eleven o'clock there was still another procession; another mass meeting with speeches; still more delirious applause. Colonel P.E. Peareson, the town's finest orator and president of the Straight Democratic organization, admonished them: "Every man present must do his duty and show to the world that the Democratic party is at last waking up from its long slumber and is by no means dead."

That was how the young Jaybirds went into action. Most of the white people of Richmond felt that it was about time.[14]

★

The First Murder

On the second of August, one month to the day after the organization of the Young Men's Democratic Club, an event occurred which showed how right the Jaybirds were in feeling alarm. The event was a murder.

David Nation noticed it in the "Richmond Rustlings" next day:

Mr. J.H. Shamblin, son-in-law of Mr. W.D. Fields, while sitting on his gallery at his home about seven miles below here at 9 o'clock last night, was shot in the right side by some unknown party, who rode up to the gate and fired and rode away.

Almost all the details of David's account were wrong, but in one respect he was quite correct—J.H. Shamblin had been shot and killed.

It was a hard blow to the Jaybirds, for Shamblin was one of their bitterest and most active partisans. Handsome and aristocratic in appearance, connected with the first families of the county, and a man of strong personality, he swung plenty of weight and used all of it in the Jaybird interest. All through July and August he had made speeches, talked privately with Negro voters, and stretched his patience to the limit trying to win support for his party. Some say he turned the scale against himself by running a bunch of electioneering darkies off his plantation with a cowhide whip. A better explanation comes from J.A. Ziegler, who was a cotton buyer in those days. Shamblin walked into Ziegler's office one morning and identified a stolen bale of cotton which had been brought in by a Negro named Hudson Caldwell. Ziegler asked Shamblin to have the man arrested on his return to Richmond and he promised to do so, but the thief got wind of it and disappeared for good. "Two other negroes, however, were found who were involved in the theft; and one of them turned state's evidence. En route to the trial, as he passed by Caldwell's home, the wife of Caldwell gave him a cup of coffee. In it she had placed a liberal dose of strychnine. Drinking it, the negro was stricken but managed to crawl over to Mr. Shamblin, then Justice of the Peace, and gave him his dying declaration of the poisoning and cotton theft. This evidence Shamblin brought to the court in Richmond." [1] Naturally, somebody was interested in suppressing Shamblin's testimony.

All this took place in July. On August 2, a Sunday, just between darkness and moonrise, Mr. Shamblin was sitting in his living room reading. His daughter was playing on the floor beside him. Laying his book aside, he got up from his chair and started to walk across the room. At that moment somebody fired a charge of buckshot through the window and stretched him on the floor, mortally wounded. His father-in-law, Mr. W.D. Fields, heard the shot at his home a mile away and hurried over. As soon as the moon came up he searched the grounds; and on the gatepost he found a piece of paper—a crazy, badly spelled blast against Shamblin, concluding with these words:

> . . . the Republican parties is going to hold up their heads if they die hard we will have no democrate to mislead the ignent negro Race astray. You are a man to lead them a stray and then cut their throats and suck their blud. I am a republican and have no use for a dam democrat this is a lesson to all dam cut throat democrats to hold noe more meetings with the ignorent negro race of people.

Mr. Shamblin was still alive and conscious when this document was found. He looked at it and said it was written by William Caldwell, one of the men implicated in Hudson Caldwell's cotton stealing. Sheriff Garvey found William hiding in the woods, matched the writing paper, the gun wadding, and the buckshot picked up at the scene of the murder with similar articles in the Caldwell house, and accumulated other scraps of incriminating evidence. By the time Shamblin drew his last breath Caldwell was on his way to Richmond, where he was held until he could be transferred to a safer lodging in the Houston jail.[2]

While he was there the young Jaybirds had serious thoughts of lynching him. Some of them told H.H. Frost, "If we had had you to lead us and tell us what to do, we would have done it." So at least Mr. Frost said in a letter to his brother which was published in the Houston *Post*.[3]

It was due to Sheriff Garvey's firmness and coolness that nothing regrettable happened. When the boys began to collect in front of the jail, he told them they couldn't have Caldwell without killing the sheriff and his deputy first. "Garvey and Dickenson kept so cool," said Caldwell in an interview, "it sort of gave me courage." He got safely off to Houston, was not molested when he was brought back for his preliminary trial, and eventually took his case (in 1891) to the United States Supreme Court. Turned down by the highest authority, Caldwell was hanged at last, and it is said that the Jaybirds who went to witness the execution came home with little pieces of rope in their lapels.[4]

All this came later. At the time of Shamblin's death most people were wondering if the Negro had planned his own crime. The Jaybirds printed a proclamation in the Houston and Galveston papers resolving that "the assassination of J.M. Shamblin is laid at the door of the Republicans of Fort Bend County." The indignant Republicans, in two proclamations of their own, declared that the accusation was the result of "blind partisanship and the outgrowth of narrow-minded prejudice." [5]

Not a Jaybird in the whole county believed a word of this denial. It was impossible for anyone to think reasonably of the political situation, and all that was needed was an incident to set fire to the powder keg. The big barbecue at Pittsville on August 16 was as good an excuse as one could ask for.

N. H. Rose

Creed Taylor as an Old Man

Mr. and Mrs. William E. Sutton

Some Taylor Faces

Scrap Taylor

Courtesy Alfred Hays Day and Mrs. C. T. Taylor

Pitkin Taylor
and wife,
Susan

Dr. and Mrs. Philip Brassell

Courtesy Mrs. Pansy Reed

Jim Hester

Two Generations of Suttons

Courtesy **Ed P. Cox**

James W. Cox

N. H. Rose

Capt. Lee H. McNelly

Capt. Lee Hall, 1898

John Selman while on
the El Paso Police Force

Christopher Taylor (Kit) Hunter

John Wesley **Hardin**

Figures in the Sutton-Taylor Feud

Judge Henry Clay Pleasants

Senator B. J. Pridgen

★

Thunder in the Air

In those days the barbecue was as much a part of politics in South Texas as the ballot box. The long pit was dug the day before, and all night long the preparations went forward in the red glow of the coals. Quarters of beef, mutton, and goat's meat cooked on the heavy green timbers and were gradually transmuted from mere meat into ambrosia as Mr. John Ryon—most famous barbecue artist in those parts—dipped his mop from time to time in the pot of sauce and anointed the flesh with his mysterious oil.

In the morning, not too early, people began to come in. By noon there was a good crowd. As the afternoon progressed, the buggies and hacks continued to accumulate until it seemed the countryside for miles around must be depopulated. They came to eat and to talk—and how they ate, and how they talked! The talking was done from a platform, and the flowery oratory of early America still lifted the listeners to emotional peaks where we shall never climb.

The barbecue which was held at Pittsville on August 16, 1888, was the real old-time article.[1] It was started by the Jaybirds, but nobody expected the Woodpeckers to stay away. In fact, there was still some doubt as to which side certain prominent citizens were on. The evidence of this was the Cleveland and Thurman Club, named for the Democratic presidential nominees in the coming election, which came into being shortly after the founding of the Young Men's Democratic Club. It had about sixty members, mostly Woodpeckers, and all Democrats. "One club organized and took it upon themselves to say who were the democrats, and we organized another democratic club," explained Judge Parker when he was on trial in 1889.[2]

Thus there were two Democratic clubs, and some overlapping of membership. A few of the best men among the Jaybirds, probably hoping for a compromise and peaceful settlement, were members of both. Clem Bassett was the most prominent of them. Others were Dr. H.A. Stone, Yandell Ferris, and Keane Ferris. Many of these fence riders were at the Pittsville barbecue, and there was talk of getting up a joint white man's ticket for the coming election. The younger Jaybirds were not pleased by all this shuffling, and it is said that Frost threatened to tear Clem Bassett's badge off him if he did not stand up for his side.

They almost had trouble about it when Judge Parker began holding forth on the virtues of the Cleveland and Thurman Club, and Frost challenged him to explain why he considered himself a Democrat. Parker had his hand on his pistol and Frost was about to pull a knife.

"There would have been a little hell prized up," wrote Jaybird Volney Gibson to his brother Guilf in California, "but the jaybirds were a little too thick. Frost told them to go on they could settle it another time and that he had no intention of raising a row & Parker proceeded." [3]

When it became obvious that nobody was going to get shot or stabbed, the crowd turned its attention to food and dancing—the celebration going on till three· the next morning.

Hostility grew bitter after the barbecue. H.H. Frost added a little fuel by walking past Deputy County Assessor "Happy Jack" Randal and calling him Henry Ferguson. Ferguson was the Negro assessor and Randal was his appointee. Randal was stung to the soul. [4]

On August 30 a Negro named Jim Bearfield from the Sartartia settlement came to town in a panic with a small wound in his neck and a badly mangled hand. Someone had fired at him through the door of his house the night before, but he had burst out, hidden in a cornfield, and escaped. He thought he was in demand because he knew the identity of the men who had whipped two Negroes the week before. Having so declared himself, he swore out a warrant for H.H. Frost as one of his attackers. Frost got even by having Bearfield arrested for perjury. Nothing was done in either case, so what actually happened to Bearfield has never been revealed.[5]

Four days later Jim Garvey, in an illuminated mood, announced that he was King of the Woodpeckers and insulted several old and young Jaybirds, but he later apologized[6] and there was no real excitement until Monday night, September 3, about nine o'clock.

On Mondays in a small Southern town even a place of business as flourishing as the Red Hot Bar had no excuse for keeping open after nine, and Mr. Frost had just locked his doors. His way home lay along a dark and quiet street bordered by high weeds and bushes. When he was within twenty steps of his own gate, someone let fly at him twice with a shotgun. The first charge struck him in the right arm. The second tore away the brim of his hat. He neither fell nor wavered, but marched on through his own door and coolly informed his horrified family that someone had nearly shot him to death.

Bloodhounds were immediately sent for to the Ellis Plantation, which used convict labor, and the dogs followed a trail to a Negro cabin a mile south of town where John Ewen, his son Mitchell Ewen, and a schoolteacher named Donovan were taken out and lodged in the county jail

Nobody was sure they were the guilty men, and therefore nobody was sure there ought to be a lynching. Just to keep it an open question, however, the Jaybirds posted thirty men around the jail to be sure the officers didn't take the prisoners away.

In the morning Happy Jack Randal was arrested for complicity in the attack, apparently because of an indiscreet remark which he had dropped. He was released on bond, and a little later disappeared permanently from the Richmond scene.[7]

The Frost affair did serve to bring the Negro question into the open. In a few hours the county was aroused and serious-faced men began to come into Richmond. On Wednesday, September 5, four hundred of them assembled at the courthouse. Clem Bassett presided, and the upshot was a determined and successful effort to rid the town of seven of its undesirable Negroes.

C.M. Ferguson came first. He was the district clerk—educated, wealthy, and aggressive. Maybe he was dangerous. The others on the list were J.D. Davis and H.G. Lucas, Negro schoolteachers; Peter Warren, a restaurant keeper; C.M. Williams, a barber; and Jack and Tom Taylor from Kendleton, the Negro settlement on the San Bernard River eighteen miles west of Richmond. Tom Taylor, it was said, divided his time between cattle stealing and his work as county commissioner.

As the meeting at the courthouse broke up, most of the participants fell in, two and two, ready to make the rounds. Only one man gave trouble. That was Peter Warren, who appeared at a second-story window with a shotgun; but when Kyle Terry mounted the outside stairway and kicked on the door, he came down without argument.[8]

A committee of six hardy Jaybirds rode out to Kendleton to read the riot act to the Taylors, and met defiance. "We are not going to leave," said the Negroes, "until we are packed out in our coffins." So the six hardy Jaybirds rode back to Richmond.

Their story caused a mighty upheaval. Telegrams were sent to neighboring towns. The governor called out the Peareson Guards. The adjutant general ordered out the Rutherford Guards of Houston. Rumors flew that the Negroes were massing for a last-ditch stand. The citizens themselves got up a military company with Colonel

Peareson in command and under him three lieutenants, five sergeants, and five corporals. No privates were mentioned. When a special train arrived from Houston at five o'clock, September 6, with twenty-five men and two newspaper correspondents, all the ingredients for a first-class war seemed to be assembled.

Meanwhile a band of fifty had gone out to the Colony, as Kendleton was called, and dispersed a mob of thirty Negroes, after which they rode back in triumph and starvation to Richmond, where they arrived on Friday afternoon. Adjutant General King came in on the ten-thirty train and was met by a committee of citizens who told him with much compliment that he was neither needed nor wanted. In the afternoon there was a mass meeting which arrived at the same conclusion. Colonel Peareson made a speech. General King made a speech. The heroes were fed and praised; and with the departure of the contingent from Wharton on the next morning's train, life became normal again. The Houston *Post* reporter exaggerated considerably, however, when he announced that "Perfect Quiet Reigns Supreme in Fort Bend County."

★

The Terry-Gibson Feud Begins

Only a few weeks now till election. The Jaybirds had a full slate of nominees and were hopeful that they would beat the Woodpeckers out at the polls and so get the upper hand. The Woodpeckers lined up behind their own "white man's ticket" (including three former Jaybirds), held on like grim death, and dug their toes in for the final tussle.

On October 18 there was one last barbecue, this time at Duke's Station some miles down the Brazos from Richmond. It was a joint Jaybird and Woodpecker affair, for

Clem Bassett and the older heads were still hopeful that a compromise might be arranged. Mr. C.O. Fenn provided the pickles and light bread and cigars, but the young politicians of the county provided the fireworks.[1] Before the day was over the Terry-Gibson feud, an offshoot of the Jaybird-Woodpecker trouble, was well under way.

On one side, all alone, was Kyle Terry. He was the

youngest son of the famous organizer of Terry's Texas Rangers, a regiment which fought brilliantly and lost heavily in the Civil War. All the Terrys were dangerous men in a fight. An uncle of Kyle's, Judge David Terry, had already finished a man in a notorious duel and was within a few months of his own death in a shooting scrape in California. Kyle himself had been in some bad fights and had killed a man in Houston some time before. He was a big fellow, powerful and well proportioned, with a heavy face which he adorned with a large mustache, waxed on the ends. At the time of this trouble, he was in his early thirties; had been married, but his wife and one of his two children were dead. Originally he was a Jaybird but had joined the Woodpeckers because they promised him a place on their ticket and because he had looked with interest upon Parker's attractive nineteen-year-old daughter Mamie. Mamie Parker was not for him, but he did get on the ticket as the Woodpecker candidate for county assessor.[2]

On the other side were the Gibson boys. There were four of them, sons of Dr. Gibson who lived on a farm near Richmond and cultivated race horses. Volney, Ned, and Jim were in Richmond and closely associated with the Jaybirds. Guilf was in California. They were all blond and rather slight in build, Ned being the heaviest and Volney (to quote an old lady who knew him) a "mere shadow." To compensate for his shadowy physique Volney was the best pistol shot in those parts. In society the Gibson boys were jovial and well-mannered Southern gentlemen. In the saloons of Richmond they were known as cool customers in an argument.

Volney Gibson and Kyle Terry were at the barbecue at Duke's Station and Terry was on the list of speakers. Halfway through his remarks he referred to Ned Gibson, employing the picturesque but offensive phrase "paper-collared dude." The speech ended exactly there. Volney

Gibson called out, "Ned isn't here, but I'll represent him!" Terry turned red and jumped down off the platform, pistol in hand. Clem Bassett seized him just in time; others stepped in to assist; and trouble was headed off for that day.[3] But now the most hopeful began to despair. Terry and Gibson left the grounds looking black as thunderclouds, and Clem Bassett told Judge Parker sorrowfully that there would be no more joint meetings. Each side would have to back its own men, and the people would decide.

The few days remaining before election passed without incident, and both parties went to the polls confident of success. The Jaybirds were confident because they had done everything they could think of to win. The Woodpeckers were confident because they had persuaded some charter members of the Young Men's Democratic Club (including Kyle Terry) to run for office on the Woodpecker ticket.

Under the circumstances there was not much hope for a peaceful day at the polls, but strange to say the voting was very light and was not marred by so much as a cross word. To the Jaybirds' chagrin the Woodpeckers won. Judge Parker remarked sarcastically that "the darkies were nearly fattened on Jaybird beef, light bread, cigars, and whiskey," but they voted as they always had before.

It was a severe blow and the Jaybirds were naturally gloomy about it, but instead of retiring to sackcloth and ashes, they gave a superlatively elegant supper and ball, duly noted by David Nation in his column:

> Last night the members of the Jaybird club celebrated their defeat in the local election by a grand supper and ball. Though deprived of the spoils of office, they were evidently in possession of the sympathies of their lady friends, if the abundance and variety of edibles provided be any test thereof; to all which it is needless to add, they did full justice.[4]

As the fame of the Jaybirds' entertainment spread, the Woodpeckers caught the infection and determined to have one too. Their guest list was a little more liberal, however, and included some Jaybirds The Jaybirds were not touched with gratitude. They tore up some of the invitations, defaced others, and remailed the rest to some of the Negro prostitutes living over north of the tracks.[5] The Woodpeckers heard about it, of course.

The morning after the ball, Kyle Terry met Volney Gibson at the Southern Pacific depot and hot words were spoken

"The Jaybirds have been doing things I won't stand," Kyle said.

Volney pretended ignorance. "I would like to know what I am accused of doing."

"Someone has sent out invitations to Negroes. If you did not send them, you know who did." Terry put his hand on his big nickel-plated pistol as he spoke.

"Anyone who accuses me of such a thing is a damned liar," Gibson blazed. And Terry knocked him down, at the same time drawing his gun.

Gibson was unarmed, or there would have been a finish fight then and there. Having no weapon, he began talking instead of shooting. They had not walked ten steps together before Terry slapped him again, and the result was an agreement to fight it out down in the river bottom by the railroad bridge. Tom Smith, the Woodpecker deputy sheriff, arrested Volney as he left Frost's saloon with a Winchester, and Sheriff Garvey took Kyle's gun away as he waited by the bridge.

From then on existence for Terry and the Gibsons was a succession of skirmishes. Both sides were, of course, too proud to leave and too stubborn to forget their grudges. The closest brush they had came on a Sunday morning near the end of 1888 when Terry came to town on legitimate business. First he got himself shaved and then went over to Dickerson's shop on Railroad Street for a pair of shoes he had left to be repaired. Deputy Mason, who was abroad with a weather eye out for trouble, saw Volney and Ned Gibson in an alley five or six hundred feet from the cobbler's shop. He said, "Boys, what are you doing? Do you want to raise a difficulty?"

"We are just watching," they told him.

Mason was well aware of what was about to happen. He heard Kyle Terry's voice taking leave of the cobbler and in a second was halfway to Dickerson's door. He was still six feet away when Kyle appeared in the doorway, holding his cane and a bundle of shoes in one hand and brushing some ashes from his coat with the other. Mason took the six feet in a dive, for the Gibsons were not far behind. He struck his man in the chest hard enough to knock him ten feet back into the shop, at the same time shouting at him to get out of the line of fire. Terry had just time to ejaculate "What. . . ." when he stumbled over a coil of rope placed there by a thoughtful providence. He fired his pistol into the floor as he fell.

The Gibsons, reinforced now by brother Jim, had come opposite the door, and Jim fired at Terry just as he stumbled over the rope. Seeing him fall, he swore and remarked sympathetically, "I have killed him, I hope. I have shot him in the bowels." He and Volney started in to see if his hopes were justified; but Mason and Ned Gibson held them back. It would have been better for Ned if he had not yielded to his better nature.[6]

Both sides now began to talk of the only recourse left two Southern gentlemen—a duel. But neither of the principals had much confidence in the honorable intentions of the other, and the affair proved difficult to arrange. After much futile negotiation Terry is supposed to have written a note offering to meet Volney at Wharton where they would encounter each other in the street and shoot it out.[7]

It was not Volney, however, who came to grief on the streets of Wharton.

At 3:56 A.M. on the morning of January 21, 1889, the Southern Pacific train stopped at Walker's station, some miles from Richmond, and picked up a solitary passenger. It was Kyle Terry carrying a shotgun, unjointed and wrapped in paper, under his arm. He said a few words to Tom Smith, the deputy sheriff, who was on the rear platform, and then disappeared into the water closet to be seen no more until he got off at East Bernard at five o'clock.

From East Bernard he went to Wharton, on whose streets he appeared in the early morning riding a borrowed horse. He went immediately to Malitz and Barber's saloon, remaining till 1:00 P.M. At that time a party from Richmond, including lawyer Ned Gibson, left the Fort House. They were on their way to the county courtrooms, where cases were being heard, and their road lay in front of Malitz and Barber's place. Mr. Barber and Terry were sitting on the front gallery. Barber was well acquainted with the situation and sent one of his henchmen to tell the oncoming party to look out. They never hesitated, but came steadily on. Terry stepped inside and got his shotgun. Bob Stafford said to him, "My God, Kyle, are you going to kill your friends?"

"No, I am only after those who have been waylaying me." And he carefully leveled his double-barreled gun.

The charge of buckshot took effect in Gibson's shoulder, mouth and arm, and he died in about an hour, leaving his bride of a few months and an unborn child.[8]

Many people have wondered why Terry singled out Ned Gibson when his quarrel was really with Volney. It was said later that Parker had remarked to Kyle, that "Venison is better than no meat," meaning that any Gibson was better than none. The judge later denied this under oath, but the remaining Gibsons always regarded

Parker as an accomplice in the crime. Otherwise the next chapter of this history might never have been written.

From now on there was no talk of peace. Practically everybody in the whole countryside fell into line with one party or the other, and the young Jaybirds, impetuous and eager, began to get ready for open war. Even the ladies were aroused. It was said then, and is repeated now by people who were on the ground, that the Jaybird women had prepared about forty little bags of sand to send to lukewarm men. On the bags was inscribed: "If you haven't any grit, we are sending you some." Judge Parker said he could name the ladies, though the cross-examining attorney at his trial gallantly refrained from asking him to do so.[9]

★

The Nation Family Moves Out

David Nation was walking down the railroad tracks toward the station one night in the spring of 1889. He always met the midnight train and thus combined two sorts of business with a small amount of pleasure—he was able to take care of the patrons of his wife's hotel, pick up morsels for his column in the Houston *Daily Post*, and watch the strange behavior of his fellow creatures for his own amusement.

Not that David was often amused. To be the husband of Carry was a matter serious enough, but David was a preacher of the gospel besides and took the wickedness of his neighbors very much to heart.

He knew the young men called him a black Republican and a damned Woodpecker, and that puzzled him a little, for neither the Jaybirds nor the Woodpeckers had thrown him any crumbs of friendship or respect. He may have felt a little flattered at being classed as one of the ruling clan, but as a matter of fact he was just an outsider trying to please a town full of people who preferred his room to his company.

The black looks he was getting were more Carry's fault than his. She was the one who got up praying parties to ask the Lord to break a dry spell and so made people wonder if she ought to be at large. She was the one they accused of opening the Jaybirds' mail which passed through her post office and revealing the contents to the Woodpeckers.

The day before, David himself had taken a step which was giving him a good deal of worry. He had sent a letter to the *Post* in which he raised his voice mildly against the hell-raising activities of some of the young bucks of Richmond. He knew there was resentment against him about that letter. He could feel it in the air.

As he came up to the station he noticed that a small crowd was assembled—young men, mostly. He wondered what they were up to now. They were lounging around with such elaborate carelessness that David's suspicions were aroused. His heart came up to the top of his chest when Henry George sauntered over and said he wanted to have a talk with him. They walked over to a bale of cotton and sat down.

In an instant two other boys were behind the little preacher. He was pulled backward off the bale. Everybody produced a cane and struck him—just once—wherever it was convenient. One blow each! But there were twenty-one young men. David took a beating.

When it was over he crept home to Carry. Fourteen years later she remembered that homecoming and wrote of it in her autobiography:

> The next night after the article appeared in the *Post*, he came in and I was asleep. He woke me up saying: "Wife get up; I have been beaten almost to death;" and lighting a lamp

I found that his body was covered with bruises. I bathed him in cold water and otherwise tried to relieve him. He was too faint to tell me the trouble, only the boys had beaten him. I knelt down by the window to pray to God, I began calling on God to send a punishment on people that would do such a mean, cowardly act. I prayed until I received perfect deliverance from that kind of a spirit, and when I got up from off my knees it was four o'clock in the morning.[1]

At breakfast David and Carry talked it over, and they agreed that it was time to go. If they stayed, David's life might be the price.

So David Nation cast about for another congregation and found a prospect in Kansas. By the summer of 1889 he had gone north to inspect his new location. Carry went with him, shaking the dust of Richmond from her feet like a lady prophet of ancient Israel.[2]

She got out just in time. In August the storm broke, and then, no doubt, Carry felt justified.

★

Battle, Murder, and Sudden Death

July passed and August settled down over the land, hot and oppressive. The weather was almost too warm for business or politics and the showdown which had been so close a few months ago had apparently swung away like a thunderhead and was now lingering on the horizon giving off low, sullen rumblings.

Stray bits of testimony indicate that a patched-up truce was in effect and both groups had agreed not to carry arms. The agreement was probably respected in the letter. No member of either side felt that it was good form to loaf around town with a Winchester in the crook of the arm. A gun within arm's reach is practically as good as a gun in the hand, however, and everybody had a favorite spot where he stowed his heavy artillery. The Woodpeckers made a stronghold of the new courthouse. The Jaybirds scattered their weapons out in the stores along Morton Street. Many of them used Frost's saloon. Guilf Gibson (who had returned from California when trouble seemed inevitable) and Keane Ferris had a corner reserved in McCloy's drugstore.

All this, of course, had nothing to do with small arms. In Richmond in 1889 the well-dressed man wore pistols just as he wore a shirt and suspenders. The truce naturally said nothing about laying six-shooters aside.

And so one day followed another with deceptive calm, but outside of Fort Bend County the rumor was going around that hell might break loose in Richmond at any moment. Even the officials in Austin were for once aware of what was going on, and Governor Ross, who was a famous Ranger and Indian fighter himself, did what his experience told him ought to be done. After Ned Gibson's assassination he sent Ranger Sergeant Ira Aten with seven privates to take charge of the situation.[1]

There was absolutely nothing stirring when Aten and his men rode in and set up camp. A good many of the citizens were, in fact, thinking about leaving town on a beach party and were absorbed in the somewhat complicated arrangements necessary for such an affair—horses, carriages, provisions, tents, and so on. About the beginning of the second week in August they left town—forty of them. For the most part they were young Jaybirds, though a few older people were part of the necessary paraphernalia.

The Woodpeckers had forebodings as soon as the dust of departure had settled. They figured that the beach party was just a blind, and those young men were out hatching up some new devilment. Nevertheless the community atmosphere became calmer when the forty were out

of sight; Sergeant Aten was reassured and allowed half
his little force to ride off and pour oil on other troubled
waters many miles away.

Immediately after the division of the Ranger force, as if
Fate or the Jaybird leaders had arranged it so, the beach
party clattered back into town. This was on the afternoon
of the sixteenth of August.

That same afternoon Judge Parker had a visit from
his nephew, W.T. Wade, and asked him home for the
night. It was about seven o'clock, perhaps half an hour

before sundown, when they mounted their horses to ride to the Parker establishment a half-mile south of town. Sheriff Garvey was sitting in front of McGhee's saloon and he called Parker over, probably to tell him that he smelled trouble. The Judge had been smelling it for months past, but according to McCloy, whose drugstore was just across the street, his sense of smell must have been somehow strengthened, for he went back to his office, opened his safe, and took out something. When Parker was later asked if he got his guns ready at this time, he snapped that he always had them ready.

A moment later he and Wade were riding down the street toward the courthouse, and it was then they got their first sight of the Gibson boys. Guilf was standing in front of Winston's store. A little farther down the street was Volney Gibson on a large sorrel horse. As was usual in this town of many relationships, the actors in the scene were close kin, the Gibsons being first cousins of W.T. Wade, who was a nephew of Parker.

The two men proceeded south, away from the center of town, and immediately saw Guilf Gibson riding down a parallel street to the west of them with Volney Gibson close behind and hurrying to overtake him. Just when Parker and Wade turned west into a cross street, the Gibsons turned east into the same street and both sides began shooting. There was much conflicting testimony later about who fired the first shot.

At that moment Clem Bassett and his wife were upstairs in their house a few blocks away. They looked at each other with startled eyes as a volley of shots rang out nearby. With the town's emotions in their present condition this could mean only one thing. A clatter of hoofs came through the open window. They looked out and saw Parker on a frantic horse flying up the street toward the courthouse. Now and then he turned in the saddle and fired at the two Gibsons who were in close pursuit.

Mr. Bassett had only one gun in the house. It was a double-barreled shotgun with one hammer gone, but he picked up his poor weapon and went out to the battle-field.[2]

The Jaybirds were up at last. While Parker's horse carried him back toward the courthouse, they were coming out of Frost's saloon. Just as he half-fell from his rearing mount and stumbled up the courthouse steps with a bullet hole through his back, a knot of them were moving up the street, walking rapidly. H.H. Frost was in the lead. Behind, strung out a little, were the younger Jaybirds—the Gibson boys, Yandell and Keane Ferris, Jeff Bryant, Will Andrus, Charles Parnell, and Rugeley Peareson—and apparently a few were at one side of the road among the trees around an old boiler which lay near the southeast corner of the courthouse square.

Garvey and his deputies Smith and Mason were already near the courthouse, having just arranged for Albert George to spend a comfortable night in jail. Parker called to them as he tumbled from his horse that the cursed Jaybirds had assassinated him and added, "A lot of these people are coming up the street with guns; let's go down and stop them." He raised his voice and shouted to the two deputies to "come on"—the Rangers were there and would help to stop any trouble. Then Parker, Garvey, and Judge Weston, who was a doctor, went inside to have a look at Parker's wound. The inspection was necessarily hasty. Garvey looked out of the window and exclaimed, "Yonder they are; the street is full of them; they will riddle you." Then he took his rifle, walked out of the building and stood in the road. Parker got back into his clothes as fast as he could but it was several minutes before he could join his party.

When the first shot was fired, Ranger Sergeant Aten was in camp fixing a dose of quinine for one of his men who had the chills. He dropped everything, got on his horse and headed for the courthouse. Garvey was out in front, and Aten begged him to go back inside and let the Rangers handle it. "Never, Aten," he replied. "I am sheriff of this county and am going to handle this situation myself. You keep out of this."

Aten turned his horse at once and went to work on the Jaybirds, but when he took hold of Volney Gibson's gun barrel, Vol jerked it away, pointed it at him, and said, "I don't want to hurt you, Aten, but you can't take my gun or stop this crowd. We are going to clean them all out of the courthouse this time." Aten and his two men could do nothing but get out of the line of fire.[3]

In that instant Frost and Garvey were face to face. "Trot out your brave Woodpeckers," said Frost as he came on, "the cowardly Jaybirds are coming." Judge Ballowe called to Frost to stop. Someone else shouted (a witness thought it was Guilf Gibson), "They've been assassinating us long enough. We'll kill them as they come." And a roar of gunfire followed.

Each side was anxious to finish the leaders of the other. The Jaybirds wanted Parker and Garvey, and the Woodpeckers wanted Frost. Parker had not emerged from the courthouse when the first volley was fired, so that Garvey and Frost bore the brunt of the bullets, and both were seriously hit. Garvey fell beside a hitching post. He pulled himself by means of it into a kneeling position and fired two or three times more before he slumped down, unconscious, and twisted about so that his back was against the post.

Frost was not so near the end. Beside him was Yandell Ferris with his pistol in hand, about to fire. Judge Parker's wife had rushed up in an agony of fear when the shooting began. Now she seized Ferris's arm and pleaded with him: "Oh, Yandell, don't do it; you know it's wrong."

As he hesitated, the Woodpecker ex-sheriff Jake Blakely rounded a corner and came in sight of the Jaybirds. He was an old man now and his hearing and eyesight were bad, but the Jaybirds' feelings were not changed by his weak eyes and gray hair. He was Garvey's uncle; he was a Woodpecker; he deserved the worst. That was why Frost, wounded as he was, seized the gun from Yandell Ferris's wavering hand, exclaiming, "Give me the gun; I want to kill Blakely." Calvin Blakely said, "Yes, go on. I can't; he's my uncle."

Frost fired twice and Blakely fell. Five minutes before, he had been sitting in his house reading the paper. He heard the shots, stepped outside, and his wife and children never saw him alive again.

Colonel Peareson was only a block away when the firing started. He came up in time to hear Frost say, "I am killed, I am dead; but I killed Blakely." Another friend approached the fallen leader and asked if he didn't want a doctor. "No," said Frost, "let me die; go on and fight."

By now Parker had got his shirt back on, seized his pistol and reached the courthouse door. As he stepped out he was met by a bullet which came from the upper windows of the McFarlane residence directly across the street. Deputy H.S. Mason later testified that he had seen Dolph Peareson, Earle McFarlane, and Syd Peareson enter the McFarlane gate, and had heard Earle say: "Go upstairs; we can shoot out of the windows upstairs." Earle was a boy in knee breeches at the time, and his companions were not much older, but their move was a fine bit of strategy. Mason and Smith (Garvey's other deputy) were behind the iron fence which shut off the courthouse from the road. Through it they could fire with telling effect. The Jaybirds, on the other hand, were approaching from the side; their bullets struck the iron fence at a sharp angle and rebounded, singing and whizzing, into space. By getting into a second story window across the street, these youngsters took command of the situation. Only one shot was fired from their direction but it was enough to put Parker out of the fight. He was hit in the groin, shot through, and fell again, groaning and cursing as he dragged himself back inside.[4]

There was still another boy in the Jaybird ranks. As C.W. Parnell, later sheriff of the county, stood in the midst of the smoke and confusion he looked down and saw Bassett Blakely, in knee pants, at his side.

"Son, what on earth are you doing here?" he asked in surprise.

"I was going to pick up your gun if they shot you." [5]

In a matter of minutes it was finished. The shots scattered out and stopped and there was quiet except for the groans of the wounded men.

★

The Day After

Now that the excitement was over, the post-mortem began. Everybody was surprised at the way everybody (including himself) had acted, and the comparing of notes went on until most of the eyewitnesses had aired their impressions at the examining trial of the Jaybirds, which was held on August 27, eleven days after the fight.[1]

They all agreed that everybody in town seemed to be shooting, that several hundred shots were fired, and that the men cursed and shouted as they fought. Almost every witness told of strange behavior. Some who were ordinarily timid and shy marched fearlessly down the street with bullets buzzing past their ears. Two or three women ran into the line of fire and pleaded with the men when they were fighting hardest. Mrs. Parker was one of these, and so was Mrs. Jennie Mason, who said she would have accosted Frost himself, but he "looked so much like a demon" she dared not stop him.

Another who surprised himself was Mr. Jeff D. Bryant, the orator of the Young Men's Democratic Club who a year before had accepted the "beautiful banner" from Miss Charlie Woodall with so much gallantry and vocabulary. When the hour arrived for Mr. Bryant to march forth beneath those folds, he was in the bathtub. He heard the shots; he cast modesty to the winds; in two minutes he appeared on the streets protected only by a linen duster and a rifle. The duster is rumored to have been much less effective than the Winchester.[2]

The black citizens suffered most from fright. At the first explosion of gunpowder every Negro within hearing "hit for the Brazos bottom," and not a colored nose showed itself until all was quiet. Mrs. Albert Kochan was in her back yard with a Negro laundress hanging out clothes. A high stone wall surrounded the yard, broken by only one door; and this the mistress locked.

"Oh, Miss Mary, let me out," shrieked the laundress.

"I wouldn't open that door for anything on earth," replied Miss Mary. And the next instant, Mrs. Kochan never quite knew how, a hundred and seventy-odd pounds of dark flesh had heaved itself over the stone wall and disappeared instantly.[3]

As soon as the gunfire stopped, both men and women rushed in to do what they could. Carry Nation was not there to leap into the breach, but her daughter was. Mrs. Alec McNabb was the first to get to Garvey where he lay slumped against a post, dying. Her husband was close on her heels; he picked Garvey up and carried him down to Blakely's store. They put poor old Jake Blakely on a cot outside the courthouse. Frost and Parker, alive but, seriously hurt, were taken care of inside the building.

Garvey and Blakely were the only fatalities so far, but Robbie Smith, a Negro girl, had been killed earlier by a stray bullet in the Parker-Gibson encounter. Frost was fatally wounded. Parker was shot through, but would survive. Deputy Mason, W.T. Wade, Volney Gibson, Will Andrus, and Ranger Frank Schmidt were all more or less damaged.[4]

Not many minutes after the smoke drifted away from the battle ground, the outside world knew that something frightful had happened. A dispatch reached Houston and Mr. Floyd of the *Post* had a freight train held up on which he was soon "thundering," to use his own verb, toward Richmond. At 2 A.M. he wired his paper that the town was quiet.

Other messages which left the telegraph office were not so reassuring. County Judge Weston telegraphed the Governor: "Troops needed." Sergeant Aten was not much behind with the entreaty: "Send militia." Governor Ross did what he could. He ordered out the Houston Light Guard and instructed three other militia companies to stand by. A special train brought the Light Guard at three o'clock in the morning, and they at once took up guard duty around the courthouse inside which seven or eight Woodpeckers, armed to the teeth, had been keeping watch and ward.

The morning dawned hot and sultry as people began to flock into Richmond. Soon the village was overrun with curious or morbid citizens who inspected the bloodstains in the street and milled about the courthouse. A few of the stores opened, but they did little business. The men on the sidewalks just stood around and talked.

The reporters were all surprised at the peaceful appearance of the place. One of them wrote: "The town looked the typical slow, lazy country village." Another newspaper man, however, knew Richmond better and expressed himself with all the vigor of bad grammar:

There is probably one fact about Richmond that will not be disputed by any sane man and that is that there are more men there who will stand up before shotguns and pistols

than in any town of its size in the United States, and if anybody don't believe it, just let the doubting Thomas go over
and proclaim himself "Bad Medicine from Bitter Creek" and
make a gun play and if somebody don't call him, it won't be
at this time or generation.[5]

Early in the day it was discovered that "there was no
justice." The machinery of the law was paralyzed. Months
before, Mr. Sullivan, justice of the peace for the precinct,
had resigned on account of ill health. Now the sheriff was
dead, and there was no coroner.

And so it was that about six in the evening, without inquest or official sanction, Garvey and Blakely were buried
in the little cemetery across the railroad track, little more
than a stone's throw from the spot where they died. The
sky was red with sunset as the mourners and the morbid
filtered away. At seven o'clock the Governor of Texas
stepped from the train, followed by the Brenham Grays,
whom he had picked up on the way. He went directly to
the National Hotel, which was to be his headquarters, and
so the day ended.

★

The Cleanup

It seemed to all concerned that a settlement would be comparatively easy, now that two militia companies, the Rangers, and Governor Ross were there to take charge. The
Governor was one of those who thought so, but he didn't
know Richmond. He met a committee of leading citizens at
the hotel on Sunday, August 18, and gave them a good
talking-to, fatherly but firm. He discussed all sorts of proposals with them, including the imposing of martial law and
the disorganization of the county, but he couldn't get them
to agree to any positive action.

That evening he called on Frost, who was expected to die at almost any moment but was still conscious and rational. They talked for half an hour about the troubles, mentioned some old times that both men remembered, and then the Governor went away. At four o'clock in the morning, having discussed everything calmly with his wife, Frost passed quietly out of the world where he had finished his fight.

Monday morning the committees went back to work and the matter of a new sheriff was taken up. The Jaybirds mentioned as acceptable to them Clem Bassett and Sergeant Aten of the Rangers. The Woodpeckers, for their part, would have none of Clem Bassett and thought Aten was too young.

Meanwhile both factions were taking legal action against each other. On Monday Deputy Mason made out a complaint against Volney and Guilf Gibson, and some of the Jaybirds swore out another against Judge Parker and William Wade. Captain Sieker of the Rangers arrested all four, and it was noted that they seemed glad to give themselves up and let somebody else do the worrying.

Still no way had been found to arrange a peace. Both sides were in conference continually, but the decisive stroke was not made until Tuesday afternoon when the Jaybird committee, Clem Bassett in the lead, called at the hotel. The governor had stepped out, but Captain Sieker was there, and to him the Jaybirds stated that they had no further proposals to submit. This was, in effect, an invitation to the Woodpeckers to make concessions or look for trouble— the Jaybirds were through talking. In a way that was the most dramatic moment of the whole affair. There had been daring deeds before, but now, in cold blood, a decision had to be made.

The distracted Woodpeckers went into a huddle and struggled with fate from late in the afternoon until almost midnight. Assistant Attorney General Harrison and Captain Sieker were there and witnessed the death struggle. In the end it turned out to be a matter of money. The sheriff's bond was forty thousand dollars and the small group of Woodpeckers knew they would have trouble raising it. At last, exhausted and despairing, they gave up and agreed to the appointment of young Ira Aten as supreme peace officer of the county. The crisis had passed.[1]

Next day Aten was formally appointed and Mr. Floyd of the *Post* called on him for an interview. He found a young man with seven adventurous years in the Rangers behind him, though he was only twenty-seven, and a reputation as a detective to his credit. "I fully appreciate the unusual responsibilities thrown upon me," he said. "Should there be any mistake made at any time, it will be an error of judgment and not of the heart."

After that there was nothing for the Woodpeckers to do but move out. Judge Parker went to Houston and then to the Texas Panhandle, where he died. Judge Weston resigned. All the county commissioners but one were already absent or hastened to become so. One by one the chief Woodpecker families drifted away, and it is said that only one of the emigrés has ever returned to visit his relatives—and he waited twenty-five years.[2]

On August 27 the preliminary hearing of the Jaybirds began. Judge Hightower of Beaumont, who had been agreed on by both sides as a fair and impartial judge, was of the opinion that bail might be granted and fifteen men were bound over in the sum of five thousand dollars each. They were Volney, Jim, and Guilf Gibson, Yandell and Keane Ferris, Rugeley, E.A. and Syd Peareson, Jeff Bryant, C.W. Parnell, Harris Mitchell, Will and Earle McFarlane, Will Andrus, and S.J. Winston. The bonds were quickly raised among the county's elders and wealthiers, and the young men went free.

It was lucky that the Jaybirds had plenty of money, for a month later they ran into more trouble from an unexpected source. Two of the Negroes who had been driven

out after the first shooting of Frost (C.M. Ferguson and
J.D. Davis) had brought suit in the Federal Court at Galveston against forty-three of the richest Jaybirds. They
had established residence outside the state and spent a whole
year there so that they could legally sue in Galveston and
so avoid the necessity for trying the case in Fort Bend
County. They were asking damages as a result of having
been "Unlawfully and maliciously driven" from their
homes. The Jaybirds, of course, stood by the forty-three
and assumed joint responsibility with them. They even
canvassed the county and asked each white voter where he
stood, finding only seven men who refused to stay with
them. On October 3 they had another big mass meeting in
Richmond and resolved that the expulsion "was the act of
the entire white citizens of Fort Bend County and not the
act of the said forty-three persons sued in the Federal Court
by the said Ferguson and Davis." [3]

In the evening of the same day, a few sparks of the mass-
meeting spirit still glowing brightly, another rally was held
at which the proposal originated to provide a monument
for the fallen Jaybirds. The idea was apparently suggested
by the new county judge, M.J. Hickey, who made a richly
embroidered speech in memory of the dead, dwelling particularly on "the knightly Frost." "Had he lived in ancient
Rome he would have ranked with Caesar," said Mr. Hickey.
"His private and public character was pure and upright—
as stainless as the polished scimeters of Eden's sentinels."
Before the evening was over, several hundred dollars had
been subscribed toward the purchase and erection of the
Jaybird monument which stands now at the southeast corner of the old courthouse square. The names of Shamblin,
Gibson, and Frost are engraved on it with a flowery verse
for each to keep his memory green. [4]

That same day Sheriff Aten wrote to Captain Sieker,
"We will have a Jaybird government here after a little,
whether for the best or not will remain to be seen. The

other pecker woods intend resigning soon, so they say. Everything very quiet, and have been ever since you left." [5]

To keep things quiet, the Jaybirds took one final step. On October 22 they assembled once more and organized the Jaybird Democratic Association. Clem Bassett was elected president with D.P. Coulson and Yandell Ferris as vice-presidents, J.W. Eckman as treasurer, and F.M.O. Fenn as secretary. A long and carefully worked-out constitution was presented and adopted. It contained this significant clause:

Article 15. The object of this Association is to combine and unite the white people for the advancement and prosperity of this county. . . . We, therefore, declare that any white man now residing in this county, or who shall hereafter acquire citizenship in this county, who shall undertake to lead against this Association any political faction or voting population opposed to the principles and objects of this Association, shall be considered and treated as a *social* and *political outcast.*[6]

For seventy years the Association dominated county politics. It met at stated times in a "pre-primary" which nominated a white man's ticket—thereby keeping the government out of the hands of political adventurers and preventing even the most incorruptible incumbent from remaining more than four years in office. During those times the best citizens were behind the organization heart and soul, and their influence was so great that the Jaybird slate was elected as a matter of course. In a few cases a party member not on the ticket triumphed over the official nominee, but outsiders never had the remotest chance of holding office.

So came the day before Christmas, 1889, and with it came Deputy Dickson from Galveston. Dickson was a former Woodpecker county clerk of Fort Bend County and he was there to arrest all the Jaybirds for running Ferguson and his colored friends out of the country, interfering with a congressional election, and otherwise misbehaving. He had a special coach sidetracked near the station and from it he dismounted with a small army of deputies and a little arsenal of pistols, Winchesters, and sawed-off shotguns. It was the last attempt of the Woodpeckers to get even.

Working rapidly, Dickson and his gang cornered all the Jaybirds they could lay hands on. Then Clem Bassett good-humoredly sent off for such of the brethren as were missing. Dickson herded them all down to the station and set about disarming them before shipping them off. Few of the men left unarmed, however, for as soon as Dickson handed a man's pistol to a wife or sister for safekeeping, she would step around to the other side and pass the weapon back to its owner. Nearly a hundred men were absent from Christmas dinner that year. Dickson expected them to enjoy the fellowship and good cheer of the Galveston jail, but Sheriff Tiernan put them up in the Galveston courthouse and made them as comfortable as he could. In a few days, with the help of Houston and Galveston businessmen, bail was raised for everybody and the men went home. The suit was eventually settled out of court, but it cost the Jaybirds a good deal of money to buy off Ferguson and Davis, the negro plaintiffs.[7]

For all but a few Richmond people the war was over and there were other things to think about. A new school building was purchased and the system was reorganized, one of the new teachers being the lovely Miss Charlie Woodall of Huntsville. The young men and women of the town carried on by organizing a dramatic society "for the purpose of giving entertainment to assist in buying furniture for the new academy." The president of the society was Volney Gibson, who was approaching the final scene of his own version of *Hamlet* in real life.[8]

If those things were not enough to keep people's minds occupied, there was the following news item in the Houston *Post* for September 13:

Mrs. Carrie Nation arrived from Kansas today on the late train. She has been spending the summer months with her husband, Rev. David Nation, of that State.

★

The Last of Kyle Terry

The Terry-Gibson affair came to its climax in the Galveston courthouse on January 21, 1890. On change of venue several Fort Bend cases had been moved to Galveston. Judge Parker and his nephew Wade were to stand trial for killing Robbie Smith, the little Negro girl who was accidentally shot when they met the Gibsons. Their hearing was to be followed by the state's case against Kyle Terry for the murder of Ned Gibson.

Many people expected and feared that there would be trouble. They whispered that Kyle had sent word to Volney that he would shoot him on sight; and friends of the Gibson family said that Volney considered himself bound to do the same for Kyle.

The witnesses from Fort Bend County, who were to appear in both cases, arrived in Galveston the night before the trials under the eye of Sheriff Aten. Volney came in the next morning, remarking that he did not want any night play in his. He was met at the station by a number of young Jaybirds who were having forebodings about what might befall them. They all agreed to keep together and ask the sheriff to prevent anything unfortunate from happening.

Terry also felt that there was trouble brewing. With Parker and some other friends he sought out Attorney Lovejoy, of the staff defending Parker, and asked him to take steps to keep the peace. Lovejoy, according to his own tale, did ask for police protection but got none. The officers "scouted the idea of there being any danger." Sheriff Tiernan later denied emphatically that any request for protection had been made to him or his deputies, except by Volney Gibson, who had reported to him at the courthouse a little before ten in the morning and asked that a meeting between himself and Terry be prevented. Tiernan offered to keep the two parties in separate rooms if they should come to the courthouse at the same time, but just as he was about to lead the Jaybirds to a place where they would be to themselves, he was approached by an attorney with a paper for his signature. "Just a minute," he said to Volney, and stepped into his office.

At that moment Kyle Terry entered the courthouse. He turned to the left in the direction of the stairway leading up to the criminal courtroom on the second floor and partially faced back to the right as he began to mount the steps, which cut diagonally across the rotunda. Gibson was standing in the far corner to Terry's right. Calvin Blakely had just taken him aside and warned him to look out, for almost every Woodpecker in town was in the building. Volney must have seen his enemy first, but as Terry's foot reached for the third step, their eyes met. Gibson got his pistol out, aimed it with both hands, and shot Terry through the heart. Kyle fell, clutching at the railing and attempting to get his own pistol into action.[1]

A rumor is still in circulation that it was not Volney who fired the fatal shot, but another young Jaybird who was standing near him. The story cannot be verified, of course. Gibson seems to have been convinced that the deed was his.[2]

The firing lasted only a few seconds, but a good number of cartridges were exploded; and almost with the speed of the bullets, men dashed for doors and windows. Gibson did not move, however, until Sheriff Tiernan put a hand on his arm to arrest him. Then Volney suddenly came to life, twisted away, and broke for the rear of the building. He ran into Detective Cahill, who was coming down the back stairs, however, and the two officers led him off to the vault of the county attorney's office where they locked him up, first removing from him an improved Colt's revolver and a double-edged bone-handled knife.

At that moment F.M.O. Fenn of Richmond was straightening out Kyle's body on the floor of the rotunda downstairs. He found the hammer of the man's pistol caught in the loop of his drawers. His was one life that had literally hung by a thread.

A few minutes later David Terry, a brother of Kyle's who had come back from California to be with him during the trial, was brought upstairs by one of the deputies. He had stopped for a moment outside the courthouse to speak with an acquaintance, allowing his party to precede him. When the shooting began, someone thrust a pistol into his hand and a vigilant officer picked him up for carrying arms. They locked him up in the vault with Volney Gibson.

It was the sort of situation that happens once in a million times; and to make the thing even more weird, neither knew who the other was. They paced the floor of the vault, passing and repassing each other, in silence. Terry was on the point of speaking once or twice, thinking this might be a friend of his brother's, but he thought better of it. One unspoken word was probably all that stood between them and still more death and destruction.[3]

Finally Gibson and his party were removed to the county jail and held there while hundreds of morbid people surveyed the bloodstains and bullet holes; gazed at Terry in his "beautiful casket," clad in a "dark diagonal suit with a beautiful and fragrant buttonhole bouquet in the lapel of his coat"; and discussed theories of how it all happened.[4] Next morning the trains disgorged new hordes of the curious—some from Fort Bend County—and the height of notoriety was reached when the *National Police Gazette* took up the subject and displayed pictures and paragraphs dripping gore to horrify peaceable citizens all over the country.

The last act of the play was now approaching its final

scene. The trial of Judge Parker for the murder of Robbie Smith and for attempting to assassinate the Gibson boys was postponed one day because of Kyle Terry's death and occupied most of the court's time on January 23. The great sensation was Volney Gibson's testimony. He was brought directly from the jail to the courthouse and "the audience rose to its feet as one man to get a look at him who has of late become so consequential." He admitted that the Gibsons were not averse to trouble the day they met Parker on the streets of Richmond. "I wanted to give him a chance to do what he was going to do. There was deep enmity between us; at least there was on my part."

After that there was little chance of a conviction and the state practically abandoned the case. Nobody could prove that Parker attacked the Gibsons; in fact, his witnesses made out a good case for his having been the object of an assault. As for the dead Negro girl, she probably never knew herself who fired the bullet that killed her. Certainly nobody else did. By seven o'clock the trial was over.[5]

Only the Terry-Gibson matter was left to be settled. The young Jaybirds who had been with Volney Gibson at the time of Terry's death were held until January 31. Then William McFarlane, J.R. Mitchell, William Andrus, William Little, Dan Ragsdale, and Calvin Blakely were released under bond of twenty-five hundred dollars each. Gibson had to raise a bond of ten thousand dollars, and was not released until April 2, 1890. The names of Clem Bassett, Colonel Peareson, and S.J. Winston appeared on his bond. He lived only a year longer and was never brought to trial for killing Terry. On April 9, 1891, he died of tuberculosis.

★

Last Words

If you go out to Richmond looking for relics of the great feud, you will probably be disappointed. You turn off the highway and drive a block north to Morton Street, down which the Jaybirds marched, and look first of all for Frost's saloon with its club rooms overhead and its memories of the Rosebud Club and the Young Men's Democratic organization. You will find only a vacant lot. The building went down in the great storm of 1900.

The old National Hotel, where Carry Nation supported her family, taught her wildcat Sunday school, and thanked God for her troubles, has been replaced by a brick store building. The structure across the street, now called the National Hotel, was never hallowed by Carry's footstep. The old courthouse is gone likewise. It was moved away some years after the big fight and became the headquarters of the local fire company. A few years ago it burned down in spite of the fire department, and where it originally stood is now a vacancy surrounded by trees. A glass-eyed pony is tied to one of them, drooping one hip and letting its lower lip hang slack. A Negro boy sits on the curb and amputates round hunks from an ample watermelon. At the west side of the vacant space, across brown wisps of grass, is a community swimming pool where a few children splash and squeal.

At the southeast corner of the square is the Jaybird monument, a stone shaft fifteen feet high dedicated to "Our Heroes." On March 18, 1896, the Houston and Galveston papers were full of the story of its unveiling the day before. Herb's Light Guard came down from Houston; the new Lamar Guards turned out bearing the banner of the old Peareson Guards; and the Honorable Jonathan Lane appeared as speaker of the day, bearing his sheaves of oratory with him. There was a parade, of course, and a formal unveiling by juvenile relatives of Frost, Shamblin, and Gibson, the fallen warriors.

The memorial still stands, but the cause it represents has fallen on evil days. The power of the Jaybird Association was challenged effectively for the first time in 1953 when John Terry and several other colored citizens sued in the Federal District Court at Houston, complaining that their civil rights had been infringed. The case went to the Supreme Court of the United States, and the Jaybirds lost.[1] In 1954 the Executive Committee voted to allow negroes to participate in the Jaybird Primary "as per the decree of the Supreme Court." [2]

After that there was not much use in keeping the Association going, but it took five years more for the membership to accept defeat. On October 15, 1959, in a final brief meeting, the Executive Committee voted to recess indefinitely.[3] "It now appears," says one loyal member, "that the flag of the Association has been folded and reverently laid away." [4]

By "recessing," however, the Jaybirds let it be known that in case of future need the banner might be raised again to call them to battle.

There will probably be no more banners or battles in the streets of Richmond. The place grew quiet—deathly quiet —after those days of wrath in 1889. Carry Nation noticed the change when she paid the town a visit in 1902. "I never saw such a difference," she said. "A pall of death seemed to be over the whole place, and one coming into the town would feel a desire to leave it as quickly as possible, if there was not some interest independent of the town. God said: 'They shall eat the fruit of their own doing.' "

Memories of the feud have never died, and will be a long time dying, but most of the old people do not care to talk about it. They twist in their chairs and wonder why these old scandals can't be left in peace. Sometimes one of them will tell you what he remembers, and you listen on the shady gallery while the breeze blows through the house from open front door to open back door. He will be a Jaybird, of course. You have to go to Houston, or Galveston, or even farther afield to find anybody connected with the Woodpeckers. And they are less willing to talk, if possible, than the remaining Jaybirds. An outsider can hardly imagine what a sore, unhappy subject the trouble is to anyone whose relatives were in it.

The whole situation has been overlaid with a crust of myth and legend. In Houston you will be seriously told that the Jaybirds are a desperate lot and if you go to Richmond you must not ask questions—that even to be caught examining the Jaybird monument is to ask for trouble. Incidentally, the marble jaybird was blown off the top of the monument in the great storm of 1900, but the myth says that a Woodpecker shot it off, and that the Jaybirds are still looking for him.

The best story of all is about a Methodist minister who stopped off at Richmond in the discharge of his pastoral duties some years after the riot. He was waited on at his hotel by a committee of Jaybirds and asked if he were a Jaybird or a Woodpecker.

"Why, gentlemen," he answered, "I'm neither one, and I don't know what you are talking about."

"You'll have to declare yourself if you stay here," they told him. "We don't have any neutrals in this town."

After they were gone a delegation of Woodpeckers called and posed the same question. By now the preacher had had time to think it over, and knew what to say.

"You don't allow anybody to be neutral?" he asked.

"No sir."

"And I have to declare myself?"

"Yes sir."

"Well, gentlemen, I'm a minister of the gospel. I've come here to save souls and not to meddle with politics. I'm neither a Jaybird nor a Woodpecker; but if I have to be some kind of a bird, I'm a turkey buzzard and it's ten dollars fine to shoot me."

From the Nervous Nineties to the Present

★

One of my mother's stories dealt with a friend of hers who married and went to some Wyoming town. There, after some years, her husband was murdered, "on the very steps of the courthouse." The misdemeanor may not have had social sanction but there was no thought of arresting the misdemeanant. The widow was acquainted with the usages: before the corpse was carried away she dipped a token in the thickening blood. She would save it until her son grew up; then, my mother said, she would give it to him and bid him "wash the stain from your mother's handkerchief." The tale sounds a theme from the border ballads of all ages but it is quite true. To a boy growing up in that culture it had solemnity but nothing of the inappropriate.

BERNARD DEVOTO, Forays and Rebuttals

> This, by his voice, should be a Montague.
> Fetche me my rapier boy. . . .
> Now, by the stock and honor of my kin,
> To strike him dead I hold it not a sin.
> SHAKESPEARE, *Romeo and Juliet*

"Damn all family feuds and inherited scraps," muttered Ranse vindictively to the breeze as he rode back to the Cibolo.

O. HENRY, The Higher Abdication

OTHER DAYS—
OTHER WAYS

By 1890 the days of great feuds were over in Texas, but the casualty rate showed no sign of dropping off. Several of the big troubles which began earlier were kept alive into the nineties, and there was a rash of smaller ones which amounted to a revival of the customs of the seventies. The type of feud was changing, however. Gone were the old days of carpetbagger abuses, quarrels over the Negro vote, and vigilantes out to hang all the horse thieves. Political shenanigans could provoke organized fighting, particularly in the Lower Rio Grande Valley; the Negro vote still had a hangover or two to be cleared up (as in the troubles at Columbus); mob feuds were apt to break out (for instance the San Saba trouble); but the feuds of the nineties and early 1900's, though numerous, are not so big, bitter, and baleful as their predecessors. They are more apt to involve personal or family quarrels. And as time goes on they are more apt to smolder than blaze.

Underneath, the old revengeful spirit was as strong as ever, and Texans never hesitated to take up for themselves whenever the occasion called for action. Anything would do for an excuse, just so two groups of people could fall out over it. There were simple personal difficulties like the Kelly-Smothers-Stubbs business at Hallettsville which started when W.A. Stubbs, a peace officer, killed Bob Kelly at a dance and took his own turn on August 4, 1890, when the Kellys and their kin caught him sitting in the window of a saloon.[1]

There were family split-ups like the Houston-Boothe trouble at Gonzales in 1899 when the heirs of old Bob Houston quarreled over the division of his property.[2]

In 1905 two small feuds broke out over the Prohibition issue—one at Groveton in the piney woods of East Texas when an intrepid preacher named Jesse Lee led the embattled citizens in a successful attempt to eliminate the saloons and with them a prize collection of toughs, gamblers, and murderers[3]—and another at Hempstead where four men, including Congressman John M. Pinckney, were wiped out at a "Dry" rally.[4]

Ranger trouble caused another bad situation at Brownsville in 1902, resulting from the sudden death of a prominent local youth who was caught red-handed stealing King Ranch cows. The climax was reached in a pistol duel on the streets between Ranger A.Y. Baker (later a famous sheriff) and Alfredo de la Cerda. Alfredo lost.[5]

More bizarre than any of these was the Brann case at Waco, in which religious loyalties played a major part.

Texas will never forget W.C. Brann, though he originated in Illinois and never gave the Texans any peace after his arrival in 1886. He was a good newspaper man and held some fine jobs, the best being the editorship of the San Antonio *Express* from 1892 to 1894. He was a mental porcupine, however—always had his spines out for somebody and never gave the soft answer which turneth away wrath. Much of his prickliness, it must be admitted, was honest indignation against all sorts of sham, graft, humbuggery, pomposity, and corruption. About fifty per cent of it, however, was the result of his equally honest delight in stirring up the pious brethren with revelations of the foulness he accused them of taking for granted and the frauds he believed they encouraged.

His particular gift was invective, and he was a master of words that cut, burned, and bludgeoned. He could use slang like O. Henry and Latin polysyllables like Samuel Johnson, but he always seemed to be talking personally to his reader. At the time of his death in 1898 he was just beginning to make an international reputation in his specialty.

In 1894 he decided to give up orthodox journalism and make his living by stripping the husk off the viciousness and meanness of his fellow men. He moved to Waco, the seat of Baylor College and a center of Baptist publishing and training, where he started his magazine *The Iconoclast* and went to work at making his Baptist neighbors uncomfortable.

His great opportunity came in the spring of 1895 when a nasty scandal broke out in the very sanctum of the Baptist denomination. An adolescent Brazilian girl named Antonia Texeira had been brought to Waco for training and had been received in the home of Dr. Burleson, the president of Baylor. There she became pregnant and accused the brother of the president's son-in-law of being the father of her child.

This was Brann's sort of special interest and he knew exactly what to do with it. In the July *Iconoclast* he gave his version of the affair, using such phrases as "lousy and lecherous male mastodon" to describe the seducer, and even more colorful terms for the Baptist leaders. From time to time after that, as the case went to the courts, he revived the subject.

In the issue for October of 1897 he picked up his bludgeon again and took the name of Baylor University in vain, calling it a "manufactory of ministers and magdalenes." This was too much for the young men of Baylor's two literary societies—the Philomathesians and the Erisophesians. They dragged Brann across the college campus with a rope around his neck and made him sign a retraction.

This brought out the friends and enemies of Brann in full cry. His intimate acquaintance Judge George B. Gerald wrote an article protesting against the indignities visited upon Brann and tried to get it published in the Waco *Times-Herald*. J.W. Harris, the editor, had declared himself on the other side, however, and refused to give Gerald any space. When the judge came by the office to pick up his manuscript, he and Harris came to blows over the matter and everybody who knew them was sure there would be further trouble, especially after Gerald had his article distributed as a handbill, including some bitter personalities about Harris.

Then on October 6 three men caught Brann and gave him a terrible public beating. Two were Baylor students and the third, the father of one of them, was a prominent judge. This brought tempers up to the boiling point and increased the hatred between Gerald and Harris. On November 19, 1897, as Editor Harris and his brother W.A. Harris were standing on opposite corners of Austin Avenue talking to friends, Judge Gerald appeared on the street. As soon as the men saw each other, the firing started.

They say that Gerald, a veteran of Gettysburg, calmly put on his glasses before he began to fight. He was badly hit himself, and was heard to remark that he did such a thorough job because he thought he was mortally wounded and did not wish to leave anything for his son to finish.

It dragged on for a few months more. Brann, of course, kept adding fuel to the fire instead of trying to put it out. People told him he was fixing to get himself killed, but he refused to back down or be silent under any circumstances. It was no particular surprise to anybody, therefore, when he got into a pistol fight with Captain Tom Davis on April 1, 1898, and was fatally wounded. Davis was killed too.

People still wonder why Davis had to be the man. It is true that his daughters were students at Baylor and that he and Brann were supporting rival political candidates, but they had not been particular enemies. It still seems queer.[6]

Of the feud history of Texas in times approaching the present it is impossible to say much. The principals in many cases are still living. Their friends hesitate to open their mouths. And feeling is sometimes so warm that much harm can be done by raking up the coals again.

Some day an insider will write a history of the Lower

Rio Grande Valley; and if he tells the whole truth, the story will have some incredible chapters about the political warfare which has smoldered and blazed in that region since Civil War days. My friends in Brownsville say it will be a long time before the whole truth can be told.

It is too soon also to talk about the "Coahoma Shootin'" which embroiled the Black, Johnson and Echols families in the little town of Coahoma near Big Spring in 1910—or about the Boyce-Sneed affair at Amarillo in 1912—or about the feud between the Johnson and Sims families at Snyder in 1916.

The few "live" feuds that I know about can hardly be mentioned. I asked a Longview lawyer about two oil-rich families who are popularly supposed to be carrying guns for each other in his home town. He replied that both clans were "too robust and too quick-tempered and too good shots for either of us to fool with."

Occasionally a press item shows that subterranean activity is still going on and may break through the crust at any moment. The Texas papers for December 15, 1943, carried a story about the culmination of a family feud near Victoria in which three men were killed and a fourth was badly hurt. The ages of the three dead men were given as eighty-five, seventy-nine, and eighty-one. "Two revolvers, two automatic pistols, a bloody hammer and a bloody pair of tin snips were being studied today as authorities tried to solve the slayings."

Again in January of 1950 Associated Press dispatches broadcast news about the death of James Alfred Bailey, shot to death from across the street as he stood in front of a store building in the East Texas town of Hemphill. Officers arrested Buren Butler, brother of J.M. Butler for whose death Bailey was to answer in the District Court in February.

There is certainly feuding blood in Texas yet, but since it takes about fifty years for a real shooting feud to cool down, it is better not to stir up the hot ones. The feuds of the nineties are just beginning to be cool enough to handle.

BULLETS FOR UNCLE BUCK'S BOYS
The Broocks-Wall Feud

The last big trouble in the old haunts of the Regulators and Moderators took up the final half of the nineties and made news in Texas for something like six years. The storm center was the little East Texas town of San Augustine, in the heart of the Redlands, where the old pioneer stock had settled seventy-five years before and put its roots down deep into the soil. Things had changed a good deal since 1842, but sometimes a man or a family would crop up as rugged as the first settlers. Such people went their own way, righted their own wrongs, thought it was better to die than to put up with insult or injury, and regarded a Winchester repeating rifle as the best judge and jury.

Uncle Buck Wall was a good example. He lived seven miles from town down the Geneva road on a farm where he could do pretty much as he pleased. Some of the old neighbors say that he was a high type of citizen, and others think he was a rough old specimen with a habit of getting into trouble. He certainly cherished his own opinions. When the Civil War broke out he said he was a Union man and refused to go and fight for either side. Ordinarily such conduct would have been a form of suicide, but Uncle Buck stuck to his guns and got away with it. It has been said that his political perversity was exceeded only by his personal courage, which no doubt explains why he lived so long.

His family was worthy of him. Mrs. Wall was as sturdy as her husband and is said to have taught her sons to fight their own battles and never let anyone run over them. Their three girls married into families of good old stock, thereby adding to the clan. And their five boys grew up with their father's disregard for other people's ideas. Even their names were peculiar, for Uncle Buck called them after his favorite historical characters. The oldest was George Washington Wall. One of the brothers was "Pez" Wall (for Lopez, a Cuban filibuster). And Uncle Buck's Napoleonic enthusiasms appeared in Ney, Brune, and Eugene Beauharnais Wall. He must have done a good deal of reading to prepare himself for fatherhood.[1]

Closely related to the Walls were the Robertses and the Tuckers, and they had dozens of friends they could call on when need arose.

Living in the same neighborhood was the Border family, a fighting clan likewise. William Border of Lincolnshire, England, migrated to America in the early days and fathered sons named John and George, who came to the Southwest. George married into the pioneer Broocks family of San Augustine. In the third generation were two more boys, George and Lycurgus, who with their cousins John, Ben, and Moses Lycurgus Broocks, gave Uncle Buck Wall his first real opposition since the Civil War.

Lycurgus Border—"Curg" was the usual abbreviation— was the fighter of his clan, and he must have been a pretty bad specimen. Rather small and never a strong man physically, he was nevertheless a murderous opponent in a fight and went after blood when he got angry. In justice it should be added that he could be very generous with people he liked—"Would give them his shirt" say his old acquaintances. While still not much more than a youngster he took on the wrong man and was permanently crippled by a bullet in the leg. Some say he even had to wear an iron brace afterward, but that did not make him any less dangerous.[2]

The Wall boys and Curg Border were enemies from their school days on, and fought each other more than once. But the really bad blood between them began with the political campaign of 1894 which made things sizzle all over Texas. The People's Party or Populist group was at the peak of its influence. Preachers and stump speakers of great lung power and enthusiasm whipped up a tremendous amount of feeling. Seventy-five weekly newspapers trumpeted Populist principles, and all the poor folks, reformers, and radicals fell into line, crying for a new deal for the little man. Over in San Augustine County Uncle Buck Wall and his sons took up the banner. The old man ran for county commissioner and George was a candidate for sheriff. They both won, too, but the campaign aroused hard feelings all over the county which didn't help matters when the feud broke out.[3]

There is more than one story about what brought it on, but they all boil down to trouble between Sheriff George Wall and Curg Border. Some say Curg got in bad with the law by developing very unusual ways of extracting money from farmers who were trying to get out of town with the price of a bale of cotton. Others tell that storekeeper Lynch hired him to handle his collections and that he used offensive tactics toward the Negroes on George Wall's farm.[4] The two of them and their kinsfolk were soon ready to fly at each others' throats, and at least once they traded shots. Brune and Pez Wall encountered Curg Border and his brother George on the road and exchanged bullets but did each other no special damage.

This state of affairs had gone on for nearly six years when something happened that gave a final squeeze to the trigger: Sheriff George arrested Curg Border for disorderly conduct of some kind and took him before a justice of the peace. The newspapers later got hold of a story that he also locked Border up and would not allow him a chance to give bail.[5] In Texas this was enough to start hostilities, and the friends of both sides were present with arms in their hands. "Great excitement prevailed," says the Reverend George W. Crocket in his unpublished notes on the feud (Mr. Crocket

was a beloved rector of the San Augustine Episcopal church for many years), "and a serious difficulty was anticipated, but the affair passed off without a clash."

It may have been this arrest which gave Curg Border his final push toward the blood-spattered existence he was to lead thereafter. He vowed to get even, and some weeks later he had his chance when he caught George where he wanted him on the streets of San Augustine and shot him dead. This was in April of 1900.

Immediately the gossiping and the rumors started, all centering on Border's cousins, the Broocks brothers. One story said that a member of the family, a storekeeper, had handed

Curg a shotgun out of the back door of his place of business and told him to "go the limit." Another whisper told how one of the brothers had said Curg did just what he should have done in shooting Wall.[6] More than once talk like this has kept a feud going if somebody wanted to believe it, and in this case the man who took it seriously was Eugene Wall, the youngest of the brothers. On June 2, 1900, a few weeks after George was killed, he met Ben Broocks on the street and hit him with four out of the five shots in his six-shooter. Broocks was armed but seems not to have had a chance to get to his gun. Curg had left town and gone to Beaumont when it happened, and nobody else cared to call Eugene to account. He walked up and down the streets of San Augustine waiting for somebody to try it, but the merchants closed up their stores and went home, leaving him in complete possession. A new sheriff had been appointed by this time—Noel G. Roberts, a nephew of the Wall boys—but he did nothing at the time of the shooting. Next day he rode out to the Wall home and placed Eugene under nominal arrest, allowing him to remain at Uncle Buck's house.[7]

After these two assassinations there could be no peace. Before Ben Broocks was cold, a telegram went from San Augustine to Beaumont and two days later, about seven o'clock on the morning of June 4, the two remaining Broocks brothers, a brother-in-law, and Curg Border came into San Augustine and found their friends and supporters assembled. The brothers stopped at their father's house for a brief visit; Curg Border joined a number of other men in an old stone store building on the square. About an hour later Sheriff Noel Roberts, his brother Sid Roberts, who was Superintendent of Schools, and their uncle Felix Roberts, a notary public, rode into town from another direction. They entered the courthouse by a side door and prepared to go about the day's business. For some reason Sid Roberts stepped out of the front entrance, perhaps to see if there was any trouble in sight, and immediately the men in the old stone store building started in on him. The Reverend Mr. Crocket says "The two parties hurled defiance at each other and a shooting affray took place." Sheriff Spradley of Nacogdoches always thought Sid was fired on without warning. Whichever way it was, Sid was mortally hit at the first fire. His uncle Felix, hearing the shots, pushed a window curtain aside to have a look and dropped dead with a bullet in his head. The sheriff ran out of a back door, got on his horse, absorbed a few ounces of lead himself, and came back indoors to barricade himself inside the county clerk's office. There he remained for several hours until his kinsman Dr. Felix Tucker and the Reverend Mr. Crocket came in and persuaded him to try once more to get out. He mounted his horse again and dodged slugs as far as Dr. Tucker's home, stayed there overnight while Mrs. Tucker and her two boys stood watch, and was taken to Nacogdoches in the morning.[8]

Correspondents for the city dailies dusted off their most potent adjectives as they tried to convey the excitement and fear which gripped not only San Augustine but every town in the region. From Nacogdoches one of them wrote: "This town at once went wild and many flew to their arms. . . . All people who know the parties predict more killings. Nacogdoches is in the direst dread and deepest gloom as if an awful fate were impending. Men gathered in crowds on the streets here and discussed the trouble in the most excited manner. Officials had to clear the sidewalks for ladies to pass. Interested parties rushed around and got ready to rush off to the combat. Horses, teams, arms, and ammunition were quickly procured. Relays of horses were telephoned for use on the way. One man made the ride in less than four hours riding four horses." [9]

The authorities in Austin received frantic telegrams. The governor ordered out the Stone Fort Rifles of Nacogdoches who marched and rode and pushed their wagons over muddy roads all night to place San Augustine under martial law at four o'clock in the morning. The adjutant general telegraphed that he would be there shortly with the Rangers. Everybody hoped that enough force could be assembled to head off the threatened massacre, but there was plenty of cause for worry.

Out at Uncle Buck Wall's place two hundred men had assembled and they meant business. Sheriff Spradley says they sent a note to one of their sympathizers in town telling her to get her family away because they were going to clean out their enemies. This note was shown to Adjutant General Scurry and District Judge Tom C. Davis, who had arrived not long before, and they went out to Uncle Buck's place to see what the Walls were up to.

When they looked over the grim-looking band assembled around that house, they knew the case was pretty bad but they went to work to talk the men out of their resolve to fight. Eugene was the one they tried hardest to persuade. He ought to give up, they told him, stand an examining trial, and ask for bail. He agreed, but said he was afraid he would be taken out and lynched if they put him in jail at San Augustine. Finally he yielded to reason when they promised to take him somewhere else. So the threat of open war passed.[10]

Uncle Buck and his boys were brought to Nacogdoches and then to Rusk where on June 17, 1900, Eugene and Brune went on trial for the killing of Ben Broocks. They were acquitted. Eugene was tried last and his lawyer, Judge Stilwell Russell (a famous pleader), let go at the jury with everything he had, including a lovely young girl who was going to marry Eugene in the courtroom if they set him free. Needless to say, they set him free.

Everybody else was set free likewise. Two men were indicted for shooting the two Robertses in the battle of the courthouse, and Curg Border was tried for shooting George Wall. None of them was convicted.[11] It was about this time that Brune Wall left the country, became a doctor, and settled in Oklahoma. He did not come back to join in the later troubles.

It took a year more for the threads to spin themselves out. San Augustine was an armed camp where war could be expected to break out at any time. Some of the best members of the Wall party moved out to keep the trouble from getting any worse. His friends told Uncle Buck that he ought to go. But Uncle Buck hated to do it. His conscience did not bother him, and those hills and thickets had been home for a long time. He waited until two more of his boys were gone before he made up his mind.

The first to go was Pez, probably the most peaceful of the brothers. He was on his way to Nacogdoches with some cattle he wanted to sell when he was shot from ambush.[12] A few months later it was Eugene. He was thinking about getting away by now, and while he was busy making some of the arrangements, his wife went to visit Uncle Buck for a few days. She had a day or two of illness during their separation, which made her want to see Eugene. He had been living down toward Geneva, more or less out of harm's way, but he came when she sent for him, stayed a while, and started back. He was hardly out of sight of the house, just passing the old Roberts cemetery, when the ambusher put a bullet through his heart.[13]

Both his father and mother heard the shot. Old Buck grabbed his shotgun and ran out, but it was too late; nobody was in sight. While he searched, his wife stayed by her son's body, where she was seen by a Negro mail carrier who happened to be passing by. She begged him to stay with Eugene while she went for help, but the colored boy rolled his eyes and said, "No. Ma'am!"

Again the feverish fears and rampant rumors began. The Nacogdoches *Sentinel* asked "Where will it end?" and urged its readers to "be guarded in their expressions. For God's sake let's not let it break out here." [14]

There was really not much cause for worry. The fight

had almost all gone out of Uncle Buck and he was ready to go. He dropped in to see his old friend W.H. Whitton (still alive and hearty at the age of ninety-nine when I saw him), and Mr. Whitton had never seen him so downcast. "Brother Whitton," he said, "I don't know as I'll ever see you again. This trouble is going to kill me. I can't bear it. They've murdered all my boys. The only one I've got left is Brune and I've chased him off to Oklahoma. They'll murder him too if he stays around here."

Uncle Buck and his wife followed Brune, settling in Oklahoma, where they died some years later. Brune Wall had Frank Tucker come to Shreveport in November of 1901 and turned over all his affairs to him. They both knew there would be a man behind a bush if Brune came back to San Augustine.[15]

The man who was blamed for all the bushwhacking was, of course, Curg Border, but no scrap of evidence was ever brought forward to connect him definitely with the crimes. He lived only a few years after the Walls were gone. Once he was elected sheriff of the county, but before his term was up his bondsmen withdrew and he had to resign. He was very bitter about it and is reported to have sworn that if he couldn't hold the office, nobody else could either.[16] Nevertheless the commissioners appointed a vigorous young man named Sneed Nobles to take his place. He was told about the talk that Border had been making and didn't waste any time one day when he saw Curg near the courthouse with a big, blue-barreled six-shooter. When the echo of his shot died away, one of the strangest characters who ever figured in or out of a feud was a part of San Augustine history, and the whole county breathed easier.

ALL IN THE FAMILY
The Feuds at Columbus

The big news at Columbus in 1890 was the new courthouse. It was going to be a big brick structure with a silver dome rising up in the midst of the magnificent moss-hung live oaks on the square. It was to be finished in a style worthy of a rich cattle-and-cotton county where millionaire ranchers divided the land with thrifty German and Bohemian farmers. And it was to cost sixty thousand dollars. To make sure they got their money's worth the county commissioners gave the contract to Marlin, Byrne and Johnson, professional courthouse builders, who sent their best construction man, W.R. Grimes, to superintend the job.[1] Mr. Grimes found a house near his work, sent for his family, and became for the time being a citizen of Columbus.

His three children, Allie, Etta, and Ralph, had a good time getting acquainted with their new home. It was a pretty town on a bluff overlooking the Colorado River with rows of neat white frame houses under the massive live oaks. The people were kind and hospitable in the old Southern tradition and made the newcomers feel at home immediately. Mr. and Mrs. Grimes sometimes felt that something was going on under the surface of community life, and after a while they learned that there had once been "hard feelings" between some of the first families, but it didn't seem like anything to worry about and they went about their business.[2]

Mr. Grimes wanted to lay the cornerstone on the Fourth of July and he worked mightily at his foundations and excavations. The children played near by in a patriarchal oak with a wonderful overhanging limb, underneath which they rigged up a flying jenny. Mrs. Grimes kept house and made friends with her neighbors:—Mrs. Lite Townsend, the sheriff's wife; Mrs. Bob Stafford, whose husband was a millionaire and owned the bank at the southwest corner of the square with a palatial three-story house next door; Mrs. John Stafford, who lived on a big ranch three miles south of town; Mrs. Marcus Townsend, whose husband was a leading lawyer. It seemed that there were innumerable Townsends and Staffords about, all kind and courteous to her, but not so friendly among themselves. It was hard for her to understand. They all had plenty of everything— what could they find to disagree about?

What Mrs. Grimes probably never knew, since these were family matters and not to be discussed before strangers, was that trouble between the Staffords and Townsends dated back almost twenty years. They were the two great families in Colorado County. The Townsends had a history which went back to the time of the Texas Revolution and they had been cattle barons and Important People for a long time. Old Asa Townsend had brought up half a dozen boys to follow the cattle business and run the county, the best known being Sheriff J.L. (Lite) Townsend. Mose Townsend, Asa's brother, was the father of lawyer Marcus, or Marc Townsend. The third member of the older generation was Spencer Townsend, who had a son named Jim.

For many years Lite and Marc Townsend ran Colorado County. The Negroes were still voting and the Townsends told them how. They were tall, handsome, blond men with strong wills and much personal force. Marc Townsend was thought by many people to be the smartest lawyer in South Texas.

But it was really the women of the family who were the unlucky instruments of tragedy, for they married and had sons, and it was their sons who got into difficulties from which there was only one exit. Asa Townsend's daughter Mary became the wife first of a man named Hope by whom she had two boys, Marion and Larkin; later she married Joe Lessing and had a third son, also named Joe. Spencer Townsend had two girls, Louise and Keron. Louise married Gus Clements and had Jim, Will, and Hiram. Keron (or Keetie) married Sam Reese of the Oakland district in the western part of the county and became the mother of two sons and three daughters. Thus the younger generation of Townsends, Hopes, Clementses, Lessings, Reeses, and others besides were cousins.

The Staffords were likewise a powerful clan with a good many branches. They had been in Texas since 1858 when four brothers came out from Georgia and went into the business they knew best, which was cattle. They took time out to help fight the war, and then came home to get rich as ranchers, trail drivers, meat packers, bankers, and real estate operators. The Stafford brothers were an unusually vigorous and enterprising set of men, sketchily educated and inclined to be a little more rough-and-tumble than the Townsends, but well schooled in the art of getting along. They had big ranch houses, ran big herds, occupied big tracts of land, and had big bank accounts. Captain Bob Stafford, the powerhouse of the family, soon became a millionaire and had his finger in half a dozen financial pies. Captain Bob was a red-bearded, hard-fisted, six-foot-two cattleman who could be as tough as a boot and as generous as the soil of Texas. His brother John, who was a partner in several of his enterprises, was much younger and much milder than Captain Bob, though he was not one to let himself be run over, either. Ben was ordinarily pretty quiet, but sometimes he flared up quickly and subsided just as fast. There was also Bill Stafford, who kept out of trouble and need not be mentioned further. They were the open-handed, outspoken type of Westerner who is apt to go to heaven or go to feuding, depending on the circumstances.[3]

In the days of the cattle boom every big stockman had his enemies, big and little, and Bob Stafford was the kind who accumulated his full share. He had a sort of private feud with Shanghai Pierce for years. They even carried guns for each other for a time, but neither one of them wanted to bring the quarrel to an issue. They just talked and tried to outsmart each other in business deals, and refused to sleep in the same hotel.[4]

It was cattle that caused the first break between the Staffords and their neighbors the Townsends, but they could not or would not dodge each other as Captain Bob and Shanghai had been doing. By 1871 they were definitely at outs and ready to fight about it. Henry Thomas, who was brought up by Ben Stafford and worked for years for Captain Bob, says "accommodation" branding was at the bottom of it. When one rancher got ready to gather stock he expected to brand odds and ends of his neighbors' herds, and the neighbors expected to pay him fifty cents a head for doing it. A little carelessness plus a few cases of doubtful ownership could cause hard feelings wherever the system was used. Just what specific grievances existed between the two families at the beginning of their trouble is not clear, but by the fall of 1871 they were all stirred up against each other and Ben Stafford had taken it up. Some of their friends tried to make peace between them. Lite Townsend's father-in-law, Mr. Cummins, went to Sumner Townsend about the first week in December when both sides were in town and told him he ought to speak to Ben when he came out of the barber shop and make friends. About that time Ben appeared, and they went for their guns. The Texas papers reported that "words brought pistols from their scabbards, and pistols brought firing, and the six or seven shots resulted in the serious wounding of Sumner Townsend in the arm and shoulder, and of B.F. Stafford in the ankle severely. We do not pretend to say who was to blame in the matter." [5]

Those who like the bloody details of these old-time gun fights may care to know that Ben shot Sumner in the arm just as he threw down. This deflected Sumner's aim and he wounded Ben in the ankle. Both of them recovered, but Ben took a couple of years to get well and had to wear a special shoe as a result of his injury.

After that there was no further open warfare for a long time. The two families got along, mostly by letting each other alone. They wouldn't do business with each other but they would speak, and one or two of the Staffords seemed to think a good deal of one or two of the Townsends. Things might have remained in this state of balance indefinitely if some of the next generation had not grown up.

In 1890 Larkin and Marion Hope were young men and acting as peace officers under their uncle, Sheriff Lite Townsend. The Hope boys were not of the same caliber as their uncles. They were handy with guns but were undersized and had not picked up much education. Larkin had the force to carry out his duties as a deputy but Marion was just a sort of human echo who did whatever Larkin said. Nobody paid them much attention, favorable or unfavorable, until the seventh of July, 1890.

Mr. Grimes had not been able to get ready for the cornerstone laying on the Fourth, but the people of the county were willing to go by his schedule and a big celebration had been arranged for the seventh. There were to be speeches and food and a grand ball in the evening; visitors were expected from all over the country; and everything was done that could be done to make the day memorable. Sheriff Townsend, however, was uneasy. He had heard, or thought he had heard, that there was some kind of plot against his life. Somebody may well have dropped a remark which put him on his guard, for there was much dissatisfaction with his handling of the sheriff's office. He and Marcus stayed in power by controlling the Negro vote and the county was getting tired of it. The result was that the sheriff and his deputies were on edge the day of the celebration and perhaps that was why Warren Stafford, Captain Bob's son, got into trouble.

Bob had an understanding with the Hope boys that if Warren outdid himself a little, he was not to be bothered and his father would pay the fine or otherwise see that no damage was done.[6] The arrangement had worked before, but this time the Hope brothers arrested Warren and took him through the streets in handcuffs. They probably meant to lodge him in the jail, but friends of the family interfered and Warren was spared that last indignity. Captain Bob heard of it, however, and began to rumble like a volcano.

It may be hard for non-Texans to comprehend why he was so upset, but it should be understood that cautious peace officers just did not do those things to important people. A gentleman expected to be notified courteously that he was under arrest and he would set a time when he could conveniently come in to answer charges. If he happened to be overtaken in the pursuit of joy, the officer who followed the unwritten code would ask his friends to take care of him. To be dragged off like a common thief was an insult, and Bob Stafford was not the man to put up with it without an eruption of some kind.

About seven o'clock that evening he had a chance to speak his mind when he ran into the Hope brothers, who had just emerged from Nicoli's saloon at the southwest corner of the square. They were leaning up against the door jambs when Captain Bob and his brother John came along the street. Just before the Staffords reached the corner, Ralph Grimes came by with his little wagon on the way to get a watermelon for the evening celebration. Bob asked if he could have a ride. "Sure, get in," said Ralph, and Bob put one foot in the wagon. He and Ralph had a good laugh together, and then his face grew stern as he saw the Hopes.

Constable York, bartender Hugh Smith, and a number of other witnesses saw Captain Bob start a heated conversation with them. He "shook his fingers" in Larkin Hope's face and Larkin stepped back, drawing his pistol. Constable York, C.T. Hancock, and John Stafford tried to break it up, and Mrs. Larkin Hope, who drove by in a buggy just then, added her own entreaties. Larkin walked over to the buggy and told her to go on home—he was all right.

At that moment Stafford called Larkin a particularly unflattering name, insinuating that the Negro race had been enjoying a little too much of his company. Hope said that was more than he could take and started shooting.

For some reason he shot John Stafford first—some say because he feared him more. John backed away and sat down in the door of the saloon while Hope turned his gun on Captain Bob. It was a bad business. Bob staggered into the saloon after he was hit, and Larkin ran around to a side door and shot him again. Then he came back to the front and made sure of John.

"Larkin and Marion Hope walked to the other side of the street," testified Constable York at the inquest. "I caught up with them and told them I would have to arrest them, and they said all right. About this time J.L. Townsend came up with his Winchester and said that he would take them." [7]

Mrs. Grimes and her little girls were on the sidewalk near by when the trouble began, but a clerk pulled them into a store when pistols were drawn. As soon as they dared venture out, they went back to the street, and met Mrs. Bob Stafford and her daughter, Mrs. Early, who were just passing. They begged her to tell them what had happened, and Mrs. Grimes had to take the two hysterical women to where the bodies were lying on the floor of Nicoli's saloon. Mrs. Grimes never did get over it.

The death of the Stafford brothers was about the worst shock Columbus had ever had to stand. Captain Bob was the wealthiest citizen of the county and the most enterprising. He had property all over South Texas and had just set up a cold storage and packing business with John as a partner. For such men to be shot down on the street was almost unthinkable. They had dozens of relatives and hundreds of friends who were all aroused to the highest pitch. When the brothers were buried in the family plot seven miles south of Columbus, a procession a mile long followed the bodies to the grave and the Townsend clan was spoken of more sternly than ever before.[8]

The Hope brothers went on trial several times at various near-by towns, but hung juries and postponements wore the case out and nothing was ever done to them. Ten-year-old Ralph Grimes had seen the whole thing and was carted around to all of the trials, quizzed by attorneys for both sides, and kept in such a state of excitement that he was almost a nervous wreck before it was over.[9]

In between times he and his sisters continued to play under the big oak tree across from the courthouse square as the new building put up rafters and sprouted scaffolding for the dome. The new jail, which went with the courthouse, was about finished and ready for the jailer to move in. Lite Townsend should have been the one to take charge, but on September 25, 1890, the general dissatisfaction with his conduct of affairs came to a head, a citizens' meeting was held, and he was asked to resign his office.[10] He stepped down for a while, and the new man who moved in to take his place was S.H. Reese of Oakland, a handsome, black-haired young man who was the husband of Lite's cousin Keetie. Sam Reese was a well-to-do landowner, but he had had some experience as constable in his own precinct and was willing to serve as sheriff. One sunshiny morning in the fall of 1890 he drove into Columbus and stopped in front of the new jail, bringing his family with him.

The Grimes youngsters were playing under the big tree when the Reeses drove up. They watched four children dismount (one of the Reese girls was away on a visit and didn't come along until later). The four children stopped and looked back at them. And in a matter of seconds they had formed a friendship which was to last as long as they lived. The boys, Herbert and Walter, were of an age to play with Ralph; and the three girls, Nuddie, Lillian and Keron, got down to doll business and other little-girl concerns with Allie and Etta Grimes.

The Grimes children, no longer young now, like to remember what kindly, home-loving people Mr. and Mrs. Reese were in the days before their troubles began. They enjoyed music and laughter with the children, and they were good to their prisoners. Mrs. Reese cooked great pans of beans and vegetables and corn bread for them and saw that they were warm on cold nights. When Mr. Reese came home tired and lay down on the sofa, the girls would rub his head until he went to sleep, and then they would get Mrs. Reese to tell them one of her famous stories. Everybody was happy—but all the while trouble was brewing.

The next few years brought changes. The Grimes family went on to other courthouse jobs but corresponded with their Columbus friends and sometimes visited them. They heard that Mr. Reese continued as sheriff for some time— then worked as a deputy, and in 1894 was elected for a full four-year term. Everybody thought he made a good officer but it seemed that he was not getting along with his wife's relatives, the Townsends. He was having trouble with Constable Larkin Hope; something about court costs or other county business. In 1898 Larkin ran against him for sheriff with the blessing of Marc Townsend and his political machine.

It was a hot campaign and both sides began to hate each other over it. Some people said "I told you so" when Larkin Hope was killed on Milam Street just north of the square on the night of August 3. A mysterious gunman rode into the dark alley behind Brunson's saloon, tied his horse, and came through a narrow passageway between two buildings until he could command the street. He put two charges of buckshot into his victim, went back to the alley, loaded his shotgun again and rode out of town at a long lope. He was seen getting on his horse and leaving the alley.[11]

Allie Grimes was back in Columbus that night, visiting some of her friends. She had gone out early in the evening with a party of young people to attend a revival service in the country, and a little after dark they were coming back. As they approached the town they heard a furious clatter —the sound of a running horse crossing the bridge—and a horse and rider went by them so fast their own teams shied off the road. It was the assassin getting out of town.

Allie and her friends had been looking forward to attending the ice cream social which a group of church people were planning to hold on the square, but nobody ate ice cream that night. After crossing the bridge they drove on into town, where not a light was showing, and came to a sudden stop when a man with a rifle stepped out in front of them. "Get home as fast as you can," he said. "This town is about to explode. Larkin Hope was killed a little while ago on this very spot and everybody in town has guns."

Allie hurried to the house where she was staying, wondering why it was her fate to be in Columbus every time something terrible happened.

The Stafford-Townsend feud had now been replaced by the Reese-Townsend feud. Jim Coleman of Alleyton was arrested for the murder of Larkin Hope and the whisper began to go around that Sheriff Reese was responsible for the whole thing. One man told another that Coleman had been tracked to Reese's house, though the sheriff and his family indignantly denied having anything to do with the man. It seemed to them that the whole affair was a cleverly managed undercover campaign to discredit Sam Reese before the election,[12] and they were not much surprised when

Marc Townsend's brother-in-law Will Burford, a substantial farmer from Osage, was put on the ticket and beat Reese at the polls.

It is typical of such feuds that nothing was ever done to Coleman. His case was transferred to Fort Bend County and finally to San Antonio, where he was acquitted.[13]

The matter could not end there—not in Columbus. Burford appointed Willie Clements as his deputy and thereby widened the breach between the factions. Willie was a nephew of Mrs. Reese and she had been a second mother to him and one of his brothers—but he was Marc Townsend's man now.

The bitterness between Sam Reese and the Townsends came to an issue on March 16, 1899, about five-thirty in the evening. It was as sudden and unexpected as an earthquake. Henry Thomas had just sold Mr. Reese a bull, received his check, and gone into the bank to get his money. Reese had got on his horse and ridden up to the horse rack in front of Brunson's saloon, half a block north of the square, and was tying his pony up. Marc Townsend was sitting on a barrel in Bob Farmer's grocery store next door to the saloon eating cheese with a friend. Ed Scott, a local citizen just released from jail by action of the grand jury, was beginning a conversation with Deputy Willie Clements. Other townspeople and peace officers were going about their regular business in the near vicinity. At that moment, out of a clear sky, everybody began shooting. Fifteen or twenty shots were fired, and when it was over, Sam Reese was dead, shot through the neck; a farmer named Boehm was killed by stray bullets as he was getting into his wagon for the drive home; and John Williams, a small boy who had come to his father's gate to watch the fight, was hit in the hip and crippled for life.

Walter Reese, now about twenty years old, ran out of one of the stores when he heard the shots, dodged the bullets and picked up his father's gun. It was empty. He knelt down in the road, took the dead man's head in his lap, and vowed that he would get the man who had killed him.[14]

The Reese family was distracted—in fact the whole town was stirred up as never before. Willie Clements, Marion Hope, and Marc Townsend were arrested. They were glad to go to jail for a few hours to get away from Sam Reese's angry friends. Later they were let out on bond, and Marc Townsend moved to San Antonio, where he lived until his death in 1915. Meanwhile Judge Kennon had wired Governor Sayers for the Rangers, describing the emergency in a superb understatement as "pressing." So Captain Bill McDonald came in from the Panhandle on the twenty-second and was met by four privates from other parts of the state. McDonald found the town divided into two armed camps breathing slaughter at each other and meaning every word of it. Sheriff Burford had deputized a great many of his friends and supporters and was keeping them together. A small army of the opposite faction were on the other side of the square, watching every movement.[15]

Captain Bill's biographer, Albert Bigelow Paine, gives him credit for great courage and firmness on this occasion. Before his men arrived he presented himself, solo, to Judge Kennon and said he was ready to stop the riot. The Judge was appalled at the thought of turning such an affair over to a lone man, even a Ranger captain. "Come on," said Captain Bill. "I believe I can stop it. We can see a mighty good fight, anyhow." [16]

There was no fight. McDonald persuaded both sides to disarm, and when his men arrived, he put them to patrolling the streets and disarming everybody who appeared with any kind of weapon. That made things seem a good deal more peaceful, the only disturbance during the rest of the Captain's visit being an attempt to shoot Willie Clements through his own window on the evening of March

28. Four days later McDonald thought the worst was over and he went off to attend to more important business.

At Columbus, however, quiet was the most deceptive thing in the world. Just when life was beginning to seem normal, there would be a new flareup, more bloodshed, more telegrams, more Rangers, and more excited dispatches in the papers. It was a long and weary road that the people of Columbus had to travel for the next few years— a monotonous series of clashes which gave the town a bad name and ruined the lives of many good people. The Grimes family read about these encounters and grieved for their friends living in the fear of death in the little town on the Colorado. Two months after Mr. Reese's death, for instance, they were shocked to see this announcement in the Galveston *News:*

"Columbus, May 18—Dick Reese of Orange and Dick Gant, colored, of Alleyton, were shot and killed about 9 o'clock last night by Deputy Sheriffs Step Yates and J.G. Townsend. The deputies were stationed over the Colorado river by order of Sheriff Burford to intercept pistol carriers who have become numerous and bold of late. . . . The deceased was a brother of ex-sheriff Sam H. Reese, who was shot and killed two months ago in a street battle with Deputy Will Clements, a nephew of Deputy Townsend. Trouble has ever since been expected between the relatives of the parties. . . . County Judge Mansfield, upon solicitation of many citizens, telegraphed the governor for Rangers. . . ."

Other details appeared later. Dick Reese, who had one paralyzed arm, had come from his home in Orange to join the family when his brother Sam was killed. The two deputies said he had drawn his pistol when they tried to make him halt at the bridge, but his friends and relatives thought he had been the victim of a cold-blooded ambush. Both Reese and his driver were instantly killed. The horses turned around and ran away down the Alleyton road, making it necessary for a search party to hunt until three o'clock in the morning before they found the bodies, which were still in the buggy.[17]

Again the temperature of the town went up above boiling, and again friends of both parties gathered from all over the county and beyond. Judge Mansfield sent off the familiar telegram, and once more the Rangers arrived, headed by Captain Sieker. For the next month they held the lid on with some difficulty. Ranger W. L. Wright was left in charge of the detachment, and his reports show what a tinder box the town had become. On June 10 he wrote to Captain Rogers, his superior officer:

"Things have been a little rockey for the past 3 days but think I have it under controle now. The other day when I was out of town a young man let a double barrell shotgun go off in a saloon and caused a terrible excitement and the 2 crowds liked to have run together but Coley and a deputy held them down but they are just waiting there chance. . . . After this trouble these 2 boys [Herbert and Walter Reese] wrote to there relatives at Hallettsville and Yoakum and yesterday eve 8 men came in to the Reece House and last night at 1 o'clock 6 more men came to Reece heavy armed. Taylor and I went down there this morning and talked to them. . . . I think Taylor and myself can handle them down but if anything changes I will wire you and if I do you will know things is beyond our controle. . . ."[18]

The Rangers stayed around for weeks this time, and quieted the place down so effectively that there was no bad trouble for five months. Then came January of 1900, and the Columbus feud was in the headlines again. January 15 was the day set for the trial of Jim Townsend, one of the two men accused of killing Dick Reese at the bridge (Yates was already dead of tuberculosis). The trial was to be held at Bastrop since in Columbus there was little chance of a fair trial and some likelihood of a massacre. Three hundred people took the train around by LaGrange. Some were witnesses, some were clansmen ready to stand by their kin, and some were just curious.

The authorities were determined to prevent any fighting and a detachment of Rangers was very busy, very thorough, and sometimes very unpleasant in confiscating firearms. Doc Houchens of Hallettsville was there to be with his cousins the Reese boys, and he relates that some of his friends, unwilling to be caught without weapons, tied strings to their pistols and let them down their pants legs. In that way they passed inspection by the Rangers and were able to leave their arms at a convenient barber shop.[19]

The legal proceedings took only a few minutes. A motion for continuance was granted before any evidence was presented. Everybody left the courthouse and walked downtown, laughing and chatting but keeping an eye out for trouble. In one group was Willie Clements, walking with Sheriff Burford's son Arthur, just back from the university where he had completed a law course. He was a bright and promising boy, the pride of his parents and a friend of practically everybody. As the two were passing the Golden Rule Saloon, a burst of gunfire struck them. The six-shooters were aimed at Clements but he dodged behind Burford. Arthur was shot through the head, dying instantly, while Clements ran through a store building and got away with a bullet hole through his lungs. It was a bad wound, but he eventually recovered.

Walter Reese, Jim Coleman, and Tom Daniels were arrested for this unfortunate killing and held in Bastrop to answer to the grand jury. The cases against them eventually went to San Antonio, as did the one against Jim Townsend, and all were dismissed.[20]

By now Walter Reese had made up his mind to get away from the trouble which had been following him around like a faithful dog. He moved to Rosenberg, fifty miles closer to Houston, where he had friends. The Townsend party sometimes went through on the train and both sides watched each other like hawks. Finally, on July 31, 1900, they had their fight out. Jim Coleman and Walter Reese were on the station platform when Willie Clements, Marc Townsend, Frank Burford, and A.B. Woolridge rode through in a passenger coach, and both sides burned considerable powder. Coleman and Reese were badly wounded. Townsend and Burford were arrested when they reached Houston but there is no record of any further proceedings against them.[21]

There was one more fight, and that was all. It happened on June 30, 1906. The Reese family was back in Columbus again, where a new roller skating rink had just been set up near the square. About ten-thirty that night trouble broke out between Herbert Reese and Marion Hope. As the story is sometimes told, Hope leaned out of a window with a lighted cigar in his hand and burned Herbert's face as he passed the rink. This started a fight out in front of the place and in a few minutes both parties went off after their guns. They were all back very shortly and everybody commenced firing. Much of the shooting seems to have been pretty wild. A mule was hit in the head, several show windows were punctured, and the awning posts around the square suffered severely; but only one man was seriously hurt. This was Hiram Clements, who later died of his wounds. The two Reese boys and their brother-in-law, Dr. Joe Lessing, were arrested and tried for killing him, but nothing could be proved against them.[22]

This was the last act in one of the most irrepressible of the feuds of Texas. It was many years before the feeling died down, and even yet there is grief and bitterness. When Carrie Townsend married Joe Stafford, the first breach between the big Columbus families seemed to be healed, but there has been no such amalgamation of the Reeses and the Townsends.

Almost all the participants in the feud died unhappy deaths. Jim Coleman was killed in San Antonio. Will Clements was shot by a Bohemian blacksmith. Herbert Reese was accidentally killed when he dropped an automatic pistol in his own home.[23] Walter Reese died in an automobile accident near El Paso.

Again Allie and Etta Grimes were there when misfortune came. They were married now and both working in the El Paso post office. Walter Reese had come out to West Texas and was chief of detectives on the El Paso police force when his fate overtook him. In November of 1919 he was coming back from Ysleta with a party of friends one night and his car failed to make the turn at what was known as "suicide bridge." He was fatally injured but lingered for several days while the Grimes girls telegraphed his mother and sisters and did the best they could to help the family through another time of grief.[24]

More than once during those days they thought of a sunny autumn morning thirty years before when they made friends with the five Reese children and so began a long familiarity with tragedy.

THE PATTERN, THE FOLKLORE, AND TOMORROW

What does it all add up to? Do these feuds follow any standard pathway? Can a blueprint be constructed for the typical Texas feud? The answer is yes and no. Each feud has its individual features, just as every human being has; but every feud resembles every other feud in certain ways, just as men resemble each other.

First, how does a feud get started? Intolerable conditions have been behind all of them. Outraged honor, which we usually think of as the determining factor, may set the feudist going—but so may fear, political abuses, or heavy property loss. Any highhanded invasion of what a man considers right or just is enough to start a feud when conditions are right.

Even then trouble may be averted if there is any chance of getting redress at the courthouse. But feuds occur especially when law and order cannot be appealed to and a man has to right his own wrongs. "There are times when patience ceases to be a virtue," he says, and goes for his gun.

Once the feud is under way, other figures in the pattern may be made out. One of these is the decision everybody has to make as to whether he will fight or run. It will surprise some readers to learn that when feuds were common many people did run and kept on running. It was no particular disgrace to leave the country, especially if the runner was not too close to the center of disturbance. A witness, an innocent bystander, a not-too-closely-related kinsman, or an ordinary peace-loving man could run and still keep his credit—and it should be noted that in most cases running was the only way out. Seldom could anyone stay on the ground and remain neutral. Tom Elder was a fourteen-year-old boy when he stood on the store gallery at McDade and saw the shooting on Christmas Day, 1883. He knew he would be called as a witness and maybe get himself into more trouble, so he went home as fast as he could, packed up, and pulled out for the Panhandle. He stayed for sixteen years. "And I didn't get any letters, either," he will tell you today. Whenever a feud broke out there was an exodus of people like him.

For most Texans, however, the compulsion to stay and fight was too strong to resist. They still say in DeWitt County that John Wesley Hardin had to take sides with his relatives by marriage, the Taylors, or "he could not have held up his head in the county." And men like David Terry and Guilf Gibson left everything and came home from California when the Terry-Gibson trouble endangered the lives of their brothers.

The community approved of this sort of loyalty—even demanded it. Today storytellers recount with admiration how the six Taylor boys made their vow of vengeance at the funeral of poor old murdered Pitkin; or how Walter Reese knelt beside his father's body in the dusty street at Columbus and vowed to even the score.

How kindly Christian people could give countenance to such deeds seems puzzling at first, but that is part of the pattern too. They always argued that the greatest deterrent to crime is the well publicized readiness of every citizen to right his own wrongs. You think twice about killing a man if you know that his brother will be on your trail with a Winchester right after the funeral. There may be some truth in the idea, at that.

What a few years of feuding does to these same kindly Christian people is one of the darkest figures in the pattern. They grow used to the thought of killing and lose all compunction about how it is done. Shooting an unarmed man or killing from ambush does not seem dishonorable any more than "commando" tactics seem dishonorable to a seasoned soldier. A feudist is brave enough to stand up to his enemies in fair fight, usually, but waylaying ("laywaying," they call it in some sections) conserves manpower. After all, though our party is composed of honorable gentlemen, those cutthroats on the other side are bushwhackers and assassins—you have to fight fire with fire. And pretty soon both factions are shooting from the roadside, surrounding houses at daybreak, taking prisoners out of jail, and killing each other like wild animals.

"I don't like that shooting from behind a bush. Why didn't you step into the road?" Colonel Grangerford asked his boy Buck, as Huck Finn tells it.

"The Shepherdsons don't, father. They always take advantage," Buck replied. And the old man made no more objections.

As a consequence of this loss of scruples some pretty obvious blacks looked snow-white to people involved in a feud. Burning people out of their houses was just a "scorched earth" policy—necessary and therefore right. Running them out of the country was a generous act, for it gave them a chance for their lives. Killing a man who refused to get out according to orders was defensible because the man had a chance he willfully would not take—he really committed suicide. Even the inhuman whooping, laughing, and singing which sometimes followed an atrocious feud killing seemed natural to the people who did it, for a menace had just been removed from their lives—they had done what they had to do—they felt happy and righteous.

The matter of broken treaties comes in here too. Many times, at the behest of district attorneys or Ranger captains, feudists have signed an agreement to cease fighting. Usually these documents, like other treaties we have heard of, were just scraps of paper. Why? Because each side reasoned that the other was unworthy of trust or honorable treatment.

Perhaps the most important thing about the pattern is the fact that it seldom stops or dies out of its own accord. Like a cancer, it eats deeper and deeper. More and better people are drawn in, even the women being involved. Business is paralyzed; property values go down; non-combatants, if there are any, stay in their houses or go back to Arkansas to visit their wives' people; armed bands gather in the streets; and telegrams go out to the adjutant general, to the governor, and sometimes to the President of the United States. Unless one of these officials brings in sufficient force to overawe the men on both sides, there will be one riot after another until there is nobody left to fight.

Then comes the litigation, which is also part of the pattern. Sometimes the feud stays alive for years as the lawyers apply artificial respiration. Continuations, postponements, appeals, changes of venue, and hung juries are the tools usually used, but in special cases witnesses have been corrupted, intimidated, or even killed, records have been altered, and perjured testimony has been used. The record of convictions for feud killings is appallingly short.

Many of the threads in this web of death were arranged thousands of years ago when the law of feud was the only law; and that fact puts feuding into the realm of folkways and folklore.

The taboos and compulsions which make folkways may be observed in a feud, operating at full strength. The rule against "talking," which has led to so many deaths, is one of them. So is the feeling that any sort of fraternization with the other clan is treason.

That brings up the favorite folk story in feud lore— the tale of Romeo and Juliet. Fraternizing being forbidden, it naturally becomes more attractive, and before long there is a midnight elopement. It has happened several times in Texas. A Townsend married a Stafford at Columbus; an Arnold married a Foster after their feud in Bosque County; and there are rumors of half a dozen other alliances "over the moor." O. Henry used this theme in one of his Texas stories, "The Higher Abdication."

The real appearance of folklore is in the stories that grow up about a feud. They start before the fighting is finished and keep on spreading. The horrors of each killing grow more revolting; the character of the enemy becomes blacker; the Great Men grow greater. There is always a Great Man—a John Wesley Hardin, a Bill Mitchell, a Curg Border, a Pink Higgins. Ordinary mortals regard them with awe, and every one of them has the making of a legend.

In Sweet and Knox's book *On a Mexican Mustang through Texas* the authors tell about a visit to Cuero in 1874 at the height of the Sutton-Taylor trouble. They asked a citizen how John Wesley Hardin stood in the community and were told that nobody would talk about him, the reason being Hardin's habit of killing anybody who mentioned his name. If he found that the dead man had spoken kindly of him, he would "apologize to the widow and orphans for his thoughtlessness, and make a solemn vow never again to shoot a man until satisfied that he really needed shooting. This course, however, made even his warmest friends appear cold and reticent."

Sweet and Knox were trying to be funny, of course, but they had caught an echo of the horrified fascination felt by the public for a successful desperado—in this case a feudist.

Another bit of folklore that gets around where there has been a feud is the story that the trouble is still smoldering and may break out at any minute. Years ago, when I first began looking into feud history, I stopped off in Houston to inquire about the Jaybirds and Woodpeckers out at Richmond and was told that the thing was still warm—that the Richmond ladies had to be careful not to ask the wrong people to their card parties—that the feud was never allowed to come up in casual conversation. I found that all the Woodpeckers had left town in 1889 and had never come back, making a revival of trouble a complete impossibility.

Likewise there is the whisper that it is dangerous to go into an old feuding community and ask questions. Stories still circulate about men who have stopped off in Cuero to see about the Suttons and Taylors and have been run out of town. As a matter of fact, nobody could be kinder or more helpful than the people of Cuero, and if anyone there ever suggested to an investigator that his work was uncalled for, the suggestion was probably made in a spirit of pure friendship.

Other strange tales get started. There is often an argument about who actually killed somebody. The "Whodunit" interest makes mysteries of what may not have been mysteries at all. Did Calvin Blakely kill Kyle Terry, or was it really Volney Gibson? Nobody is sure—but people like to discuss the possibilities.

Another familiar question is: "Did he really die?" Like Jesse James and Billy the Kid, many an important feudist is supposed to be alive and well somewhere though the funeral service was read over him in all solemnity.

A small feud broke out in Richmond after the Jaybirds had won their battle, in which one of the Mitchells was involved. He moved to the northern part of the county where he eventually died of pneumonia. They brought him back to Dr. Gibson's house, where a hearse and coffin were provided, and all the Gibsons saw that he was really dead. The other party, however, was suspicious, and used to ask the Gibsons (who were related to both sides) if they were sure a log had not been buried in that coffin. Years later, when it became necessary to move the body, it was found that somebody had already opened the coffin—just to make certain.

A few humorous stories have been handed down in connection with the feuds of Texas, though there was nothing much to laugh about, as a rule. For instance there is the legend of the young Taylor who had part of his cheek and jaw shot away in a fight with the Suttons.

"Is there anything I can do for you?" one of his friends asked.

"Well, I *would* like a drink of water," said the wounded man, "but I haven't the face to ask for it."

Will the law of feud and revenge ever cease to haunt the dim caverns of the human mind? Probably not—at least as long as man continues to be man as we know him. While we have wars we may expect to have feuds. War itself is a form of feuding with the same psychology, the same tearing up of treaties, the same loss of peacetime compunctions, the same hatred of a supposedly inhuman or subhuman foe, the same betrayals and ambushes. But the real feuds will come during the aftermath—the Reconstruction—whether it be in Poland or Greece or China or the United States.

There is discouragement in the thought that after all these thousands of years of painful progress, we still revert to the law of the cave and the jungle. But there is another way of looking at it. Many feuds originate in a strong if mistaken sense of justice—and a sense of justice is a good thing to have. Others begin with an offense to personal honor—and a feeling for personal honor is a good thing to have. Feuds operate on loyalty and devotion to a clan or a cause—and loyalty and devotion are good things to have. In the long run we are probably justified in believing that the feuds described in this book were the result of bad times working to pervert some of our best instincts, and one proof of it is the fact that nine times out of ten the descendants of the vigilantes and feudists of seventy-five or

eighty years ago are among the best people in Texas. I
know, because I know them.

And finally there is the matter of courage. In the midst
of the ambushing and waylaying and poisonous hatred
which has filled these pages there is an occasional gleam of
heroic bravery, reminding us that the thing which made
Texas feuds was one of the things that made us a nation.
Think of Mart Horrell, wounded and alone, standing up in
the road and running off a whole gang shooting from behind the creek bank. Think of the Marlow brothers,
shackled and unarmed, taking the Winchesters away from
their guards and putting the lynch mob to flight. It takes

men to do that. When they do it in the air force or the infantry, we pin medals on them. When they do it in a feud, we put them in jail.

But there is one thing we can all be certain of—as long as this country lasts, there will be times when we need a man who will die before he will run.

Sources and Notes

The average reader does not pay much attention to bibliographies and notes, but somebody is going to pay particular attention to those included here. People who have family reasons for being interested in one or another of these feuds are apt to develop fixed ideas about how the story ought to be told, and any variation from the facts as they understand them may generate considerable heat. For that reason the source of every important statement made in these pages is indicated in the notes which follow. I hope that those who question my facts will have the patience to see where I got them before taking any drastic steps.

Many people have helped with the making of this book. Specific obligations are mentioned in connection with each feud, but I owe special thanks to a number of people and organizations:

The Texas State Historical Association obtained a grant-in-aid from the Rockefeller Foundation for me in the summer of 1944, enabling me to dig farther into libraries, newspaper files, and the recollections of men and women all over Texas.

Mr. G.B. Dealey, Mr. Stuart McGregor, and Mrs. Marie Peterson of the Dallas *News* arranged for me to go through their unique file of the Galveston *News* from 1865 to 1877.

Librarians have put me deeply in debt—especially Miss Harriet Smither, late of the Texas State Library; Miss Winnie Allen, formerly University of Texas archivist; Miss Marcelle Hamer, formerly librarian of the Texas Collection, University of Texas Library; the late Mr. E.W. Winkler, Bibliographer of the University of Texas; the late Mrs. Maude L. Sullivan and Mrs. Helen Kister, former librarians of the El Paso Public Library; Mr. Baxter Polk, Miss Hilda Cole and Miss Frances Clayton of the Library of Texas Western College; Miss Susan F. Horn, Reference Librarian at the University of New Mexico.

Friends who have mulled over questions of Texas local history with me include the late W.H. Burges and the late Major Richard F. Burges of El Paso; former Dean J.L. Waller and Dr. Rex Strickland of Texas Western College; Dr. H. Bailey Carroll and Dr. Mody C. Boatright of the University of Texas; Dean C.S. Potts of Southern Methodist University; Mr. C. Stanley Banks of San Antonio; Mr. Chris Emmett of Santa Fe.

Those who have had the kindness and patience to read parts of the manuscript include Mr. J.R. Webb and Mr. W.G. Webb, Sr., of Albany, Texas; the late Judge and Mrs. C.W. Webb of Elgin, Texas; Mrs. J.F. Lessing and Miss Lillian Reese of Columbus; Mrs. C.T. Traylor of Cuero; Mr. and Mrs. W.F. Mace of Lampasas; Miss Margaret Bierschwale and Mr. Roscoe Runge of Mason; Miss Barbara Groce, the late Mrs. R.E. Tompkins, and the late Mrs. M.T. Crook of Hempstead; Mr. LeRoy Echols of Coahoma; Mr. Shine Philips of Big Spring; the late Mrs. Clifton Rice of Fort Worth; the late Judge W.C. Linden of San Antonio; Mrs. Lillian Hague Corcoran, Mr. Lester Horrell, Mrs. Allie Wetteroth, the late Mrs. Etta Longnecker, Mr. Ralph Grimes, the late Mrs. Paul Heisig and the late Mr. Heisig of El Paso.

A list of source materials appears with the notes for each feud. Two fundamental sources of information—the reports of the Texas Rangers and files of Texas newspapers—may be mentioned now to save repetition. The official reports and private correspondence of the Ranger officers are preserved in the adjutant general's files in the State Library in Austin. Much of this material was transcribed by Dr. W.P. Webb for his monumental work on the Texas Rangers and the transcripts are now available to students in the Webb Papers, University of Texas Archives. I have used both the original materials and the transcripts. Information from the Ranger material is indicated by the letters AGF (Adjutant General's Files).

Newspapers quoted from are as follows:

The Austin *Weekly Statesman*
The Austin *Daily Statesman*
The *Weekly Austin Republican*
The Bay City *Tribune*
The Bastrop *Advertiser*
The Dallas *Weekly Herald*
The Dallas *Daily Herald*
Norton's Union Intelligencer (Dallas)
The Elgin *Courier*
The El Paso *Evening Post*
The El Paso *Times*
The Galveston *Weekly Civilian*
The Galveston *Daily News*
The *Daily National Intelligencer* (Galveston)
The Graham *Leader*
The Houston *Chronicle*
The Houston *Daily Post*

The Houston *Telegraph*
Flake's Semi-Weekly Bulletin (Houston)
The *Frontier Echo* (Jacksboro and Albany)
The Nacogdoches *Weekly Sentinel*
The Richmond *Democrat*
The Richmond *Opinion*
The Richmond-Rosenburg *Herald-Coaster*
The Roswell *Daily Record*
The San Angelo *Morning Times*
The San Antonio *Daily Express*
The San Antonio *Daily Herald*
The San Saba *Daily News*
The *Western Chronicle* (Sutherland Springs)

The Theory and Practice of Feuding

1. A similar and better-known story is in *Huckleberry Finn*.
2. T.D. Clark. He admits that behind the trivialities were more serious things: "the greatest single cause for dispute . . . was the division of sentiment over the Civil War." Light is thrown on this question in *The Hatfields and the McCoys*, by Virgil Carrington Jones, The University of North Carolina Press, Chapel Hill, 1948.
3. *Popular Tribunals* (2 vols., *Works*, Vols. XXXVI and XXXVII, The History Company, San Francisco, 1887) Vol. I, p. 10, and "Preface," p. 7. James G. Leyburn (*Frontier Folkways*, Yale University Press, New Haven, 1935) and J.E. Cutler (*Lynch Law*, Longmans, Green and Co., New York, 1905) agree that Lynch Law was an "efficient system."
4. Historians of the law have devoted many pages to the change from feud law to the criminal codes of today. See William Seagle, *The Quest for Law*, Alfred H. Knopf, New York, 1941, p. 36.
5. Leyburn, p. 215.
6. Leyburn, p. 215, and Cutler, p. 42.

7. *Life on the Mississippi*, Heritage Press, New York, 1944, pp. 238, 272.
8. "The Southerner and the Law," *Journal of Southern History*, February, 1940, Vol. VI, pp. 2-23.
9. Several famous cases have tested the doctrine of "retreat" in Texas. W.H. Burges and C.S. Potts called my attention to Horbach vs. the State, *Texas Supreme Court Reports*, XLIII (1883), 242-261; and to Brown vs. the U. S., 256 U. S. 335, 41 S. Ct. 501, 65 L. Ed. 161, 18 A. L. R. 1276, decided by Justice Holmes in 1921.
10. Cutler, p. 91.

★

From Regulation to Reconstruction

1. The Regulators and Moderators have accumulated a long bibliography. For a full discussion of the feud and the documentary material dealing with it see C.L. Sonnichsen, *Ten Texas Feuds*, The University of New Mexico Press, Albuquerque, 1957, pp. 11-57; 219-224.
2. R.N. Richardson, *Texas the Lone Star State*, Prentice-Hall, New York, 1943, p. 228.
3. Walter Prescott Webb, *The Texas Rangers*, Houghton Mifflin Company, Boston, 1935, Ch. VIII.
4. J. Fred Rippy, "Border Troubles along the Rio Grande, 1848-1860" *Southwestern Historical Quarterly*, Oct., 1919, Vol. 23, pp. 91-111; J. Frank Dobie, *A Vaquero of the Brush Country*, Southwest Press, Dallas, 1929, Chapter V, "The Bloody Border."
5. John Warren Hunter, "Heel Fly Time in Texas," *Frontier Times*, April, 1924.
6. *Ten Texas Feuds*, 67-78; 226-227.
7. *Ibid.*, 79-83; 227-228.

★

The Hunting of Bob Lee

Two people who had intimate knowledge of the background have written about the Lee-Peacock trouble. Dean T.U. Taylor, late of the University of Texas, grew up in the neighborhood, knew the Lees, and even served papers on them. Sixty years after the feud died out, he looked up the last survivors and published his findings in the *Frontier Times* for May, 1926, and March, 1928. Later the articles were reissued as a pamphlet (*The Lee-Peacock Feud*, The Frontier Times, Bandera, Texas, n. d.). Page references which follow are to the pamphlet. More recently G.B. Ray, the historian of the Red River Valley, has done more exhaustive research and published it under the title *Murder at the Corners* (The Naylor Company, San Antonio, 1957). These two sources, plus additional material from contemporary newspapers, must form the basis for any discussion of the subject.

1. For Bob Lee's military record see Ray, *Murder at the Corners*, pp. 2-4.
2. Dean Taylor describes Bob Lee, using local tradition and a story published in the *Weekly Harrison Flag* for June 17, 1869, and copied by the Bonham *News* (date not given). The same article was printed with alterations in the Galveston *News*, June 11, 1869.
3. *Murder at the Corners*, p. 5.
4. *Ibid.*, p. 25 (material on Peacock).
5. *Ibid.*, pp. vii, 23-24.
6. *Ibid.*, pp. 10-13.
7. *Frontier Times*, March, 1928; Bright Ray, *Legends of the Red River Valley*, The Naylor Company, San Antonio, 1941, pp. 167-180.
8. The sketch of Lee's life (Galveston *News*, June 11, 1869) says the jail was broken open for the Peacock party after Lee had them arrested.
9. Dallas *Weekly Herald*, March 30, 1867; Taylor, p. 2.
10. Dallas *Weekly Herald*, April 20, 1867.
11. *Murder at the Corners*, pp. 33-35.
12. *Ibid.*, pp. 35-36.
13. *Ibid.*, pp. 37-39.
14. Dallas *Weekly Herald*, July 4, 1868; Galveston *News*, June 27, 1868.
15. *Weekly Austin Republican*, Jan. 20, 1869; Dallas *Weekly Herald*, August 29, 1868.
16. Galveston *News*, Dec. 31, 1868.
17. Taylor, pp. 3-4, from the recollections of Miss Pierce (Mrs. John Hancock of Trenton, Texas).
18. Galveston *News*, April 24, 1869.

19. *Ibid.*, June 3, 11, 1869; *Murder at the Corners*, pp. 69-72; Taylor, pp. 3-4. The sister-in-law was Mrs. John Lee of Upland, California.

20. Galveston *News*, Feb. 5, 1870.

21. Taylor, pp. 6-7.

22. *Ibid.*, pp. 7-8; *Flake's Semi-Weekly Bulletin*, June 28, July 26, 1871.

23. *Flake's Semi-Weekly Bulletin*, Oct. 11, 18, 1871; Taylor, p. 8.

24. Taylor, p. 2.

★

Thirty Years A-feuding

1. Jack Hays Day, *The Sutton Taylor Feud*. Press of Sid Murray and Son, San Antonio, 1937.

2. Lewis S. Delony, *Forty Years a Peace Officer*, Cuero, n. d.

3. James T. DeShields, *Tall Men with Long Rifles*. The Naylor Company, San Antonio, 1935.

4. Chris Emmett, *Shanghai Pierce, a Fair Likeness*. The University of Oklahoma Press, Norman, 1953.

5. O.C. Fisher, *It Happened in Kimble*. Anson Jones Press, Houston, 1937.

6. Thomas W. Gamel, *The Life of Thomas W. Gamel*. Mason, Texas, n. d.

7. Mrs. Augusta Keller Grunder, "Indianola Storm Survivor Recalls Night of Terror." *Frontier Times*, August, 1933 (reprinted from the San Antonio *Express*, May 21, 1933).

8. John Wesley Hardin, *The Life of John Wesley Hardin, from the Original Manuscript, as Written by Himself*. Smith and Moore, Seguin, Texas, 1896.

9. James Hatch, "Lest We Forget the Heroes of the Alamo." Typed copy in the *Indianola Scrapbook*, University of Texas Archives.

10. J. Marvin Hunter, editor, "Goliad Man Recalls Wild Frontier of Lone Star State," *Frontier Times*, September, 1932.

11. J. Marvin Hunter, editor, "Story of Indianola Hurricane." *Frontier Times*, November, 1930 (quoted from the Victoria *Advocate* for September 24, 1875.

12. N.A. Jennings, *A Texas Ranger*. The Southwest Press, Dallas, 1930.

13. L.W. Kemp, "Was Creed Taylor at San Jacinto?" *Frontier Times*, April, 1936.
14. G.E. Mayfield, "Capt. W.L. Rudd of Yorktown, Ex-Ranger," *Frontier Times*, September, 1932.
15. J.B. Polley, "Historical Reminiscences." The San Antonio *Express*, January 26, February 2, 1908 (Reprinted as "The Taylor Boys," *Frontier Times*, June, 1928.
16. Dora Neill Raymond, *Captain Lee Hall of Texas*. University of Oklahoma Press, Norman, 1940.
17. Victor Rose, *The Texas Vendetta; or, the Sutton-Taylor Feud*. J.J. Little & Co., New York, 1880.
18. A.J. Sowell, Early Settlers and Indian Fighters of Southwest Texas. Ben C. Jones & Co., Austin, 1900.
19. Coke R. Stevenson, Jr., "Kimble County History Tells of Pioneer Struggles." *Frontier Times*, September, 1930 (reprinted from the Junction *Eagle*).
20. Alex Sweet and J. Armoy Knox, *On a Mexican Mustang through Texas from the Gulf to the Rio Grande*. Rand, McNally and Co., Chicago and New York, 1892.
21. Walter Prescott Webb, *The Texas Rangers—A Century of Frontier Defense*. Houghton, Mifflin Company, Boston, 1935.

The Sutton-Taylor trouble was the worst of the Texas feuds but nobody is left to tell about it. A few survivors were alive in the thirties when I was collecting material. I talked to Lewis Delony, who sided with the Suttons, and communicated with Jack Hays Day, a Taylor, through our mutual friend Mrs. C.T. Traylor of Cuero. Others who had special knowledge which they were willing to share included Judge Sam D. Lackey of Cuero, W.H. Burges of El Paso, Mrs. Mattie Hardin Smith of Fort Worth, R.R. Smith of Jourdanton, E.D. Spellman of Burnet, Ralph Calhoun and S.R. Weisiger of Victoria, Mrs. Tim B. Cobb of Del Rio, E.P. Cox of Anthony, New Mexico, Mrs. J.F. Lentz of Marshall, Mrs. Max Weinert of Seguin, Chris Emmett of Santa Fe, Newton Crain of Cuero, Dean C.S. Potts of Dallas, former Assistant Attorney General David Heath of Dallas (who helped me find material in the State Capitol), George Isbell of San Antonio (who lent me *The Texas Vendetta*), G.P. Day of Cuero (who helped me find the Taylor cemetery and the old McCrabb burying ground), Mrs. Edith Pridgen and Mrs. Leonard McDonald of El Paso (who told me about Bolivar Pridgen), Mrs. Georgie Brassell Alford and Mrs. Pansy Reed of Los Angeles, descendants of Dr. Brassell. Mrs. C.T. Traylor has my special gratitude for constant help and advice.

★

The Root of the Matter

1. Galveston *News*, Nov. 12, Dec. 1, 1865; July 26, Oct. 27, 1866.
2. *Ibid.*, Nov. 4, 1866.
3. *Ibid.*, Aug. 16, 1866.
4. *Ibid.*, Nov. 25, 1869.
5. *Ibid.*, April 5, 1867.
6. *Ibid.*, Dec. 31, 1867.

★

Creed Taylor's Boys

1. Sowell is the best source for Creed Taylor's family background (p. 805 ff.). DeShields covers the Mexican War service, but Kemp's article takes issue with him. The San Antonio *Express*, April 7, 1904, and June 28, 1905, contains first-hand biographical material. Dr. Robert S. Giles of San Antonio, a Taylor descendant, has made extensive researches into the pioneer history of the family. He says that the first Josiah returned to Texas to settle in 1827-28 (R. S. G. to C. L. S., Sept. 18, 1953).
2. J.B. Polley describes the Taylor boys in the Galveston *News*, Jan. 26, 1908.
3. Gamel, p. 11.
4. Galveston *News*, Jan. 26, 1908.
5. *Ibid.*, Nov. 27, Dec. 3, 1867.
6. Mrs. C.T. Traylor, Cuero, Texas, Aug. 16, 1944.
7. Galveston *News*, Feb. 2, 1908.
8. Rose, p. 15. More on Bell: *Weekly Austin Republican*, May 6, 1868.
9. Rose, pp. 13-14.
10. *Ibid.*, pp. 15-19.
11. Galveston *News*, Aug. 13, 1869.
12. Rose, pp. 23-26.
13. Galveston *News*, Aug. 24, 1869.
14. Rose, p. 19; Galveston *News*, August 29, 1869.
15. Gamel, pp. 11-12; Galveston *News*, February 2, 1908.
16. Galveston *News*, September 4, 14, 1869, February 2, 1908.

17. Coke Stevenson, Jr., describes the ruins of Creed Taylor's house, built in 1872 on the James River.
18. San Antonio *Express*, December 13, 1871; Galveston *News*, February 2, 1908; Rose, p. 28. The *Frontier Times* for December, 1931, p. 122, has more on Holstein.

★

Bill Sutton Takes a Hand

1. S.R. Weisiger of Victoria, Texas, to C. L. S., June 28, 1961, quoting his grandfather Reed Nelson Weisiger. I learned about Bill Sutton from the late Ralph Calhoun, his grandson, and from Mrs. Tim B. Cobb, his first cousin once removed. Rose, p. 13, also describes him. The Sutton genealogy has been worked out by Mr. S.R. Weisiger.
2. Jack Hays Day and other Taylors declare that Charley was no relation of theirs (Mrs. C.T. Traylor to C. L. S., July 2, 1949).
3. September 27, 1874.
4. Rose, p. 12.
5. Buck's tombstone bears the dates November 1, 1837-December 24, 1868.
6. Delony, p. 8.
7. Day, pp. 10-12.
8. Raymond, p. 59. See also Jennings, p. 248, and Galveston *News*, September 27, 1874.
9. June 28, 1905. Dr. Robert Giles of San Antonio says, "There is strong reason to think . . . that Mary Ann Hepsebeth Smith Taylor came from Georgia. My own family tradition places the origin of Josiah Taylor I as in Tennessee. It is possible that he lived in four states before finally arriving in Texas for settlement" (R. S. G. to C. L. S., September 18, 1953).

★

The State Police

1. Ramsdell, *Reconstruction in Texas*, pp. 295-313; Texas newspapers, April-July, 1870.

2. San Antonio *Herald,* July 27, 1870.
3. Cox family records in possession of the late Ed P. Cox of El Paso.
4. Austin *Daily Statesman,* September 2, November 12, 1874.
5. Chris Emmett, Shanghai Pierce specialist, says Helm assisted at the Lunn hanging, for which see his *Shanghai Pierce,* pp. 57-58, 66; also the *Weekly Austin Republican,* July 20, 1870, and the San Antonio *Herald,* July 21, 1870.
6. The Kelly murder: Day, pp. 13-14; Rose, pp. 38-50; San Antonio *Herald,* Sept. 4, 1870. Mrs. Kelly's story: *Weekly Austin Republican,* Sept. 14, Nov. 2, 1870. Tradition in the Sutton family says that the Kelly boys were not innocent. They had been "raiding" the Taylors and the Sutton women had sat up nights making "turpentine balls" to cast light on the proceedings. (Mrs. Tim B. Cobb to C.L. Sonnichsen, Nov. 7, 1959.)
7. *Weekly Austin Republican,* Nov. 2, 1870.
8. *Ibid.,* Oct. 26, 1870; San Antonio *Herald,* Dec. 9, 1870.
9. Day, pp. 14-15; Hardin, p. 80.

★

The Young Men Take Over

1. Delony, p. 7; interview with Mr. Delony, Cuero, Texas, July 7, 1943.
2. Raymond, p. 179; Galveston *News,* Sept. 23, 1874.
3. Day, p. 16; Hardin, p. 80.
4. Day, p. 16, San Antonio *Herald,* June 20, 1873.
5. Austin *Daily Statesman,* Nov. 12, 1874.
6. O.C. Fisher, p. 149.
7. Hardin, p. 64.
8. *Ibid.,* pp. 78-81.
9. Houston *Telegraph,* July 27, 1873; San Antonio *Express,* July 10, 1873; Rose, p. 30; Day, p. 19; Hardin, p. 81.
10. R.R. Smith to C. L. S., Oct. 1, 1943.
11. Hardin, pp. 81-82; Day, p. 18; Houston *Telegraph,* July 30, 1873.
12. Houston *Telegraph,* Aug. 20, 1873; Austin *Daily Statesman,* Nov. 12, 1874; Hardin, pp. 82-84.
13. Day, p. 20; Rose, p. 32; S.R. Weisiger to C. L. S., June 28, 1961.
14. Austin *Daily Statesman,* Dec. 9, 1874.

15. San Antonio *Herald,* Jan. 26, 1874.
16. Day, p. 22.

Bill Sutton Checks Out

1. S.R. Weisiger to C. L. S., June 28, 1961.
2. Austin *Daily Statesman,* May 18, 1874; San Antonio *Herald,* March 17, 1874.
3. Judge Sam D. Lackey, Cuero, Texas, August 16, 1944.
4. Mrs. C.B. Fallis (now Mrs. Tim Cobb) to C. L. S. June 20, 1951.
5. Hardin, p. 86.
6. Ralph Calhoun, Victoria, Texas, August 15, 1944.
7. Rose, p. 52; Hardin, p. 87; Day, p. 23.

★

Bloody Harvest

1. Rose, p. 52.
2. Hardin, pp. 87-88.
3. E.D. Spellman, Smiley, Texas, July 7, 1943.
4. Hardin, pp. 88-106.
5. Day, pp. 28-29; San Antonio *Herald,* June 25, 30, July 1, 1874. Scrap (R.P.) Taylor's tombstone says that he was twenty-nine years old.
6. Sam D. Lackey, Cuero, July 6, 1943.
7. *Ibid.;* E.D. Spellman, July 7, 1943.
8. E.D. Spellman; Austin *Daily Statesman,* July 16, 1874.
9. Austin *Daily Statesman,* July 21, September 24, 1874.
10. McNelly's letter is in the AGF. See also *Daily Statesman,* August 8, 1874.
11. Pidge's letters: Austin *Daily Statesman,* August 8, September 2, 24, October 24, December 9, 1874.
12. McNelly to Steele, August 7, 1874, AGF.
13. *Ibid.,* November 30, 1874.
14. *Ibid.,* August 28, 1874.
15. *Ibid.,* September 2, 1874.
16. Galveston *News,* September 23, 1874.
17. *Ibid.,* September 24, 27, 1874.
18. McNelly to Steele, Sept. 30, 1874, AGF.

19. *Ibid.*, Nov. 5, 1874.
20. *Ibid.*, Dec. 10, 1874.

★

Last Battles

1. Mrs. Grunder, James Hatch, and Hunter's reprint from the Victoria *Advocate* describe the hurricane.
2. Newton Crain, Cuero, Texas, Aug. 17, 1944; Hunter, "Goliad Man Recalls Wild Frontier"; Hatch in *Indianola Scrapbook*.
3. Ralph Calhoun, Victoria, Texas, Aug. 15, 1944.
4. Dallas *Weekly Herald*, Nov. 27, 1875; Day, p. 31.
5. Austin *Daily Statesman*, Dec. 2, 1875.
6. Day, pp. 29, 32.
7. Delony, pp. 12-15; interview with Mr. Delony, July 7, 1943; San Antonio *Herald*, Jan. 3, 1876; Austin *Daily Democratic Statesman*, Jan. 15, 1876.
8. Delony, p. 16.
9. Telegram from County Clerk L.C. Williamson of Coleman County to the Adjutant General, April 15, 1877, in AGF.
10. *The Western Chronicle* (Sutherland Springs), June 7, 1878; Rose, p. 53.
11. Hall to Jones, Oct. 4, 1879, AGF; Raymond, p. 179.
12. Roberts to Jones, Jan. 1, 1881, AGF.
13. Jack Hays Day to Mrs. C.T. Traylor, Dec. 4, 1944, quoted by permission of Mrs. Traylor.

★

The Brassell Murder

1. McNelly to Steele, March 8, 1876, AGF.
2. Galveston *News*, Oct. 4, 1876; interview with Mrs. Pansy Reed of Los Angeles (Dr. Brassell's grand-daughter), El Paso, April 7, 1959.
3. Sam D. Lackey, Cuero, July 6, 1943.
4. *Ibid.*
5. *Texas Criminal Reports* VIII (1880), pp. 298-299; Rose, p. 61.
6. Galveston *News*, October 4, 1876.
7. Mrs. G.B. Alford to C. L. S., January 27, 1961.
8. The testimony of the Brassells is in *Texas Criminal Reports* VIII, 258-263.

9. Mrs. Pansy Reed; Mrs. Alford to C. L. S. Mayfield's article in the *Frontier Times* describes Nancy's ride.
10. Galveston *News*, October 4, 1876; Day, p. 36.
11. Hall to Steele, December 10, 1876.
12. *Ibid.*
13. Judge Pleasants: Frank W. Johnson, *Texas and Texans*, ed. Barker and Winkler, Vol. III, p. 1181. Judge Lackey told me about the sheepish Ranger.

★

Wedding Bells and Prison Cells

1. Ed P. Cox, El Paso, August 8, 1943.
2. *Texas Criminal Reports* VIII, p. 278.
3. Jennings, pp. 248-255; Raymond, p. 69 ff.
4. Hall to McNelly, Dec. 22, 1876, AGF.
5. Jennings, 257-259.
6. Galveston *News*, Jan. 6, 1877.
7. Austin *Weekly Statesman*, April 12, 1877.
8. Delony, p. 21.
9. *Texas Criminal Reports* VIII, p. 279; Galveston *News*, January 2, 1878.
10. Hall to Steele, January 1, 1878, AGF.
11. *Texas Criminal Reports* XII, pp. 665-671.
12. Fred Cocke to General King, August 26, 1882, AGF.
13. Dates are from the Criminal Minutes, District Court, Cuero.
14. *Texas Appeals Reports* VIII, pp. 254-310; Rose, pp. 62-69; Raymond, p. 76.
15. The facts about the Augustine case are in the Criminal Minutes, DeWitt County courthouse, Cuero, and in *Texas Criminal Reports* XLI, pp. 61-76. Governor Sayers' comment on the petition for pardon, October 30, 1899, indicates that there was much sentiment for Augustine (Pardons and Remissions, No. 5473, Texas State Archives, State Library, Austin).

★

Days of Wrath

1. Webb, *The Texas Rangers*, p. 287.
2. R.B. Townshend, *The Tenderfoot in New Mexico*, John Lane, London, 1923, pp. 178-188.
3. Austin *Weekly Statesman* for Oct. 12, 1876, speaks of "raids in Frio County by a band of highwaymen painted red." It happened many times.
4. Austin *Weekly Statesman*, May 3, 1877; Jennings, *A Texas Ranger*, p. 197.
5. San Antonio *Herald*, July 17, 1875.
6. For fuller treatment of this feud see C.L. Sonnichsen, *Ten Texas Feuds*, University of New Mexico Press, Albuquerque, 1957, pp. 185-199.
7. *Ibid.*, pp. 87-107.
8. *Ibid.*, pp. 108-156.
9. *Between Sun and Sod*, The Clarendon Press, Clarendon, Texas, 1938, p. 162.
10. Frank H. Bushick, *Glamorous Days*, The Naylor Company, San Antonio, 1934, p. 254.

★

Hot Heads and Hair Triggers

J.B. Cranfill, *Dr. J.B. Cranfill's Chronicle—A Story of Life in Texas Written by Himself about Himself*. Fleming H. Revell Company, New York, 1916.

C.L. Douglas, *Cattle Kings of Texas*. Cecil Baugh. Dallas, 1939.

C.L. Douglas, *Famous Texas Feuds*. The Turner Company, Dallas, 1936.

Maurice Garland Fulton, "Roswell in its Early Years." Old Timers' edition of the Roswell *Daily Record*, October 7, 1937.

James B. Gillett, *Six Years with the Texas Rangers*. Von Boeckmann-Jones Co., Austin, 1921.

Emerson Hough, *The Story of the Outlaw*. In *The Frontier Omnibus*, Grosset and Dunlap, New York, n. d. (reprint).

W.C. Nunn, *A Study of the State Police during the E.J. Davis Administration*. M. A. thesis, The University of Texas, 1931.

P.J. Rasch, "The Horrell War." *New Mexico Historical Review,* Vol. XXXI, July 1956, pp. 223-231.

William MacLeod Raine, *Famous Sheriffs and Western Outlaws.* New Home Library, New York, 1944 (reprint).

Dan W. Roberts, *Rangers and Sovereignty.* Wood Printing and Engraving Company, San Antonio, 1914.

The Horrel-Higgins feud happened over seventy-five years ago. The few remaining pioneers who could say, "I saw it myself," used to get together regularly every Saturday afternoon in the district Clerk's office in the courthouse at Lampasas where there was apt to be a breeze and where Mr. Word, the clerk (who was an old-timer himself), loved to preside over a discussion of the rocky old frontier days. When Mr. Word died, the old men kept right on using his office. I met Mr. Gus Coffey, Mr. J.H. Yazell, and others there one Saturday afternoon in July, 1944, and have to thank them for much kindness and information. Mr. and Mrs. W.F. Mace and Mrs. J.L. Culberson added much more, and so did Mr. Dave Hill, of California, who came back for a visit to his old town in the summer of 1944. Mr. Byron Wren of Colorado City, a son of Bill Wren, gave me some useful facts. The last few pages were filled out with the help of Uncle Ed. Nichols of Morgan and Meridian, Texas, who remembered everything from away back. For help with the Horrell background I have to thank Mr. L.E. Horrell of El Paso, grandson of Mart Horrell and P.J. Rasch of San Pedro, California.

1. Gillett, p. 108; Douglas, *Famous Texas Feuds,* p. 130. A story in *Flake's Semi-Weekly Bulletin,* Nov. 11, 1871, says that Derman, Wicks and West left Lampasas with a trail herd, were pursued, caught up with, and relieved of 87 out of 140 head.

2. San Antonio *Herald,* Feb. 1, 1873.

3. Gus Coffey, Lampasas, July 14, 1944.

4. Gillett, p. 108.

5. Rasch, p. 223, says the Horrells were from Arkansas and had lived before 1870 in Lincoln County, New Mexico. Roberts, p. 165, says the Horrells kept up strife over the " 'dead war' issues."

6. J.H. Yazell, Gus Coffey, and Mrs. J.L. Culberson agreed that the Horrell boys bore good characters before the outbreak

of feuding (Lampasas, July 15, 1944). Rasch, p. 224 says they were accused of rustling.

7. San Antonio *Herald*, March 22, 1873; *Norton's Union Intelligencer*, March 29, 1873; Gillett, p. 109.

8. Gus Coffey.

9. San Antonio *Herald*, March 25, 1873.

10. *Norton's Union Intelligencer*, Feb. 15, 1873.

11. Gillett adds the name of Jerry Scott to the list of prisoners and describes the jail delivery, pp. 110-111.

12. Hough, p. 201.

13. The water trouble is mentioned in an undated clipping from a Roswell newspaper in possession of L.E. Horrell of El Paso.

14. Fulton's article collects some of the information about the "Horrell War" in New Mexico. He added stories about several additional skirmishes in a letter to me dated Dec. 25, 1932. The rest is from Rasch's excellent article and the old men at Lampasas.

15. Marvin E. Reed to C. L. S., July 10, 1957, quoting from his recollections of Mrs. Harrison in whose home he spent seventeen years.

16. Austin *Daily Statesman*, March 5, 1874.

17. *Ibid.*, March 21, 1874.

18. Dallas *Daily Herald*, March 25, 1874.

19. Austin *Daily Statesman*, Sept. 20, 1874.

20. *Ibid.*, Oct. 12, 1876; Gillett, p. 113.

21. Douglas, *Famous Texas Feuds*, p. 135.

22. Byron Wren, Colorado City, Texas, June 5, 1944.

23. Galveston *News*, Jan. 30, 1877; Austin *Weekly Statesman*, Feb. 1, 1877. Douglas, *Famous Texas Feuds*, pp. 136-137, makes it appear that Pink beat Merritt to the draw.

24. Austin *Weekly Statesman*, Feb. 15, 1877; Sparks to Jones, Feb. 6, 1877, AGF.

25. Mrs. J.L. Culberson, Lampasas, July 15, 1944.

26. Gus Coffey; Gillett, p. 113.

27. Austin *Weekly Statesman*, Feb. 15, 1877; Sparks to Jones, March 30, 1877, AGF.

28. Austin *Weekly Statesman*, April 26, 1877.

29. *Ibid.*, quoting from the Lampasas *Dispatch*.

30. Galveston *News*, June 15, 1877.

31. Austin *Weekly Statesman*, June 21, July 5, 1877; Douglas, *Feuds*, p. 139.

32. Austin *Weekly Statesman*, June 28, 1877.

33. Jones to Steele, July 10, 1877, AGF.
34. Gillett, pp. 114-116; Austin *Weekly Statesman*, Aug. 2, 1877; Galveston *News*, Aug. 14, 1877.
35. Byron Wren.
36. "Operations of Detachments of Cos. 'A' and 'C' Front." Batt. for the month of July, 1877, AGF.
37. The letters: AGF and Austin *Weekly Statesman*, Aug. 16, 1877.
38. Galveston *News*, April 9, 1878.
39. El Paso *Evening Post*, Sept. 14, 1928.
40. Cranfill, pp. 221-223; Galveston *News*, May 30, June 20, 1878.
41. Cranfill, p. 222.
42. Ed Nichols, Morgan, Texas, July 18, 1944.
43. Cranfill, pp. 225-226.
44. Galveston *News*, Aug. 29, 1878 (interview with Captain Glenn).
45. *Ibid.*, Dec. 17, 1878.
46. *Ibid.*, Oct. 13, 1878.
47. *Ibid.*, Dec. 17, 1878.
48. Ed Nichols.
49. Douglas, *Famous Texas Feuds*, pp. 143-146, tells more about Higgins and adds further facts in *Cattle Kings of Texas*, p. 305 ff.
50. Cranfill, pp. 231-238, sketches Babb's later life.

★

Justice After Dark

Don H. Biggers, "Shackleford County Sketches." Albany *News*, Albany, Texas, 1908.

Fort Griffin (second edition). Albany Chamber of Commerce, Albany, Texas, September, 1936.

J. Evetts Haley, *Jeff Milton, A Good Man with a Gun*. The University of Oklahoma Press, Norman, 1948.

John R. Hutto, "Emmett Roberts, a Pioneer of Jones County," *Frontier Times*, November, 1933 (reprint from the Anson *Western Enterprise*).

Sallie Reynolds Matthews, *Interwoven*. The Anson Jones Press, Houston, 1936.

Sophie A. Poe, *Buckboard Days* (ed. Eugene Cunningham). The Caxton Printers, Caldwell, Idaho, 1936.

Carl Coke Rister, *Fort Griffin on the Texas Frontier*. The University of Oklahoma Press, Norman, 1956.

Edgar Rye, *The Quirt and the Spur*. The W.B. Conkey Co., Chicago, 1909.

J.R. Webb, "Henry Herron, Pioneer and Peace Officer during Fort Griffin Days." *West Texas Historical Association Year Book*, Vol. XX, October, 1944, pp. 21-50.

Owen White, *Lead and Likker*. Minton, Balch and Co., New York, 1932.

Don Biggers and Edgar Rye have written full accounts of the Shackleford County feud. Old residents say that the Rye version, though based on first-hand observation, has been embroidered and that Biggers is more reliable. Rye was a justice of the peace and later a newspaper editor at Albany and knew the facts, but nobody, including Mr. Rye, cared to tell too much of the story for years after it happened because it was painful to so many good people. It has been possible for some years now to ask a few questions without giving offense and to make public a few of the answers. I was able to talk to some of the old-timers in the last years of their lives and to some who are still living. Mr. Henry Herron told me about John Selman. Mrs. A.A. Clarke (ninety-one years old when I talked to her, and full of memories and old-time kindliness) described the founding of Albany and some episodes in the feud. Mr. W.G. Webb, Sr., piloted me around Fort Griffin. His brother J.R. Webb, an authority on Fort Griffin history, has read this chapter and helped me in many ways to get at the truth. The invaluable file of the *Frontier Echo*, published at Jacksboro from 1875 through 1878, and at Fort Griffin from 1879 to January of 1882, now belongs to the Albany *News* and was carefully kept, when I consulted it, at the Albany High School. Mr. J.H. McGaughey, editor of the *News*, and Mr. C.B. Downing, Superintendent of Schools, graciously allowed me to inspect the file. Next to the *Echo* the most valuable newspaper source is an article in the Galveston *News* for July 13, 1878.

1. Early days at Fort Griffin: Mathews, pp. 51-73; Biggers, "In a General Way" and "Early Settlers"; Rister, pp. 125-196; Albany Chamber of Commerce, *Fort Griffin*; J.R. Webb to C. L. S., July 29, 1945.

2. Mrs. A.A. Clarke, Albany, Texas, June 6, 1944.

3. Galveston *News*, July 13, 1878.

4. Issue of April 28, 1876.

5. For facts about Larn see Rye, p. 103; Mrs. Poe, p. 88; Biggers' chapter on "Old Camp Cooper"; Galveston *News*, July 13, 1878; interview with Mrs. A.A. Clarke.

6. Issue of March 8, 1874.

7. Matthews, p. 48; Henry C. Herron, Albany, Texas, June 7, 1944; Biggers' chapter on "Old Fort Davis."

8. Rye, pp. 104-105.

9. *Frontier Echo*, April 28, June 2, 1876.

10. More on Reddy: *Ibid.*, May 12, 1876. He was taken from the guards who were escorting him to Eastland.

11. *Ibid.*, April 28, 1876.

12. *Ibid.*, May 12, 1876.

13. *Ibid.*, June 9, 1876.

14. *Ibid.*

15. Galveston *News*, Dec. 26, 1876. The Austin *Weekly Statesman* for Dec. 28 says that the lynching occurred "ten days ago." J.R. Webb thinks that the story refers to the wiping out of the Hays outfit at Bushknob in Throckmorton County (letter, January 29, 1945).

16. Galveston *News*, July 13, 1878.

17. Rye, p. 106.

18. Galveston *News*, July 13, 1878.

19. Rye, p. 107.

20. Campbell to Jones, Feb. 28, 1878, AGF.

21. Rye, p. 107; Hutto in the *Frontier Times*.

22. J.R. Webb, Albany, Texas, June 7, 1944.

23. The arrest: Rye, p. 108; J.R. Webb, "Henry Herron," pp. 32-33.

24. Rye, pp. 109-112.

25. Mrs. Poe describes her husband's later career.

26. Webb, *The Texas Rangers*, p. 413. He says Selman was warned by "Hurrican Minnie."

27. The Fort Davis episode: Webb, *The Texas Rangers*, 406-408; Haley, pp. 61-63. Haley gives the names of the Shackleford County vigilantes as Selman detailed them to the arresting officers.

28. Cruger to Jones, July 2, 1880, AGF.

29. Galveston *News*, Aug. 21, 1880.

30. Henry C. Herron.

31. White, pp. 9-12.

32. J.R. Webb to C. L. S., Jan. 6, 1947.

★

Four on a Limb

Jeptha Billingsley, assisted by Mrs. Emma S. Webb, "McDade Lynchings Fifty Years Ago Remembered." Elgin *Courier*, May 11, 1936.

Mrs. Edward C. Garland, "History of Elgin," MS reprinted in the Elgin *Courier*, June 25, 1953.

Helen Rummel, "When Eleven Were Lynched." Austin *Daily Statesman*, July 29, 1928 (reproduced in the *Frontier Times*, July, 1930.

Mari Sandoz, *The Cattlemen*. Hastings House, New York, 1958.

T.U. Taylor, "In and Around Old McDade." *Frontier Times*, May, 1939.

The McDade feud, though it has some very interesting aspects, never has had much publicity. Helen Rummel's article has had some notice, but it is almost completely at variance with the facts. Mr. Billingsley and Mrs. Webb published their account as a corrective to Miss Rummel's, but it had only local circulation. Dean Taylor visited the old-timers and wrote a good account of the later stages of the feud. The earlier stages are here pieced together for the first time from newspaper stories and oral tradition. The climactic episodes were covered thoroughly in the newspapers but the tale could never be told without the help of people who grew up in the neighborhood. Judge and Mrs. C.W. Webb of Elgin shared their rich memories and sent me on to others. Special thanks go to Mr. J.J. Sapp of Bastrop; Tom Elder, Dr. G.T. King, and R.L. Carter of Elgin; General W.D. Cope of Austin; Judge S.J. Isaacks of El Paso; Styles Byrom of Georgetown, district Clerk of Williamson County.

1. Early history: Mrs. Edward C. Garland; Galveston *News*, April 22, 1868.
2. *Flake's Semi-Weekly Bulletin*, Oct. 4, 1871.
3. San Antonio *Herald*, May 7, 1874.
4. Austin *Weekly Statesman*, Jan. 13, 1875.
5. Tom Elder, McDade, Texas, June 26, 1943.
6. J.J. Sapp, Bastrop, Texas, June 13, 1943.
7. Austin *Daily Statesman*, Sept. 22, 1875.
8. Austin *Weekly Statesman*, Nov. 4, 1875.

9. Mari Sandoz, *The Cattlemen*, 68-76. Miss Sandoz gives a full, though fictionized and undocumented account of the Olives in Texas and Nebraska. Harry E. Chrisman in the Denver Westerners' *Roundup* (XVII, June, 1961, 13-15) defends them against her charges of extreme brutality.

10. Austin *Weekly Statesman*, Aug. 10, 1876.

11. Judge C.W. Webb, Elgin, Texas, June 6, 1943; Tom Elder, Austin *Weekly Statesman*, July 27, 1876.

12. Austin *Weekly Statesman*, Aug. 10, 1876.

13. *Ibid.*, Sept. 14, 1876. Williamson County records show that Prentice Olive was indicted for murder on Sept. 22, 1876, and acquitted on Oct. 4, 1876 (Styles Byrom, County Clerk of Williamson County, to C. L. S., June 19, 1945).

14. Austin *Weekly Statesman*, June 1, Aug. 17, 1876.

15. April 25, 1876.

16. July 20, 1876.

17. May 17, 1878.

18. Tom Elder.

19. Helen Rummel, "When Eleven Were Lynched."

20. *Ibid.*, Tom Elder.

21. The hanging: Austin *Daily Statesman*, June 29, July 4, 1877; Rummel; Taylor; Billingsley.

22. J.J. Sapp, Bastrop, Texas, June 13, 1943.

23. Galveston *News*, Aug. 25, 1883.

24. Bastrop *Advertiser*, Nov. 25, 1883; Galveston *News*, Nov. 25, 1883.

25. C.W. Webb; Jeptha Billingsley's article. I find only one contemporary account of the Wynn robbery—a reprint in the Bastrop *Advertiser*, Jan. 5, 1884, of a story in the St. Louis *Globe-Democrat*, no date given.

26. Galveston *News*, Dec. 4, 1883.

27. Mrs. C.W. Webb, notes of an interview with Sam Sanders, Aug. 8, 1944; J.J. Sapp.

28. Galveston *News*, Dec. 9, 1883.

29. J.J. Sapp.

30. Bastrop *Advertiser*, Jan. 26, 1884.

31. *Ibid.*, Jan. 3, 1884.

32. Gen. W.D. Cope, Austin, July 6, 1944.

33. Jeptha Billingsley's article.

34. Bastrop *Advertiser*, Jan. 3, 1884.

35. Tom Elder.

36. Dr. G.T. King, Elgin, Texas, June 13, 1943.

37. Bishop and the others told about the fight at the examining trial. Their testimony was recorded in the Bastrop *Advertiser* for Jan. 26, 1884. H. Goldsticker and J.W. Holloman testified that the Beatty brothers bought cartridges. Dr. Vermilion admitted on cross examination that Bishop fired the first shot. Heywood Beatty and Milton told what happened in the store. James Allen described the wounding of Goodman. Tom Elder told me about Heywood's courage. J.J. Sapp recalled the misfit cartridges.

38. Tom Elder.

39. Houston *Post*, Dec. 27, 1883.

40. Mrs. C.W. Webb, notes of interview with Sam Sanders.

41. Tom Elder; J.J. Sapp.

42. T.U. Taylor in *Frontier Times*.

43. Bastrop *Advertiser*, Jan. 19, Nov. 1, 1884.

44. J.J. Sapp; R.L. Carter; Tom Elder.

45. Tom Elder.

★

Better Days

1. For improved law enforcement in the eighties see Rupert N. Richardson, *Texas the Lone Star State*, Prentice-Hall, New York, 1943, pp. 332-339; Webb, *The Texas Rangers*, p. 425.

2. There is much material on the subject of wire cutting. Any file of Texas newspapers for 1883 is useful. Two good references are Webb, *The Texas Rangers*, pp. 426-437, and R.D. Holt, "The Introduction of Barbed Wire into Texas and the Fence Cutting War," *The West Texas Historical Association Yearbook*, 1930, Vol. VI, pp. 65-69. For sheepman-cattleman trouble see Winifred Kupper, *The Golden Hoof*, Alfred H. Knopf, New York, 1945, and T.R. Havins, "Sheepmen-Cattlemen Antagonisms on the Texas Frontier," *West Texas Historical Association Yearbook*, Vol. XVIII, 1942, pp. 10-23.

★

A Family Named Marlow

Carrie J. Crouch, *A History of Young County, Texas*. Texas State Historical Association, Austin, 1956.

William MacLeod Raine, *Famous Sheriffs and Western Outlaws.* New Home Library, New York, 1944 (reprint; first edition, 1903).

William Rathmell, editor, *Life of the Marlows. A True Story of Frontier Life of Early Days, as Related by Themselves.* Ouray Herald Print, W.S. Olexa publisher, Ouray, Colorado, n. d. (second edition; first edition, 1892).

Torrence Bement Wilson, *A History of Wilbarger County,* Texas. M.A. thesis, The University of Texas, 1938.

The fullest account of the Marlow feud is the pamphlet "edited" by William Rathmell, who met and admired the two surviving brothers after their removal to Colorado. It is, of course, heavily weighted in their favor but it gives the facts as they saw them in great detail. Raine's chapter "Texas as Was" is an excellent account. Though Raine was a writer of "Westerns," he was a conscientious historian. He went to local newspapers, consulted legal documents, talked to old-timers, and got a first-hand story from George Marlow. I supplement Rathmell and Raine occasionally by adding details from the Graham *Leader* and from the old men at Graham.

I owe thanks to Phil Luker, editor of the *Leader* at the time I was looking for information; to Uncle Bill Ribble of Graham, who knew the Marlows; to Mrs. Carrie J. Crouch, the Young-County historian; to Mr. and Mrs. C.V. Hallenbeck of Grand Junction, Colorado. Mrs. Hallenbeck is George Marlow's daughter and her husband had close and pleasant associations with him during his last years. I am indebted to Mr. Hallenbeck for a lively account of George Marlow's habits and personality.

1. Marlow background: Rathmell, pp. 7-25.
2. Raine, p. 24.
3. Graham *Leader*, Sept. 6, 1888.
4. *Ibid.*, Dec. 20, 1888.
5. Wilson, p. 156.
6. Graham *Leader*, Sept. 6, 1888.
7. Rathmell, p. 21.
8. Graham *Leader*, Sept. 6, 1888; Rathmell, pp. 21-25.
9. Rathmell, pp. 26-28. Raine quotes the telegram but is skeptical about the existence of the letter.
10. Rathmell, p. 28.
11. Graham *Leader*, Sept. 6, 1888.
12. Rathmell, pp. 28-30.
13. *Ibid.*, p. 32.

14. *Ibid.*, p. 30.
15. Bill Ribble, Graham, Texas, June 7, 1944. Bill lived near Mr. Denson.
16. Graham *Leader*, Dec. 20, 1888.
17. Rathmell, pp. 33-34. The Galveston *News*, Dec. 18, 1888, says Boone fired at the command from the deputy to throw up his hands."
18. Graham *Leader*, Dec. 27, 1888.
19. *Ibid.*, Jan. 3, 1889.
20. *Ibid.*, Jan. 10, 1889.
21. Raine, pp. 31-33; Rathmell, pp. 38-39; Graham *Leader*, Jan. 17, 1889.
22. The lynch mob: Graham *Leader*, Jan. 24, 1889; Galveston *News*, Jan. 19, 21, 1889; Rathmell, p. 40; Raine, pp. 35-36.
23. Graham *Leader*, Jan. 24, 1889.
24. *Ibid.*
25. *Ibid.*
26. Galveston *News*, Jan. 25, 1889.
27. Crouch, pp. 114-120.
28. Graham *Leader*, Jan. 31, 1889.
29. Crouch, p. 121.
30. Undated notes on George Marlow written by C.V. Hallenbeck, Grand Junction, Colorado, for C. L. S.

★

The Feud of the Pious Assassins

Sam Ashburn, "W.C. Linden, 72 Year Old Lawyer, Who Broke Mob in San Saba During Bloody Days of 1896, Is New Assistant District Attorney in Bexar County, Texas." San Angelo *Morning Times*, December 21, 1934.

J.B. Cranfill, *Dr. J.B. Cranfill's Chronicle*. Fleming H. Revell Co., New York, 1916.

Eugene Cunningham, *Triggernometry—A Gallery of Gunfighters*. The Caxton Printers, Caldwell, Idaho, 1941.

Alma Ward Hamrick, *The Call of the San Saba: A History of San Saba County*. The Naylor Company, San Antonio, 1941.

Tyler Mason, *Riding for Texas*. Reynal and Hitchcock, New York, 1936.

Albert Bigelow Paine, *Captain Bill McDonald Texas Ranger*. Little and Ives, New York, 1909.

Report of the Adjutant General of the State of Texas for the Fiscal
  Year Ending August 31, 1878. Galveston News, Galveston,
  1878.
Sergeant W.J.L. Sullivan, Twelve Years in the Saddle for Law and
  Order. Von Boeckmann-Jones Co., Austin, 1909.

The San Saba Mob feud has not had much attention from historians.
Alma Ward Hamrick dismisses it with a few paragraphs. The best
documentary sources are Sergeant Sullivan's book, the reports and
correspondence of the Rangers, and the files of the San Saba News
(opened to me by Editor M.W. Trussell). Paine's book has many
interesting details but gives Captain Bill McDonald credit for everything, besides needing correction in points of fact. Tyler Mason is
nothing more than a jazzed-up version of Paine. Cunningham likewise leans heavily on Paine in his Triggernometry. Anyone who
wants to know the real background of this strange episode has to
go places and ask questions. The answers in this case came from
Mr. W.A. Smith (postmaster) and Dave Chadwick (deputy sheriff)
of San Saba; Jim Sloan of San Saba County; and the former district
attorney of San Saba County—Judge W.C. Linden. I have to thank
them for much courtesy as well as for much information.

1. The Buzzard's Water Hole: Paine, supposedly quoting Mc-
   Donald, says that "here the Worthy Order of Assassins assembled once a month, usually during a full moon" and
   "opened their meetings with prayer" (p. 222). Judge Linden
   told me that he knew of only one meeting there.
2. I learned something about mobs from B.J. Stubbs of Johnson
   City, Texas (interview July 11, 1944), Ed. S. Nichols of
   Meridian (interview July 18, 1942), and Hervey Chesley of
   Hamilton (letter, May 22, 1945); and from Cranfill's Chronicle, pp. 296-302. Texas papers for the seventies often refer to
   mysterious mobs, as do the reports of the Ranger captains.
   For an example see G.W. Arrington to Major John B. Jones,
   July 26, 1876 (AGF), about a mob of 100 men operating
   in Comanche and Erath Counties: "One of their party has
   divulged . . . all their passwords signs oaths and everything
   connected with them."
3. Austin Daily Statesman, July 31, 1874.
4. Dallas Weekly Herald, April 5, 1875.
5. Report of the Adjutant General . . . 1878.
6. AGF.
7. Nevill to Jones, March 7, 1880.

8. W.C. Linden, San Antonio, April 26, 1945.

9. Ashburn, San Angelo *Times,* Dec. 21, 1934.

10. *Ibid.*

11. W.C. Linden.

12. *Ibid.*

13. Dave Chadwick, San Saba, July 14, 1944.

14. Austin *Daily Statesman,* Feb. 14, 1897 (testimony of Ford, Dougherty, and Murphy).

15. Jim Sloan, San Saba, July 13, 1944.

16. Information about Turner and his family is pieced together from the testimony of his wife and children as reported in the Austin *Daily Statesman,* Feb. 24-27, 1897, and in the San Saba *News,* March 5, 1897. Miss Eula Barnes a teacher at Locker, testified that she spent night after night teaching Mat Ford to read.

17. San Saba *News,* July 26, 1889; Austin *Daily Statesman,* Feb. 24-27, 1897.

18. Sullivan, pp. 43-46.

19. Martin to King, Dec. 22, 1889, AGF.

20. W.A. Smith, San Saba, July 13, 1944; Dave Chadwick; San Saba *News,* Sept. 1, 1893.

21. McDonald to Mabry, Sept. 26, 1897, AGF.

22. Austin *Daily Statesman,* Feb. 24, 1897 (testimony of J.F. Dougherty).

23. AGF.

24. Undated clipping in the Webb Papers, University of Texas Archives.

25. Dave Chadwick; San Saba *News,* July 31, 1896; letter from T.S. Johnson to "The Honorable Legislature of Texas," AGF.

26. The letters, dated June 29 and July 7, are in the AGF.

27. San Saba *News,* July 31, 1896.

28. *Ibid.,* Aug. 21, 1896.

29. *Ibid.*

30. The letter, dated July 4, 1896, is in the AGF.

31. San Saba *News,* Oct. 2, 1896.

32. *Ibid.,* Sept. 4, 1896.

33. *Ibid.,* Sept. 25, Oct. 23, 30, 1896. A list of twenty-three men killed in the feud was compiled at this meeting, of whom only eleven had been killed in San Saba County.

34. Sullivan's letters (Aug. 28-Sept. 5, 1896) are in the AGF. For more on the Sullivan case see McDonald to Mabry, Oct. 1, 1896, Sept. 27, 1897; Linden to Mabry, Nov. 30, 1896;

Hawkins to Mabry, Dec. 24, 1896. Sullivan's book, p. 197 ff.,
gives his view of the story.

35. Linden to Mabry, Dec. 7, 1896, AGF.
36. Sullivan to Mabry, Feb. 7, 1897.
37. The trial: Austin *Daily Statesman*, Feb. 24, 25, 26, 27, March 5,
1897.
38. Linden to Mabry, May 11, 1897; San Saba *News*, July 9, 1897.
39. San Saba *News*, June 18, 25, 1897.
40. *Ibid.*, Sept. 3, 1897.
41. McDonald to Mabry, Sept. 26, 1897.
42. *Ibid.*, Sept. 29, 1897.
43. Ashburn; Dave Chadwick.
44. Linden told the story; Dave Chadwick added many details.
45. Ashburn.
46. Opal Yarborough, Deputy Clerk, Travis County, to C. L. S.,
May 15, 1945, on final disposition of cases 11154 and 11155,
State of Texas vs. G.W. Trowbridge and Mat Ford.
47. Sullivan, p. 200.

★

Old Southern Style

Ira Aten, "Six and One-Half Years in the Ranger Service." *Frontier
Times*, February, 1945.

Ed Kilman, "How Carry Nation Got Her Start." Houston *Post*,
May 17, 1942.

Ed Kilman, "Jaybird vs. Woodpecker War." Houston *Chronicle*,
April 9, 1944.

Milly Kochan, *The Jaybird-Woodpecker Revolution*. M.A. Thesis,
The University of Texas, 1929.

S.A. McMillan, compiler, *The Book of Fort Bend County*, Texas.
McMillan and Rich, n. p., 1926.

Carry Nation, *The Use and Need of the Life of Carry A. Nation
Written by Herself*. F.M. Steves and Sons, Topeka, 1904.

A.J. Sowell, *The History of Fort Bend County*. W. H. Coyle and
Co., Houston, 1904.

Clarence Ray Wharton, *Wharton's History of Fort Bend County*.
The Naylor Company, San Antonio, 1939.

Pauline Yelderman, *The Jaybird Democratic Association*. M.A.
Thesis, The University of Texas, 1938.

J.A. Ziegler, *Wave of the Gulf*. The Naylor Company, San Antonio, 1938.

I began looking into the Jaybird-Woodpecker trouble in 1933 at the suggestion of Mr. F.G. Belk of El Paso. At that time a few of the participants and bystanders were still on the ground. In June and July of 1933 I talked with F.M.O. Fenn, Judge J.R. Peareson, Mrs. Clem Bassett, and Mrs. C.E. Parnell of Richmond; Clarence Wharton, Mrs. I.B. MacFarland, Mrs. W.R. Goss, and Dr. Lay of Houston. Miss Milly Kochan allowed me to use a transcript of her thesis, while her father and mother, Mr. and Mrs. Albert Kochan of Richmond, went over their memories with me. Mr. C.I. McFarlane of Houston permitted me to inspect his treasured file of Richmond papers. Mr. and Mrs. Clifton Rice, once my neighbors in El Paso, supplied me with recollections of the Gibson family, pictures, letters and a warm friendship.

★

Prelude to Trouble

1. The Nation family in Richmond: Carry Nation, pp. 37-39; Ed Kilman, "How Carry Nation Got Her Start."
2. Yelderman, p. 7, gives population figures for 1890: black, 8, 981; white, 1, 605.
3. McMillan, p. 89, describes the background of the white families.
4. Reconstruction days: Wharton, pp. 174-186.
5. *Ibid.*, pp. 178-179; Clarence McFarlane, Houston, June, 1933.
6. Richmond *Opinion*, Aug. 14, 1885.
7. Yelderman, pp. 18-22; Albert Kochan, Richmond, June, 1933.
8. Wharton, p. 192.
9. Galveston *News*, Aug. 19, 1889; Wharton, p. 195; F.M.O. Fenn, Richmond, June, 1933.
10. Houston *Post*, Aug. 28, 1888.
11. Wharton, pp. 190-192; *Texas and Texans*, Vol. IV, pp. 1674-1675 (Peareson), Vol. III, pp. 1542-1543 (Bassett).
12. Mrs. W.R. Goss, Houston, June, 1933; Carry Nation, p. 39.
13. Wharton, pp. 179-180.
14. Organization of the club: Galveston *News*, July 4, 1888; Houston *Post*, July 31, 1888; Richmond *Democrat*, July 7, 1888.

★

The First Murder

1. Houston *Chronicle*, Oct. 11, 1936; Ziegler, *Wave of the Gulf*, pp. 152-158; Houston *Post*, Aug. 3, 7, 8, 1888.
2. Galveston *News* and Houston *Post*, Aug. 3, 1888; Wharton, p. 196 ff.
3. Houston *Post*, Aug. 8, 1888.
4. Kochan, p. 6; Wharton, p. 199; Houston *Post*, Oct. 23, 25, 1889.
5. Houston *Post*, Aug. 7, 22, 1888.

★

Thunder in the Air

1. Galveston *News*, Aug. 29, 1888.
2. *Ibid.*, July 7, 1889. W.H. Gayle, Jr. says he and Parker started the Cleveland and Thurman Club because they were left out of the other Democratic organization. He makes the best statement of the Woodpecker position.
3. The letter, dated August 17, 1888, is in the possession of Mrs. Clifton Rice.
4. Kochan, p. 3; Houston *Post*, Aug. 30, 31, 1888.
5. Kochan, p. 6; Houston *Post*, Sept. 4, Oct. 13, 1888.
6. Galveston *News*, Aug. 29, 1889.
7. *Ibid.*, Sept. 5, 1888; Wharton, p. 199.
8. F.M.O. Fenn.

★

The Terry-Gibson Feud Begins

1. Houston *Post*, Oct. 19, 20, 1888.
2. Wharton, p. 205; F.M.O. Fenn.
3. Galveston *News*, July 7, 1889.
4. Houston *Post*, Nov. 16, 1888.
5. Galveston *News*, July 4, 1889 (testimony of Henry Mason).
6. *Ibid.*, July 2, 1889 (testimony of Dr. John Dillard), July 4, 1889 (testimony of John A. Ballowe and Henry Mason).
7. Wharton, p. 209; Galveston *News*, July 5, 1889.

8. Wharton, p. 210; Galveston *News*, July 1, 2, 4, 1889.
9. Kochan, p. 24; F.M.O. Fenn.

★

The Nation Family Moves Out

1. Carry Nation, p. 43.
2. *Ibid.*, p. 43 ff.; Ed Kilman, "How Carry Nation Got Her Start."

★

Battle, Murder and Sudden Death

1 Aten in *Frontier Times.*
2. Mrs. Clem Bassett, Richmond, June, 1933.
3. Aten tells his story in the *Frontier Times*. The Jaybirds thought he was sympathetic toward them (Wharton, p. 13). Aten later admitted that "the Woodpecker faction thought I had some Jay Bird leanings" (Aten to Sonnichsen, July 24, 1934).
4. The battle was reported in the Galveston *News* and Houston *Post* for Aug. 17, 18, 1889, and for Aug. 28, 29, 30 (the examining trial).
5. Mrs. C.E. Parnell, Richmond, June, 1933.

★

The Day After

1. The Houston *Post* and the Galveston *News* for Aug. 28, 1889, carried eyewitness accounts.
2. Mrs. Clem Bassett.
3. Mrs. Albert Kochan.
4. Aten says Schmidt never recovered.
5. Houston *Post*, Aug. 28, 1889.

★

The Cleanup

1. The negotiations: Houston *Post* and Galveston *News*, Aug. 19, 20, 21, 22, 1889. Aten (letter to C. L. S., July 24, 1934)

says the governor told the Woodpeckers "if they did not appoint me Sheriff of the County, he would put the County under martial law."

2. Wharton (p. 219) follows the leading woodpeckers.
3. Ferguson-Davis suits: Wharton, p. 216; Yelderman, pp. 52-55.
4. Houston *Post*, Oct. 3, 1889.
5. Aten to Sieker, Sept. 3, 1889, AGF.
6. Houston *Post*, Oct. 23, 1889; Yelderman, p. 55 ff. In April, 1944, as a result of the Supreme Court decision that Negroes could vote in Texas primaries, the Jaybirds were much in the news again (Houston *Chronicle*, May 9, 1944).
7. Wharton, p. 218; F.M.O. Fenn.
8. Houston *Post*, Oct. 14, 1889.

★

The Last of Kyle Terry

1. Houston *Post*, Jan. 22, 23, 1889.
2. Wharton, p. 17; F.M.O. Fenn.
3. Galveston *News*, Jan. 22, 1890.
4. Houston *Post*, Jan. 22, 1889.
5. Galveston *News*, Jan. 23, 1889.

★

Last Words

1. See Terry *et al. vs.* Adams *et al.*, 345 U.S. 461; 97 Law Ed. 1152; 73 S. Ct. 809; Rehearing denied June 15, 1953, Opinion of Circuit Court of Appeals 193 F. 600; opinion of the Federal District Court, 90 F. Supp. 595 (citations furnished by Mr. C.I. McFarlane).
2. Minutes of the Jaybird Association, January 25, 1954 (courtesy of C.I. McFarlane).
3. The Richmond-Rosenberg *Herald-Coaster*, October 18, 1959.
4. C.I. McFarlane to C. L. S., October 19, 1959.

★

Other Days, Other Ways

1. Paul C. Boethel, *History of Lavaca County*. The Naylor Company, San Antonio, 1936, outlines this and other local feuds.
2. Galveston *News*, Jan. 26, 1900; Dr. W.S. Warnock, El Paso, Feb. 20, 1944; Warren Taylor, Gonzales, Texas, to C.L. Sonnichsen, June 23, 1943.
3. Flora G. Bowles, *History of Trinity County*, M.A. Thesis, The University of Texas, 1928.
4. C.L. Sonnichsen, *Ten Texas Feuds*. The University of New Mexico Press, Albuquerque, 1957, pp. 167-182.
5. Correspondence between Captain Brooks and Adjutant General Scurry, September-November, 1902, AGF.
6. John Ralph Whitaker, *W. C. Brann, His Life and Influence in Texas*. M.A. Thesis, The University of Texas, 1938; *A Collection of the Writings of W.C. Brann*. 2 Vols., Hertz Brothers, Waco, 1898 and 1911, pp. 187, 213, 320; Galveston *News*, Oct. 4-8, 1897, April 2-4, 1898; *Southwestern Historical Quarterly*, Vol. XLIII, April, 1940, p. 520. Interviews with Judge J.D. Williamson and Judge William Sleeper, Waco, June 19, 1943. The most recent treatment of Brann is Charles Carver's *Brann and the Iconoclast*, The University of Texas Press, Austin, 1957—a well written but insufficiently documented study of the feud and its social background.

★

Bullets for Uncle Buck's Boys

Henry C. Fuller in his life of A.J. Spradley, *A Texas Sheriff*, Baker Printing Co., Nacogdoches, 1931, tells about this feud. The Reverend George W. Crocket left an account of it in his unpublished notes (*Crocket Notes*, State Library, Austin). Some of the events are covered in a volume of the Nacogdoches *Weekly Sentinel* (1901-1902) in the Newspaper Collection at the University of Texas. Trial records are available in the courthouse at Rusk.

For generous help and hospitality my thanks go to Mr. W.S. Sharp of San Augustine; Dr. Felix Tucker, Mr. Giles Haltom, and Miss Virgie Sanders of Nacogdoches; Mr. W.H. Whitton and his daughters Miss Hazel Whitton and Mrs. Lela Haggerty of

Timpson. Mr. Whitton was a schoolmate of Kurg Border and a friend of both sides.

1. Fuller, pp. 35-36, comments favorably on the Walls. Mr. Whitton and others were less enthusiastic. Uncle Buck's war record: Galveston *News*, June 5, 1900.
2. Dr. Felix Tucker (Nacogdoches, Aug. 20, 1944), and W.H. Whitton (Timpson, Aug. 21, 1944) told me about the Border family. Lonn W. Taylor of Manila, P. I., set me straight on William Border, a cousin of Colonel William Border of Texas (Taylor to Sonnichsen, Feb. 15, 1955, Sept. 22, 1959). All sources agree that the trouble began when the Border and Wall boys were still in school.
3. The Populist campaign of 1894: Richardson, *Texas*, pp. 360-363.
4. Fuller, p. 36.
5. Galveston *News*, June 5, 1900.
6. Fuller, p. 36; Dr. Felix Tucker.
7. Galveston *News*, June 5, 1900.
8. *Ibid.*
9. *Ibid.*
10. *Ibid.*, June 6, 7, 8, 9, 1900.
11. The trials: Fuller, pp. 41-42; *Crocket Notes;* Galveston *News*, June 16, 19, 21, 1900; Criminal Minutes, Book L, District Clerk's office Cherokee County Courthouse, Rusk, pp. 478, 479, 512, 513.
12. *Crocket Notes;* Fuller, p. 43.
13. Galveston *News*, Oct. 26, 27, 1901; Nacogdoches *Weekly Sentinel,* Oct. 30, 1901.
14. Nacogdoches *Weekly Sentinel,* Oct. 30, 1901
15. *Ibid.*, Nov. 6, 1901.
16. Dr. Felix Tucker; Mr. W.S. Sharp.

★

All in the Family

Little has been told of the Columbus feuds. Albert Bigelow Paine's *Captain Bill McDonald*, Little and Ives, New York, 1909, outlines McDonald's part in the Reese-Townsend flareup in 1899, but Paine knew nothing about the background and was chiefly interested in making Captain Bill look good. C.L. Douglas's chapter in his *Famous Texas Feuds*, The Turner Company, Dallas, 1936, is based on Paine. A biographical sketch of R.W. Stafford is printed in *The Trail Drivers of Texas*, J. Marvin Hunter, editor and compiler,

The Cokesbury Press, Nashville, Tenn., 1925. Mrs. Mabel Claire McGee, former editor, *Colorado County Citizen*, assembled notes which I gratefully used. Others who helped are Mrs. Allie Grimes Westeroth, Mrs. Etta Grimes Longnecker, El Paso; their brother, Ralph Grimes; Mrs. Liza McMahan, Woody Townsend, Henry Thomas, Columbus; Doc Houchens, Hallettsville; Chris Emmett, Santa Fe; C.H. Rhodes, Maury Kemp, El Paso. I am especially grateful to Mrs. Joe Lessing and Miss Lillian Reese, Columbus. Miss Reese edited Walter Reese's *Flaming Feuds of Colorado County* (Anson Jones Press, Salado, Tex., 1962); much of this information could have come only from eyewitnesses and participants.

1. The new courthouse: Galveston *News*, July 1, 1889.
2. Mrs. Wetteroth and Mrs. Longnecker, El Paso, Dec. 28, 1943, Jan. 2, 1944.
3. The family relationships: Mrs. Joe Lessing, Columbus, Aug. 18, 1944; Henry Thomas, Columbus, July 3, 1943; Mrs. McGee's manuscript notes; Hunter, *Trail Drivers of Texas*, p. 708.
4. Chris Emmett, *Shanghai Pierce*, pp. 87-88, 95.
5. *Flake's Semi-Weekly Bulletin*, Dec. 13, 1871; Henry Thomas.
6. Henry Thomas.
7. Galveston *News*, July 9, 1890.
8. *Ibid.*, July 10, 1890.
9. Ralph Grimes, El Paso, May 6, 1945.
10. Mrs. McGee's notes.
11. Galveston *News*, Aug. 4, 1898.
12. Henry Thomas.
13. Galveston *News*, April 30, 1899, July 1, 1906.
14. *Ibid.*, March 17, 24, 1899, July 1, 1906.
15. McDonald at Columbus: *Ibid.*, March 22, 24, 29, 31, 1899; McDonald to Scurry, March 22, 1899, AGF.
16. Paine, p. 243 ff.
17. Galveston *News*, May 19, 20, 1899.
18. AGF.
19. Doc Houchens, Hallettsville, Aug. 18, 1944.
20. Galveston *News*, Jan. 16-18, 21-26, 1900; Woody Townsend, Columbus, June 27, 1943.
21. *Bay City Tribune*, Aug. 3, 1900; Galveston *News*, Aug. 1, 1900.
22. Galveston *News*, July 11, 1906; Doc Houchens; Mrs. J.F. Lessing; Mrs. McGee's notes.
23. Henry Thomas.
24. El Paso *Times*, Nov. 8, 9, 1919; Mrs. Wetteroth and Mrs. Longnecker; C.H. Rhodes, Maury Kemp.

Index